HENRY V

HENRY V

KEITH DOCKRAY

TEMPUS

To Roger Kitching
for his encouragement, understanding
and friendship over almost fifty years

First published 2004

Tempus Publishing Limited
The Mill, Brimscombe Port,
Stroud, Gloucestershire, GL5 2QG
www.tempus-publishing.com

British Library Cataloguing in Publication Data.
A catalogue record for this book is available from the British Library.

ISBN 0 7524 3046 7

Typesetting and origination by Tempus Publishing Limited
Printed and bound in Great Britain.

CONTENTS

ACKNOWLEDGEMENTS

When writing *William Shakespeare, the Wars of the Roses and the Historians* (Tempus, 2002), I found myself increasingly ill-at-ease with Shakespeare's portrayal of Henry V and ever more sceptical about the admiration for the king displayed by so many historians. Alan Sutton and Jonathan Reeve both liked the idea of a short, historiographically-orientated but critically conceived biography of the victor of Agincourt; I was spurred on by Tony Pollard's less-than-admiring verdict on Henry V in his *Late Medieval England 1399-1509* (Longmans, 2000); and my iconoclastic inclinations were further stimulated by Michael K. Jones' compelling, if deliberately mischievous, reinterpretation of Richard III's character, motives and behaviour in *Bosworth 1485: Psychology of a battle* (Tempus, 2002).

I have drawn heavily on the work of others, especially Christopher Allmand, Anne Curry, Antonia Gransden, G.L. Harriss, H.F. Hutchison, E.F. Jacob, C.L. Kingsford, M.W. Labarge, K.B. McFarlane, R.B. Mowat, Edward Powell, T.B. Pugh and Desmond Seward. Peter Fleming and Peter Allender have endured many hours of relentless conversation about the king in *The Sportsman and Annexe Inn*, Bristol, and I am immensely grateful to them for their encouragement and forbearance. Sadly, my fabulous felines Snitch (1985–1996) and Snubby (1985–2002) could no longer disturb my labours but Smoky, my latest familiar, has striven hard to prove himself a worthy successor. The book's many faults, needless to say, are entirely my own.

Keith Dockray
Bristol, 29 September 2003

I

HENRY V
IN HISTORY

I

INTRODUCTION

[On the death of Henry IV] his son, Prince Hal, who had won all English hearts by his youthful pranks – (such as trying on the crown while his father lay dying and hitting a very old man called Judge Gascoigne) – determined to justify public expectations by becoming the *Ideal English King*. He therefore decided on an immediate appearance in the Hundred Years War... Conditions in France were favourable to Henry since the French king, being mad, had entrusted the government of the country to a dolphin and the command of the army to an elderly constable. After capturing some breeches at Harfleur (more than once) by the original expedients of disguising his friends as imitation tigers, stiffening their sinews etc., Henry was held up on the road to Calais by the constable, whom he defeated at the utterly memorable battle of AGINCOURT... He then displaced the dolphin as ruler of Anjou, Menjou, Poilou, Maine, Touraine, Againe, and Againe,and realizing that he was now too famous to live long expired at the ideal moment.[1]

Such was W.C. Sellar and R.J.Yeatman's verdict on Henry V in their classic spoof *1066 and All That*, 'the only Memorable History of England because all the History you can remember is in this book', first published in 1930. Some sixty years later John Farman, despite a long standing disinterest in history originally inspired by the desperately dull lessons of 'Basher' Bowker (during which he merely acquired 'an unparalleled knowledge of paper-dart making and the refined art of desk-top carving') penned *The Very Bloody History of Britain*. Henry V provided an irresistible opportunity to indulge in juvenile jingoism:

When he heard that the King of France had gone barmy he thought it might be quite a giggle to go a-conquering. Watch out you Frogs! He turned out to be rather good at this and, to cut a long story short (and loads of soldiers), he really knocked the stuffing out of them, particularly at Agincourt. So well in fact, that he married the daughter of mad Charles VI (known as Charles the Silly) of France and became Regent (nearly King) of all France.[2]

Clearly, such verdicts anticipate a readership only too well aware of William Shakespeare's portrayal of England's second Lancastrian king, not least his transformation from Sir John Falstaff's tavern-haunting comrade into the charismatic victor of Agincourt. Yet even the wild and headstrong Prince Hal of *Henry IV Parts 1 and 2* is a young man always rather aloof from his rumbustious companions and well aware of his future responsibilities. Long before his father's death there are strong hints of sterling qualities and, once king, they rapidly manifest themselves. In *Henry V* in fact, Shakespeare allows the new king to blossom into a veritable Elizabethan hero: an epic embodiment of Christian virtue and military valour, serious-minded, concerned for the welfare of his subjects and, above all, an archetypal man of action.

Ever since the first performance of *Henry V* at the newly opened Globe Theatre in 1599, Shakespeare's powerful portrayal of the king has certainly captured the popular imagination. Such a portrayal, moreover, very much reflects not only the Tudor sources on which the dramatist drew but also contemporary and near-contemporary estimates of Henry V. For his earliest English biographer, a royal chaplain and well-informed insider writing about 1417, he was a model Christian prince, carrying out God's wishes both at home and abroad; the St Albans chronicler Thomas Walsingham, in a eulogy penned very soon after the king's death in 1422, judged him a pious, prudent, distinguished and warlike ruler; and for the humanist Tito Livio in about 1437, he was an energetic, just and shrewd military commander who, at Agincourt, 'fought like an unvanquished lion'. Modern English historians have frequently brought in favourable verdicts as well: C.L. Kingsford in 1901, for instance, judged him 'the perfect medieval hero'; R.B. Mowat, in 1919, believed that 'in the long line of able English kings since Alfred' Henry V alone inspired at once the admiration and affection of his people'; and even the sober Oxford scholar K.B. McFarlane, in 1954, regarded him as 'superlatively gifted', 'born to rule and conquer' and, perhaps, 'the greatest man that ever ruled England'. For his most recent academic biographer Christopher Allmand, too, Henry V was 'a fine, indeed a remarkable soldier', a 'natural commander of men' when on campaign in France and, at home, responsible for 'a greater degree of political and social harmony than had been known for many years'.

Even fifteenth-century French commentators frequently praised Henry V's courage, love of justice and valiant deeds: an anonymous monk writing at the Abbey of Saint-Denis during the king's own lifetime, for instance believed 'no prince in his time appeared more capable to subdue and conquer a country'; another contemporary chronicler, Pierre Fenin, regarded him as a ruler of 'high understanding' who possessed 'a great will to keep justice'; and even Jean Juvenal des Ursins, a supporter of Charles VII of France and no lover of the English, judged him a prudent man valiant in arms and, above all, a great administrator of justice. Yet for Robert Blondel, a young French patriot at the time of Henry V's triumphs over his fellow countrymen, he was 'a ferocious and savage king'; the French chronicler Georges Chastellain deeply lamented the fact that, by his hand, so much French blood was spilt; and the Burgundian Jean Waurin believed the king was 'much feared and dreaded by his nobles, knights and captains, and people of every degree' because 'all those who disobeyed orders or infringed his edicts' were ' put to death without mercy'. Such critical verdicts were certainly echoed, indeed magnified, by the twentieth-century French historian Edouard Perroy when, in 1945, he chose to highlight Henry V's affectation of piety, hypocritical devoutness, senseless ambition, duplicity of conduct, cruelty, and utter lack of all scruples.

Most modern studies of Henry V have tended to concentrate on the man of action, the soldier-king who won Agincourt and conquered Normandy, and the master of diplomacy who negotiated the Treaty of Troyes (as a result of which his son became ruler of a dual monarchy of England and France). Yet what is most fascinating about Henry V, arguably, is his personality; how he was regarded both in his own time and since; and whether his heroic reputation, so graphically captured by William Shakespeare, can, in the last analysis, be justified.

2

FIFTEENTH-CENTURY
ENGLISH PERSPECTIVES

Henry V's character, life and achievements are unusually well recorded in contemporary and near-contemporary English biographies and chronicles and, even before the king's untimely death in 1422, the heroic portrayal later immortalised by William Shakespeare was beginning to take shape. This is no coincidence. From the very moment of his accession, if not before, Henry embarked on a deliberate stratagem of image-creation, consciously presenting himself as a dramatic contrast to his cautious and uncharismatic father Henry IV, a man not only resolved to restore harmony at home but also vigorously reassert traditional English claims to hegemony in France. A master of the art of political propaganda, he knew just how to win, and retain, the support of the secular and ecclesiastical elites and, no less significantly, the population at large. Magnates, knights and gentry, and the ruling oligarchies of London and urban communities elsewhere, soon came to appreciate his well publicised determination to placate former opponents of the Lancastrian regime, put an end to aristocratic in-fighting, promote impartial justice and tackle the perennial problem of lawlessness in the provinces. Men of the cloth could find little to fault in his personal piety and chastity, his enthusiasm for monasticism, his strict Catholic orthodoxy and, above all, his rigorous intolerance of religious dissent, especially the proto-Protestant Lollards. Since Henry V himself so frequently highlighted his possession of full divine approval for the Lancastrian dynasty's just claims across the Channel, moreover, patriotic pride in the victorious campaigns of their self-proclaimed chivalric warrior king probably became widespread throughout an ever more nationalistic (even xenophobic) realm at home.

Early fifteenth-century English literary sources for Henry V clearly need to be treated with considerable caution: they often reflect the king's own propaganda, deliberately embroider the truth, shamelessly borrow from each other and relay stories that may well be richer in myth and legend than historical fact. Latin lives of the king – most notably, the anonymous *Gesta Henrici Quinti (Deeds of Henry V)*, Thomas Elmham's *Liber Metricus (Metrical Life)* and Tito Livio's *Vita Henrici Quinti (Life of Henry V)* – are fiercely eulogistic, praising Henry's role as God's agent in all he did and focussing, in particular, on his entirely defensible diplomatic and military reassertion of traditional English rights in France. Latin chroniclers such as the St Albans monk Thomas Walsingham, the Kenilworth canon John Strecche and the Welsh ecclesiastical lawyer Adam Usk, although less concerned with Henry V personally, similarly gave pride of place in their narratives to the king's French exploits and their impact. John Lydgate, Thomas Hoccleve, John Page and John Harding, not to mention many anonymous poets and versifiers, were no less inspired by the man and his daring deeds, as were the authors of the *Brut* and London civic chroniclers. Even contemporary records and letters often reflect the propagandist aims and intentions of the king and his government.

Of surviving contemporary and near-contemporary lives of Henry V, earliest in date, and most valuable in content, is the *Gesta Henrici Quinti*. Although its author is anonymous, he was probably a royal chaplain attached to the king's household throughout the early years of his reign, writing between late November 1416 and the end of July 1417. Well informed he certainly was and, significantly, he particularly concentrates on the periods when he was in attendance on the king and events he observed first hand. For instance, he was with Henry V on the very day of Sir John Oldcastle's abortive Lollard uprising in January 1414; he accompanied the royal army throughout the Agincourt campaign of 1415; and he was an eyewitness of the spectacular London pageant staged to celebrate the king's triumphant return to England in November 1415. On other matters, notably Anglo-French negotiations and diplomacy more generally during the years 1413–1417, he obviously had access to government records. Yet the *Gesta*'s author can hardly be regarded as an impartial observer: indeed, his work looks suspiciously like a commissioned official life, shot through with clearly propagandist objectives. The chaplain's immediate purpose in November 1416, he tells us, was to record, justify and encourage support for:

> ...the king's unbreakable resolve to go overseas in the following summer to subdue the stubborn and more than adamantine obduracy of the French, which neither the tender milk of goats nor the consuming wine of vengeance, nor yet the most thorough-going negotiations could soften.

Throughout, moreover, he sought to present Henry V himself as a profoundly Christian prince enjoying the constant approval and support of God from the very moment of his accession:

> When young in years but old in experience he began his reign, like the true elect of God savouring the things that are above, he applied his mind with all devotion to encompass what could promote the honour of God, the extension of the church, the deliverance of his country, and the peace and tranquillity of kingdoms, and especially [the] peace and tranquillity of the two kingdoms of England and France.

As for Henry V's victories, particularly his rigorous suppression of the Lollards and his spectacularly successful defeat of the 'wretched and stiff-necked' French at the battle of Agincourt, they are indisputable evidence that divine providence was indeed firmly on the side of the splendidly upright and just ruler. And, since the chaplain also highlighted both the king's success in winning support from the Holy Roman Emperor Sigismund and his enthusiastic backing for English delegates at the Council of Constance, he was probably aiming to attract continental as well as domestic approval for his master's endeavours.

For the *Gesta Henrici Quinti*, then, Henry V was very much God's instrument, a man of 'great humility and trust in prayer' who enjoyed the backing not only of the Almighty but his saints as well (particularly the Blessed Virgin Mary and St George), a prince nevertheless subjected to a series of trials deliberately designed to test his faith and constancy. Even so, the king himself is presented as a ruler of great vision and ability, not only at the centre of events but the prime shaper (under God, of course) of his own destiny. He is also a man supremely confident in the pursuit of that destiny, remarking as he prepares to lead his puny force into battle at Agincourt that:

> ...by the God in heaven upon Whose grace I have relied and in Whom is my firm hope of victory, I would not, even if I could, have a single man more than I do. For these I have with me are God's people, whom he deigns to let me have at this time.

As for the English victory that did indeed result, the *Gesta* tells us:

> ...our older men [do not] remember any prince ever having commanded his people on the march with more effort, bravery, or consideration, or having, with his own hand, performed greater feats of strength in the field. Nor, indeed, is evidence to be found in the chronicles or annals of kings of which our long history makes mention, that any king ever achieved so much in so short a time and returned home with so great and glorious a triumph.

Nevertheless, the chaplain added:

> To God alone be the honour and glory, for ever and ever. Amen.

Surely, if Henry V himself ever read the *Gesta*, he must have been entirely content with so enthusiastic a verdict![3]

A year or so after the completion of the *Gesta Henrici Quinti*, Thomas Elmham put together his *Liber Metricus*. Originally a monk at St Augustine's Canterbury, he became prior of the Cluniac monastery of Lenton in Nottinghamshire in 1414. Since Lenton enjoyed royal patronage, moreover, Elmham's appointment suggests that he had forged court connections and, perhaps, become personally acquainted with Henry V: if so, this might explain why, in 1415, Henry recommended him for the post of vicar-general of the Cluniac order in England and why he, in turn, dedicated his *Liber Metricus* to the king. It is certainly a most curious compilation, not least its enigmatic preface where, Elmham tells us, his intention has been to pen an abbreviation in verse of a longer prose work (now lost) he had written earlier.

Although claiming to include what he had either observed himself or learned from eyewitnesses of events, he nevertheless acknowledged a major drawback to his endeavours: such was Henry V's pious humility and desire to attribute to God, rather than himself, credit for his achievements, he had made it very difficult for Elmham to obtain information at court! Perhaps this is also the key to the extraordinarily contrived and cryptic character of the *Liber's* verse, apt to obscure rather than elucidate its author's meaning and clearly aimed at a clerical, learned audience who, alone, might fully appreciate Elmham's complex Latin panegyrics.

The *Gesta Henrici Quinti* and *Liber Metricus* are the only strictly contemporary lives of Henry V we possess. Much of the information in the latter, however, appears to derive from the former (perhaps via Elmham's lost prose life), although the *Liber* is riddled with mistakes and misunderstandings. The two also share a similar political and religious perspective, although Elmham is even more vituperative than the anonymous *Gesta* when condemning the Lollards and Sir John Oldcastle. Like the chaplain, Elmham presents Henry V as an almost Christ-like figure who, at Agincourt, not only 'stood in his army without fear' but also, 'bearing his own arms, put his own crown on his head', 'signed himself with the cross', and thereby bestowed on his men courage almost comparable to his own; moreover, during the battle:

> …St George was seen fighting on the side of the English. The Virgin, handmaiden of the Almighty, protected the English. All the glory be given to her not to us.

Sir John Oldcastle, by contrast, is portrayed as a veritable anti-Christ, a 'satellite of hell and cursed heretic'. As for the Lollards, the 'shadows of evil', our 'Catholic prince and king' defeated them utterly 'so that his glory might be acknowledged by the people to the Lord, and cover the whole earth'. Such hyperbole hardly inspires confidence in the *Liber's* reliability as a source and only very rarely does Elmham provide information not to be found elsewhere (although, interestingly, he is the earliest writer to suggest that, during Anglo-French negotiations prior to the Agincourt campaign, the dauphin sought to ridicule Henry V by sending him a gift of tennis balls.)[4]

By the time Tito Livio penned his *Vita Henrici Quinti* in the later 1430s Henry V had been dead for over fifteen years, his legacy appeared ever more seriously threatened, and his only surviving brother Humphrey Duke of Gloucester had become, in effect, leader of the opposition to his nephew Henry VI's government. Livio probably joined Gloucester's household in 1436, one of several Italian humanist scholars who enjoyed ducal patronage over the years, and, by March 1437, he had become 'poet and orator' to the duke. Commissioned soon afterwards to write a semi-official Latin life of Henry V (probably the main reason why Gloucester had chosen to favour him in the first place), Livio had almost certainly completed his manuscript by the time he left England in late 1438 or 1439. Humphrey of Gloucester had clear political objectives in mind: convinced that a return to the bellicose policies of earlier times was now essential, what he wanted was a narrative highlighting Henry V's triumphs in France, emphasising his own role in English successes there and, perhaps most importantly, persuading the sixteen-year-old Henry VI of the urgent need to emulate his father's glorious exploits. He must have been delighted with the result, not least Livio's dedication of his work to Henry VI and urgent plea that the young king fight the French:

> ...not because I prefer you to have war instead of peace but because you cannot have a just peace. You should resolve to imitate that divine king your father in all things, seeking peace and quiet for your realm by using the same methods and martial valour as he used to subdue your common enemies.

Even more gratifying to Gloucester, no doubt, was Livio's stress on the duke's own courage and impressive contribution to Henry V's military success, particularly at Agincourt where he 'fought bravely without fear' until, 'pierced by the point of a sword, he was thrown to the ground half dead'. The close relationship between Humphrey Duke of Gloucester and his brother, moreover, is graphically underlined by Henry V's reported reaction to this dire event:

> [The] king himself now put his feet astride the legs of Humphrey. For the renowned Duke fell with his head against the king's feet but with

his feet to the enemy. In this position the king fought most coura-geously for a long time so that his brother might be carried safely from the enemy to his own men.

Obviously, Tito Livio can have had no personal knowledge of Henry V, or experience of his rule, so he was entirely dependent on the oral and written testimony of others. One major informant, almost certainly, was Humphrey Duke of Gloucester himself; he probably talked, as well, to older nobility at Henry VI's court who had served the king's father; and he appears to have obtained valuable material from early fifteenth-century chronicles (particularly the *Brut*), poems (such as John Page's eyewitness account of the siege of Rouen 1418/19) and government records. Strangely, he does not seem to have been aware of the *Gesta Henrici Quinti* but, even so, Livio's portrayal of Henry V has much in common with that of the royal chaplain. For the years 1416–1418, once the *Gesta* has ended, the *Vita Henrici Quinti* is the fullest authority we have and, for the period 1418–1422 (not covered by the *Liber Metricus* either), it is the earliest life. Livio's Italian human-ist credentials are most evident in his clearly classically-inspired Latin prose and in the speeches he frequently puts into Henry V's mouth (very much a feature of Renaissance historical writing). Moreover, although not literal records of what the king said, these orations (prob-ably communicated to Livio by Humphrey of Gloucester and fellow Lancastrian noblemen who had participated in Henry's campaigns) might well preserve their spirit. For instance, following the fall of Harfleur in late September 1415 and when planning his next moves, Henry V is credited with a notably morale-boosting address to his magnates:

[Even if the French] assemble a great army, our hope is in God that no injury will come to either my army or myself. I shall not suffer them, puffed up with pride, to rejoice in evil deeds or unjustly possess what is mine, against the will of God. They would say I had taken flight through fear and abandoned my rights. I have the spirit of a very strong man, ready to face all dangers rather than allow anyone to impugn my reputation. With God's favour we shall proceed unharmed and safe, and even if they try to stop us, we will triumph as victors.

And just prior to engaging the French at Agincourt a month later, he urged the troops in similar terms to:

> ...be brave in heart and fight with all your might. God and the justice of our cause will be our protection and will ensure that all, or at least a great part, of this proud enemy before us will be delivered into our hands and be at our mercy.

Stirring stuff indeed but, almost certainly, bearing the firm stamp of Gloucester's partisan and politically motivated recollections. The *Vita Henrici Quinti*, even more than earlier lives, does seem to have been an overtly propagandist work, deliberately praising Henry V's character and achievements in order to stir his son and his ministers into new martial exploits against England's traditional enemy. As such it, too, must be treated with considerable caution.[5]

For all its shortcomings, Tito Livio's portrayal of England's second Lancastrian king clearly exercised a great deal of influence on future generations, even before much of it was translated into English early in Henry VIII's reign. Indeed, within ten years of its completion it provided a model (and more) for a further Latin life of Henry V. According to its early eighteenth-century editor, the *Vita et Gesta Henrici Quinti* was another work by Thomas Elmham, author of the *Liber Metricus*. This was not, in fact, the case but Pseudo-Elmham (as it is now more often dubbed) certainly merits serious attention. Although the author's name is unknown, he obviously had similar credentials to Livio: another continental visitor to England, perhaps a transient member of Humphrey of Gloucester's scholarly coterie, he was a classical humanist even more prone to rhetorical verbosity; he appears to have begun work on his *Vita et Gesta* at the behest of Walter Lord Hungerford (formerly steward of Henry V's household and heavily involved in the king's military campaigns); and, by the later 1440s, his manuscript was probably circulating at the Lancastrian court. Down to about 1420, much of Pseudo-Elmham's factual content derives from Livio's life (easily available, presumably, in Gloucester's library): his own very extensive additions to what he himself describes as the Italians's 'bare draft of formless matter' are, however, largely rhetorical, not least the frequent lengthy orations put into Henry V's mouth. From 1420, by contrast, he provides much new evidence. No doubt Walter Lord Hungerford was one prime informant; perhaps Humphrey of Gloucester was another; and he may have drawn, as well, on English and French chronicles. Throughout, his perspective (like Livio's) is very much that of Gloucester and his circle, and here again we are dealing with an essentially propagandist work. This is never more evident than in his highly rhetorical treatment of Henry V's reaction to his father's death on 20 March 1413. As a young man, Pseudo-Elmham tells us, Henry was:

> ...a diligent follower of idle practices, much given to instruments of music. Passing the bounds of modesty he fervently followed the service of Venus as well as Mars: fired with torches, in the midst of his brave deeds as a soldier, he also found leisure for the excesses of untamed youth.

Henry IV's death, however, produced a 'sudden conversion of darkness into light, of cloud into clear air', once his son and successor had:

> ...spent the day in wailing and groaning, as soon as the shadows of night had covered the earth, the weeping prince, taking advantage of the darkness, secretly visited a certain recluse of holy life at Westminster and laying bare to him the sins of his whole life, was washed in the balm of true repentance and receiving the antidote of absolution for the poison he had swallowed, put off the mantle of vice and emerged decently adorned with the cloak of virtue.

When dealing with Henry V's last illness and death, despite almost certainly drawing on information from Walter Lord Hungerford (who was present in the king's entourage), Pseudo-Elmham again cannot resist extravagant rhetorical flourishes:

> Oh cruel disease! Do you not know whom you have presumed to fill with such fearful poison? Whom you have afflicted with such terrible torments? Whom you rejoice at removing from a grieving world? The king, indeed, is the glory of kings, the model of magnanimity, the mirror of chivalry, the champion of justice, the zealot of equity, the victor of France and Normandy. Now, for shame, you intend to conquer him, and do not hesitate to torture such an illustrious king, allowing, in your outrageous excesses, not one hour's rest to so great a

prince. In your blind presumption you fail to distinguish between a
prince and a pauper.

Such linguistic exuberance need not necessarily negate everything
Pseudo-Elmham reports but, even more than earlier biographers of
Henry V, he cannot be regarded as either objective or impartial.[6]

Contemporary and near-contemporary lives of Henry V specifically
focus on the second Lancastrian's personality, life and achievements;
chroniclers often have wider interests but they, too, can provide vital,
frequently detailed, information about the king's character and career.
Among them, much the most important is Thomas Walsingham, a
monk at the Benedictine abbey of St Albans from about the mid-
1360s until his death soon after Henry VI's accession to the throne in
1422. St Albans had a long tradition of historical writing and
Walsingham himself was an enthusiastic and well-informed reporter
of current events and their significance for over forty years. At least
three narratives covering Henry V's life and times, all in Latin, can
confidently be credited to him: a major chronicle for the reigns of
Richard II (1377–1399), Henry IV (1399–1422) and Henry V, termi-
nating in 1420; an abbreviated, largely derivative, version of the same
chronicle, apart from a new final section devoted to Henry V's last
years (1420–1422); and the *Ypodigma Neustriae* (*Image of Normandy*),
compiled after June 1419 but before Henry V's death, and concerned
primarily to justify and commemorate the king's recent conquest of
Normandy. Clearly, Walsingham benefited from both the prestige and
location of St Albans: England's premier Benedictine abbey, it lay near
a major road less than twenty miles from London and must, surely,
have played host to many politically well-informed visitors over the
years. On the positive side, too, Walsingham recorded events very soon
after they happened and his factual content is often impressively
detailed; he consulted official documents and, occasionally, tran-
scribed their contents; and his explanations of what was going on
often carry considerable conviction. Yet he, no less than the authors of
the lives, had a clear perspective of his own and, like them too, may
have had deep-rooted propagandist intentions. In particular, he was
anxious to justify the Lancastrian usurpation of 1399 (when Henry IV
deposed his predecessor Richard II and, probably, ordered his murder
in Pontefract castle soon afterwards); his orthodox Christian faith

underpinned, and helps explain, his bitter hostility to Sir John Oldcastle and the Lollards; and, as his treatment of Henry V's continental campaigns amply demonstrates, he was both highly patriotic and vigorously anti-French.

Thomas Walsingham was certainly a great admirer of Henry V, as a pious Christian and active defender of the faith who firmly suppressed the Lollards, and a chivalric warrior and patriot who proved the justice of his claims across the Channel by winning a string of military victories against the French. Indeed, he specifically dedicated the *Ypodigma Neustriae* to the king, declaring him to be:

> ...the most magnificent and illustrious Henry, King of the French and the English, conqueror of Normandy, most serene prince of Wales and lord of Ireland and Aquitaine, by the grace of God, everywhere and always victorious.

From the moment of his accession, Walsingham reported, Henry 'changed suddenly into another man, zealous for honesty, modesty and gravity, there being no sort of virtue that he was not anxious to display'. At Agincourt he fought:

> ...not so much as a king but as a knight and, performing the duties of both, flung himself against the enemy. He both inflicted and received cruel blows, offering an example in his own person to his men by scattering the opposing lines with a battle axe.

And when the field was won, 'ascribing all these outcomes to God as he ought', he 'gave ceaseless thanks to Him who had bestowed an unexpected victory and defeated savage enemies'. Certainly, too, in his final assessment composed very soon after the king's death, Walsingham brought in an entirely positive verdict:

> King Henry left no one like him among Christian kings or princes. His death, not only by his subjects in England and France but by the whole of Christendom, was deservedly mourned. He was pious in soul, taciturn and discreet in his speech, far-seeing in council, prudent in judgement, modest in appearance, magnanimous in his actions, firm in business, persistent in pilgrimages and generous in alms, devoted to

God and supportive and respectful of prelates and ministers of the church. War-like, distinguished and fortunate, he had won victories in all his military engagements. He was generous in constructing buildings and founding monasteries, munificent in his gifts, and above all pursued and attacked enemies of the faith and the church.

'Thinking of his memorable deeds', Walsingham concluded, 'people felt awe at his sudden and terrible death', and 'mourned inexpressibly'.[7]

Apart from Thomas Walsingham's magisterial narratives, contemporary and near-contemporary accounts of Henry V and his times in Latin chronicles tend to be slight, derivative, or both. Adam Usk, a Welsh ecclesiastical lawyer, certainly lived through the events of the king's reign and penned his chronicle (which ends abruptly in the summer of 1421) before Henry V's death. Unfortunately, by then, he was elderly, no longer at the centre of events (as he had been at the beginning of Henry IV's reign) and, increasingly, running out of steam. Usk's treatment of Henry V's reign, although an independent account, is thin and episodic, and lacks the splendid anecdotes that so enliven his coverage of Richard II and Henry IV. To begin with, he seems to have shared the enthusiasm for Henry V expressed by the more overtly propagandist writers of the time, describing him, at his accession, as 'a most admirable youth, full of wisdom and virtue'; he condemned the 'pestilential teaching' of the Lollards and welcomed the eventual fate of 'the heretic John Oldcastle'; and he exulted in the king's capture of Harfleur and victory at Agincourt in 1415. Occasionally, too, there are passages probably based on Usk's personal observations, most notably the great pageant held in London to celebrate Agincourt and the processions through the capital's streets to mark the fall of Rouen in 1419. By 1421, however, he had become thoroughly disillusioned, particularly at the sheer cost of Henry V's wars. Whereas in November 1415 Usk had judged parliament's financial generosity to the king 'no more than he deserved', by June 1421 he believed:

...the lord king is now fleecing anyone with money, rich or poor, throughout the realm, in readiness for his return to France. Yet I fear, alas, that both the great men and the money of the kingdom will be wasted in this enterprise. No wonder, then, that the unbearable impositions being demanded from the people to this end are accompanied by dark – though private – mutterings and curses, and by hatred of such extortions.

And, he concluded gloomily, 'I pray that my supreme lord may not in the end incur the sword of my Lord's fury', as had illustrious ancients such as Alexander the Great and Julius Caesar.[8]

While Adam Usk's Welsh credentials and tempestuous career are reasonably well documented, not least by himself, virtually nothing is known of John Strecche beyond the fact that he was a canon at the Augustinian priory of St Mary's, Kenilworth, during the first quarter of the fifteenth century. His short Latin narrative of Henry V's reign, however, was probably written very soon after the king's death and it does provide a largely independent account of events. Also, as a canon of Kenilworth and a regular visitor to the local castle, he must have had ample opportunity to hear news, gossip and rumour about the king, politics and the French war. Kenilworth was a favourite residence of Henry V outside London; he stayed at the castle on several occasions both before and after his accession to the throne; and, no doubt, at such times the royal entourage proved a major source of information for John Strecche. As a result his chronicle, despite a certain credulity when it came to courtly tittle-tattle and colourful stories, is not without value. For Henry V himself he had nothing but praise, describing him, indeed, as a Paris in eloquence, a Julius in intellect and a Soloman in wisdom; as a military commander, he was far-seeing and invincible; and, in battle, proved himself as strong as Achilles and as fearless as Hector. Patriotic Strecche certainly was and, as a result, inclined to let his fervour colour his judgement when recounting the king's campaigns in France. He particularly enjoyed retailing sensational stories, probably learned from members of the king's household when resident at Kenilworth, such as the tale of Henry V's narrow escape from death at the siege of Louviers in June 1418:

> ...while the king was standing talking in the earl [of Salisbury's] tent, near the central post, he bent his head, and a gunner from within the town at that moment unleashed a stone which shattered the pole but, thanks be to God, the king escaped. Then the king gratefully gave thanks to God Who had saved him.

And it is Strecche who provides the fullest early record of the insulting present of tennis balls allegedly sent to Henry V by the dauphin prior to his first invasion of France. Henry's response, he tells us, was to address these 'short, wise and seemly words' to his companions:

> If God wills, and if I remain in good health, within a few months I shall play with such balls in the Frenchmen's own streets that they will stop joking, and for their mocking game win nothing but grief. And if they sleep too long on their pillows, I shall wake them from their slumbers by hammering on their doors at dawn.

Good stories both but do they, and several others the chronicler tells, bear the stamp of truth?[9]

Another minor Latin chronicle of interest for Henry V is that written by a Benedictine monk of Westminster who, although anonymous, may well have held office in the royal household: in particular, he provides a splendidly vivid picture of the king's character and appearance at the time of his accession. Thomas Otterbourne's chronicle, probably written by an obscure northerner in the early fifteenth century, provides a further account of Henry V's reign (ending in 1420) but, unfortunately, most of its content comes from Thomas Walsingham. And as for Latin chroniclers at work many years after the king's death, such as a monk at Crowland abbey in Lincolnshire who probably wrote of 'this most able prince' no earlier than the 1470s, their narratives are even more obviously derivative.[10]

The most significant developments in historical writing in early fifteenth-century England came in London with the emergence of the vernacular *Brut* chronicle and the series of civic histories known collectively as the London chronicles. So called because its narrative began with Brutus, legendary founder of an ancient British kingdom, the *Brut* had several anonymous authors, survives in a number of manuscript versions and, when William Caxton published his *Chronicles of England* in 1480, became our first printed history. Sophisticated it is not but popular and widely read it clearly was and, for Henry V's life and reign, it certainly has considerable value. In dealing with the second Lancastrian king, moreover, the *Brut* is nothing if not patriotic, even eulogistic: he was 'a worthy king, a gracious man and a great conqueror', declares a version of the chronicle compiled about 1430; his claims to French territory were by 'rightful heritage and true title of conquest'; and, at Agincourt, God Himself was Henry V's guide, 'saving him and all his people from his enemy's intent'. The *Brut* clearly draws, from time to time, on newsletters, ballads and the reports of eyewitnesses, as well as being rich in colourful stories, whether based on truth or legend. For instance, the chronicle makes much of the notion that, after his accession, not only did Henry V make a complete break with the 'wild company' of his youth but also now dismissed many of those 'who had aided and consented to his wildness'. Following his capture of Rouen in January 1419, so one compiler reported, the poor of the city 'welcomed this excellent prince and king' since he showed 'more pity and compassion' to them than had a thousand of their own nation, while another author (albeit one not writing until the end of the 1470s) tells an even more splendid tale. Very early in his reign, so this story has it, Henry V learned of a fierce feud between two northern knights which had resulted in many deaths; promptly summoning them to his presence at Windsor, he declared that unless they settled their quarrel peacefully by the time he had eaten a dish of oysters both would be hanged! And, according to another version of the *Brut*, the sudden death of Henry V, 'once the glory' of his age, now became no less than 'the grief of the world'.[11]

By the early fifteenth century London chronicles, too, were beginning to be written in the vernacular rather than Latin. Closely related to the *Brut*, and happily lifting material from each other as well as drawing on proclamations, newsletters, ballads and the like, such chronicles are almost always anonymous and clearly written for a London audience. Unfortunately, even the most nearly contemporary of them are of only limited value for Henry V: they tend to be at their best when dealing with events in and around London and, of course, the second Lancastrian king spent well over half his reign abroad campaigning in France. Perhaps the best of them are the short chronicle known as *Cleopatra CIV* and the much more substantial *Gregory's Chronicle* (so dubbed, misleadingly, by its nineteenth-century editor). The anonymous author of *Gregory's Chronicle*, perhaps writing about Henry V in the 1440s, certainly brought in a notably positive verdict on the 'good and noble king' and 'flower of chivalry', proudly listing the many abbeys, castles and towns 'our full excellent lord won and conquered in Normandy and France'. *Cleopatra CIV*, although probably not written much earlier than 1450 (it ends in 1443), does provide a largely independent narrative for the years 1415 and 1416. At the siege of Harfleur, its author tells us, the king made a point of personally encouraging his forces:

> Fellows, be of good cheer! Save your energy, keep cool and maintain your calm for, with the love of God, we shall have good tidings.

Following the town's surrender, moreover, Henry V:

> ...kept his estate as royally as ever did any king. Never did any Christian king seat himself so royally and lordly as he.

Prior to Agincourt, in similar vein, he declared that, 'as I am true king and knight, never shall England pay ransom for me', before exhorting his men to behave like faithful Englishmen who 'would never flee from any battle'. And even this normally all too prosaic chronicler could not resist breaking into verse when describing Henry V's great triumph over the French.[12]

Fifteenth-century popular perceptions of Henry V are best captured in contemporary and near-contemporary English ballads and poems. Early in the reign anonymous versifiers certainly had high expectations of the new king, anticipating, in particular, a more vigorous enforcement of the rule of law and the ending of disorder, the rigorous defence of England's borders, and the securing of the seas. Several contemporary poems enthusiastically supported Lancastrian dynastic claims in France and the use of military power to enforce English rights there. The victorious Agincourt campaign, not least Henry V's personal resolution and bravery, and his triumphant return home, inspired a further group of ballads, most notably the so-called Agincourt Carol:

> Our king went forth to Normandy,
> With grace and might of chivalry;
> There God for him wrought marvellously...
> In Agincourt field he fought manly;
> Through grace of God most mighty...
> May gracious God now save our king,

His people and his well-willing.
Give him good life and good ending...[13]

Perhaps the most remarkable of all the popular ballads of Henry V's reign was inspired by the siege and subsequent fall of Normandy's capital to the king in 1418/9. Unusually, we even know the name of the poet: John Page, a soldier who was present throughout the siege of Rouen and penned his lively and detailed verse report of its progress and outcome between March 1421 and Henry V's death. He also vividly encapsulated contemporary attitudes towards the king:

> ...he is king most excellent
> And unto none other obedient,
> That liveth here on earth by right
> But only unto God almight,
> Within his own, emperor,
> And also king and conqueror...
> He is manful while the war does last,
> And merciful when war is past;
> Manhood, meekness, both wit and grace,
> He has, content, in little space...[14]

By the early fifteenth century so-called 'Mirrors for Princes' literature had very much come into vogue and such manuals of advice and example for rulers, highlighting the values Christian princes ought to cultivate and offering practical guidance on matters of statecraft and the conduct of warfare, were given a hefty boost by Henry V. Even before he ascended the throne, he commissioned John Lydgate to produce his *Troy Book* in 1412 while, in the same year, Thomas Hoccleve specifically dedicated *The Regement (Rule) of Princes* to him. Significantly, Hoccleve, a courtly poet and clerk of the privy seal, completed his *Regement* in 1411, at a time when Henry of Monmouth was enjoying a premature period of political power; he acknowledged that, already, the Prince of Wales had little need of an advice manual; and he may, like the anonymous author of the *Gesta Henrici Quinti* a few years later, have deliberately sought to reflect the young Henry's own views and preferred image of himself. Certainly, he particularly stressed the need for a prince to be a pillar of Christian orthodoxy and champion of the church against heresy; if required, he should aspire to perform great deeds of arms although, since war is so often undertaken 'to win worldly wealth', when possible he ought 'to purchase peace by way of marriage'; and, above all, he must strive to govern his people justly by enforcing the law and exercising the prerogative of mercy. Not surprisingly, he greeted Henry V's accession to the throne in 1413 with enthusiasm and, indeed, over the next couple of years wrote a cluster of political poems reinforcing his earlier manual. John Lydgate, a monk of Bury St Edmunds and (like Hoccleve) a courtly poet, undertook to compose his *Troy Book* in 1412 so that 'high and low' might openly know the 'noble story' of the siege and destruction of Troy 'in our tongue'. More than that, Lydgate explained, he intended that the present generation should have the opportunity of reading about great deeds of the past in English so as to encourage their own martial endeavours. For the next eight years he laboured at the work, finally presenting the completed product to Henry V on his return from France in 1421, noting that, since the king's sterling efforts had apparently assured that henceforth 'England and France may be all one', he is not only a 'worthy king of wisdom and renown' but 'our sovereign lord and prince of peace'. Soon afterwards Lydgate began work on his *Siege of Thebes*, an ambitious poem written in 1421/2. While firmly asserting Henry V's right to rule in France by means of celebratory references to the Treaty of Troyes, however, his overriding purpose here was to plead for peace since war, all too often resulting from ambition and greed, can, if not controlled, end in the destruction of everything.[15]

The verse chronicle composed by John Harding and presented by its author to Henry VI in 1457 also has a clearly didactic aim. A former soldier who probably saw action at both the siege of Harfleur and battle of Agincourt, Harding obviously admired Henry V greatly as a noble and chivalric prince who not only regained his rightful inheritance in France but also united the two kingdoms under his own rule. For Harding, however, 'the root and head of his great conquest' lay in the fact that he so rigorously 'kept the law and peace' in England. His prime objective in writing, indeed, was to urge Henry VI to emulate his father, reward Harding himself for past services to the Lancastrian dynasty and, above all, invade and conquer Scotland! Even more overtly didactic was the antiquarian William Worcester: first composing his *Book of Noblesse* in the early 1450s to whip up support for vigorous and effective military campaigning across the Channel, he then completely revised his text for presentation to Edward IV when that king mounted a major expedition to France in 1475. Specifically, he urged Edward IV to fulfil the obligations of his noble rank, emulate the feats of arms performed by his ancestors and reconquer what was rightfully his. Henry V, predictably, is cited as an excellent role model. In particular, Worcester highlighted the 'deeds of arms' performed by 'that victorious prince', personally present as he was at many sieges, assaults and battles from the second year of his reign, who:

> ...conquered the town of Harfleur, and won both the Duchy of Normandy and, after, the realm of France, conquered and brought in subjection and won by his great manhood, with the noble power of his lords and help of his commons, and so overlaid the mighty royal power of France.[16]

No doubt to Worcester's disgust, Edward IV's campaign proved an inglorious affair. Within a decade, moreover, William Caxton was bemoaning the decline of chivalric practices, and once again, singing the praises of Henry V:

> ...behold that victorious and noble king, Harry the Fifth, and the captains under him, his noble brethren, [Thomas Montagu] Earl of Salisbury, and many others whose names shine gloriously by their virtuous noblesse and acts that they did in honour of the order of chivalry.[17]

Most new material on the life and times of Henry V that has come to light in recent years has been gleaned from the vast bulk of surviving early fifteenth-century records. Pride of place must go to central government or public records, particularly the archives of great departments of state such as the Chancery and Exchequer. Chancery rolls have proved a veritable mine of information for Henry V's political patronage, while Exchequer records provide copious evidence about the financing and organisation of the king's military campaigns. Of great value, too, are the muniments accumulated by the court of King's Bench, particularly for criminal justice, law and order during Henry V's reign. The records of parliament, unfortunately, are rather sparse but they do include transcriptions of speeches delivered, on the king's behalf, by his chancellors at the opening of such assemblies. Their tone tends to be deliberately inspirational, presenting the familiar image of Henry V as God's chosen agent and clearly designed to maximise enthusiasm in parliament for his endeavours to follow the paths of justice both at home and abroad. Not dissimilar are a series of sermons preached during the king's reign, probably by a Benedictine monk, portraying Henry as a 'celestial knight' and 'peerless prince' successfully fighting God's battles, even, in 1421, as the 'master-mariner' who had deliberately 'exposed himself for the rights of his realm and the safety of his ship'. More personal glimpses of the king can be found in his own letters, such as that despatched to the mayor and aldermen of London following the surrender of Harfleur in September 1415:

> We wish you to give humble thanks to Our Almighty God for this news, and hope, by the fine power, good labour and diligence of our faithful people overseas, to do our duty to achieve as soon as possible our rights in this area.[18]

Increasingly, too, as the reign progressed, Henry V's letters tend to be written in English, occasionally in the king's own hand; while, no doubt as part of a conscious policy projecting notions of Englishness and the English nation, he actively encouraged the widest possible use of the vernacular in preference to French or Latin.

3

FIFTEENTH-CENTURY
FRENCH VERDICTS

Contemporary and near-contemporary French commentators, on the face of it, had little reason to pen favourable verdicts on a king who won a spectacular victory in the field at Agincourt, conquered much of north-western France and, but for his untimely death in 1422, seemed destined to succeed to the Valois throne. Yet, by and large, they respected, even admired, both Henry V himself and his achievements. The fact that he so regularly defeated their countrymen did not blind them to his commendable qualities and the list is impressive indeed: honourable, upright, prudent, resolute, chivalric, courageous and, as the staunch Valois loyalist Jean Chartier put it, 'a subtle conqueror and a skilful warrior'. Above all, even normally critical chroniclers such as Jean Juvenal des Ursins and Georges Chastellain enthusiastically highlighted Henry V's zeal for justice and impartiality in its administration. Such plaudits are not too difficult to understand. No doubt they reflect, in part at least, the second Lancastrian's powerful propaganda and image-projection in France no less than England; moreover, since French defeats could be rendered more palatable if Henry V really was so outstandingly virtuous a man and so exceptionally gifted a general, they found a receptive audience. Men like Jean Juvenal des Ursins probably had a further didactic purpose in mind as well: graphically to demonstrate just how dire had been the consequences for France of Charles VI's personal and regal shortcomings, Armagnac/Burgundian feuding and the sheer lack of any spirit of consistent aristocratic resistance to English imperialism.

Many fifteenth-century French chroniclers and commentators, even reluctant admirers of Henry V's military persona, prowess and achievements, nevertheless found plenty to criticise in the king and his behaviour. An anonymous chronicler of Saint-Denis, for instance, tells us that he 'worried little about divine wrath' and 'when his soldiers had looted with their sacrilegious hands churches consecrated to God, he would send home to England the relics they had stolen'; while Jean Juvenal des Ursins composed a treatise deliberately refuting Lancastrian claims to the Valois throne. As for the English themselves, a patriotic French tract dating from about 1419 declared venomously:

> They are a race of people accursed, denying virtue and justice, ravishing wolves, proud, pompous, deceitful hypocrites without conscience, tyrants and persecutors of Christians, who drink and swallow down human blood, like birds of prey who live by robbery at the expense of their simple and well-disposed neighbours.[19]

Burgundian chroniclers, while often adopting a pro-English line when covering the period of Anglo-Burgundian alliance (1419–1435), tended to mix praise and blame in their judgements of Henry V himself. Enguerrand de Monstrelet, for instance, while stressing that the king was very wise and capable, possessed an iron will and made great conquests, also empathised the fear he inspired and his merciless punishment of anyone who disobeyed him. Jean Waurin penned an almost identical verdict. As for Georges Chastellain, although a fierce critic of Henry V's tyrannical rule, even he dubbed him 'the prince of justice' and ruefully admitted that his valour 'shone forth as befitted a mighty conqueror'.

For several centuries the abbey of Saint-Denis, near Paris, had sustained a semi-official Latin chronicle of the French monarchy, court and government, a tradition still being vigorously maintained by an anonymous monk in the early fifteenth century. Notably well-informed about recent events in France, not least Henry V's campaigns and their impact, the chronicler provides an account that is both detailed and judicious. While always treating the Valois king Charles VI and his family with respect, moreover, he nevertheless recognised their shortcomings and, even more, the sheer irresponsibility of the early fifteenth-century French nobility. His sober and, indeed, didactic approach is nicely illustrated by his remark that, although he cannot contemplate Agincourt (an event which 'covers France and its people with shame and confusion') without shedding tears:

> ...I will acquit myself of my duties as a historian, however painful it is to me, and will transmit for posterity an account of that sad day so that such faults can be avoided in the future.

The Monk of Saint-Denis' verdict on Henry V himself is perhaps the most balanced of all the French estimates we have:

> No prince in his time appeared more capable to subdue and conquer a country, by the wisdom of his government, by his prudence and by the other qualities with which he was endowed, although the dissensions and discords which reigned among the French princes had powerfully assisted him in realising his projects of conquest.

The chronicler also reports, interestingly, what he has heard of the king from others:

> French prisoners [who] got to know the king's character when in captivity said that the prince, whose appearance and conversation gave every indication of pride and who was generally supposed to be very vindictive, nonetheless behaved in a way worthy of a king and, while showing himself pitiless towards rebels, treated those who obeyed him with the utmost tact and was anxious they should be shown respect and kindness. He knew how many princes have extended their dominions by that sort of behaviour.

He also tells us that, in 1418, French envoys found Henry V a prince of distinguished appearance and commanding stature, yet also notably courteous and generous; moreover, although his expression:

> ...seemed to hint at pride, he nevertheless made it a point of honour to treat everybody, of whatever rank or degree, with the utmost affability... A scrupulous dispenser of justice, he knew how to exalt the lowly and abase the mighty.

When besieging a castle, however, the king proved himself anything but affable:

> Anyone who rejected his summons [to surrender], and who fell into his hands bearing arms, was put to death as guilty of *lèse-majesté*, having first seen him loot and plunder their possessions. If they were young, not yet old enough to bear arms, or aged, they had to suffer cruel tortures before being chased into exile.

As for his own troops, he firmly discouraged 'vile prostitutes' plying their trade amongst them since 'the pleasures of Venus' might all too easily 'weaken and soften victorious Mars'! Once Henry V had proved his military superiority, though, the chronicler frankly acknowledged the fact:

> If he is the strongest, all right then! Let him be our master, just so long as we can live in peace, safety and plenty.[20]

The Monk of Saint-Denis, despite his status as a semi-official court chronicler, brought in a remarkably even-handed verdict on Henry V, his campaigns and his achievements; Jean Juvenal des Ursins, by contrast, never attempted to disguise his powerfully anti-Burgundian stance. An advocate in Paris at the time of Agincourt, he fled south to Poitiers when the Burgundians entered the city in May 1418, joined the Dauphin Charles's service and, as a staunch supporter of the future Charles VII, eventually became a bishop and, in 1449, archbishop of Rheims. And certainly, by the time he put pen to paper years after Henry V's death, his recollections of earlier events were very much coloured by his hostility to Burgundy and devotion to Charles VII. This is graphically illustrated by his insistence, largely on the basis of mere hearsay, that the dauphin had been entirely innocent of any involvement in the murder of John the Fearless Duke of Burgundy in September 1419. Clearly, too, he regarded the Treaty of Troyes as a disgraceful sell-out to Henry V and declared that, as a result, 'all the country' north of the Loire became 'black and obscene' since its inhabitants had 'put themselves into the obedience of the English'; France south of the Loire, by contrast, remained 'pure and clear' in its loyalty to the dauphin. Henry V himself Jean Juvenal des Ursins could not help

admiring as a courageous warrior and exemplary administrator of justice who, 'without respect for persons, gave as good justice to the mean
as to the great': as a result, he declared, the king was both 'feared and
revered by all his relatives, neighbours and subjects'. No prince in his
time was 'more fitted to conquer' than he, indeed, or 'guard what he
had conquered', not least on account of his ruthless single-mindedness.
During his Normandy campaign, the chronicler tells us, the king's
response to complaints about his tactics on one occasion was to declare
that 'war without fire is like sausages without mustard'; while, on
another, he incarcerated prisoners in deep ditches and, 'when they
asked for food and screamed from hunger, people threw straw down to
them and called them dogs': however, he added, such behaviour was 'a
great disgrace to the king of England'.[21]

Most French commentators, not surprisingly, were less concerned
with Henry V personally than the Armagnac/Burgundian feuding that
facilitated his invasions, the king's campaigns and their impact on
north-western France, and the significance and consequences of the
Treaty of Troyes. Supporters of the Valois dynasty, particularly those
associated with the Dauphin Charles, tended to be especially critical
of French military failure and the dire implications for the country of
English conquest and settlement. The Norman Jean Chartier, for
instance, while respecting Henry V's courage, military skill and capacity for administration, nevertheless judged him a harsh, even cruel,
dispenser of justice. The English, he declared, occupied the French
realm 'without reason'; the Treaty of Troyes unleashed 'a storm of misery on us'; and swearing an oath of allegiance to an alien invader, even
a 'subtle conqueror' such as Henry V, was 'degrading and criminal'. No
wonder so many wept at Charles VI's death in 1422, as they contemplated 'the evils that might come upon them by changing their natural
lord' and the prospect of rule 'by foreign nations and customs which
was, and is, against reason and right, to the total destruction of the
people and realm of France'. Chartier's brother Alain, a firm Valois
loyalist who served both Charles VI and Charles VII, was vehemently
anti-Burgundian and highly critical of the English as well. In his political tract Le Quadrilogue Invectif, penned in 1422, he reflected bitterly
on the present condition of the French kingdom, clearly hoping
thereby to rally support for the Valois dynasty. Alain Chartier was particularly critical of the French nobility's contribution to the nation's

ruin, blaming their 'lack of decision and lack of courage' rather than English prowess for 'our enemies' victory: a 'foreign king', in fact, has been able to 'gain glory from our shame and ignominy, plunder our people, and cast scorn on our exploits and courage'. As for the English settlement of his native Normandy, it was 'an outrageous and disloyal folly'. No less patriotic, and indignant, was Robert Blondel, whose family had chosen exile during the English occupation of the Cotentin and lost lands there (not restored until 1450). Moreover, in his *Complaint of True Frenchmen*, written not long after the Treaty of Troyes was sealed, he, too, exhorted his fellow country-men to reject Anglo-Burgundian rule and support the Valois cause. 'Captive Normandy', he lamented, 'lies under the yolk of the leopard' (Henry V) and, as a result, there are many 'who have fled the soil of their fathers', even 'despaired and died', ground down by the 'sheer weight of tyranny' resulting from Henry V's rule. The impact of Armagnac/Burgundian rivalry, and English conquest, on Paris and its surrounding region is graphically conveyed by an anonymous Parisian chronicler, probably writing piecemeal over a period of almost half a century between 1405 and 1449. But for the civil war prevailing in France, he declared, Henry V would never have dared invade the country and he certainly portrayed the English, 'our ancient and mor-tal enemy', in no very favourable light. Like Alain Chartier and Robert Blondel, however, he was even more critical of the French nobility and the fact that France's leaders, far from uniting society in resistance to the invader, fatally divided it. The Armagnacs, in particu-lar, attracted his venom; but for them, he believed:

> ...Normandy would still have been French, the noble blood of France would not have been spilt nor the lords of the kingdom taken away into exile, nor the battle lost, nor would so many good men have been killed on that dreadful day of Agincourt where the king lost so many of his true and loyal friends, had it not been for the pride of this wretched name, Armagnac.[22]

By the 1430s the Norman priest Pierre Cochon, probably resident in Rouen at the time, was both anti-English and critical of Henry V: the king, he reported, 'never slept and looked continually to his own interests'; the French defeat at Agincourt was 'the ugliest and most wretched event that had happened in France over the last thousand years'; and, as a result of his victory, Henry V's 'pride was greatly boosted by having such good fortune'. The Valois loyalist Perceval de Cagny, also writing in the 1430s, deliberately set himself the task of recording 'a little of the misfortunes, wars and pestilences which had happened in France before his days and those of which he had personal experience'. Yet, although hardly sympathetic towards the English, he did regard Henry V as an honourable fighter, stressed the speed of the king's conquests, and paid tribute to the impartial justice he adminis-tered. Pierre Fenin, who hailed from the Burgundian-dominated province of Artois and probably penned his *Memoirs* shortly before Perceval de Cagny began work on his chronicle, was clearly an out-and-out admirer of Henry as:

> …a prince of high understanding and great will to keep justice. As a result the poor folk loved him above all others. For he was prone and careful to preserve the lesser folk, and to protect them from the vio-lence and wrongs that most of the nobles had done to them.

Moreover, once he gained control of Paris, since 'he had justice strictly observed and duly rendered by all', he soon won the obedience of its citizens. As for Thomas Basin, few historians of Charles VII's reign had better credentials for chronicling the events of his times. Born in Normandy in 1412, he studied canon law in Paris prior to becoming a professor at the university of Caen (founded by the English) and, a few years later, bishop of Lisieux (also in English-occupied Normandy). When Charles VII put an end to Lancastrian rule in his native duchy in 1450, however, he soon embraced Valois governance and, indeed, became a royal councillor. Some twenty years later, probably in 1471/2, he wrote his *Histoire de Charles VII*. As a child Basin had had first-hand experience of the traumas of Henry V's conquests and, although he believed the English had restored a measure of peace and justice to Normandy in the 1420s, he declared that, in 1417, the mere mention of Englishmen had inspired terror there, as 'wild beasts, gigantic and fero-cious' invaders who would 'throw themselves' on the Normans and 'devour them'. Of Henry V's last illness, moreover, he recorded colour-fully that:

...many say that he was struck down with this malady because he had ordered, or had allowed, his troops to sack and devastate the oratory of St Fiacre and its glebe near Meaux. Indeed, one often calls his disease, which swells the belly and legs hideously, St Fiacre's Evil.[23]

Of all later medieval chroniclers, none has been more influential than the Burgundian Jean Froissart, whose magisterial narrative of England, France and the Hundred Years War c.1327–1399 was deliberately conceived as a celebration of, and perpetual memorial to, the great men and chivalric exploits of his age:

> In order that the honourable enterprises, noble adventures and deeds of arms which took place during the wars waged by France and England should be fittingly related and preserved for posterity, so that brave men should be inspired thereby to follow such examples, I wish to place on record these matters of great renown.

During the fifteenth century the Burgundian court became the most brilliant in north-western Europe and Duke Philip the Good (1419–1467) its brightest star. Not surprisingly, perhaps, it spawned a series of further Burgundian chroniclers determined to continue the tradition of chivalric historical writing Jean Froissart (who himself died shortly before Henry V succeeded to his father's throne) had pioneered. Most notably, Enguerrand de Monstrelet, Georges Chastellain, Jean Le Fevre and Jean Waurin not only served the Burgundian duke but also, like Froissart, enthusiastically set out to investigate and record for posterity the deeds of the great. As Monstrelet himself put it:

> There cannot be any more suitable or worthy occupation than handing down to posterity the grand and magnanimous feats of arms and the inestimable subtleties of war which have been performed by valiant men [for] the instruction and information of those who in a just cause may be desirous of honourably exercising their prowess in arms.

Monstrelet, moreover, took considerable pains to get his facts right:

> I enquired of kings of arms, and the heralds and pursuivants of several lords and countries, who by virtue of their office should be well

informed and able to give a true account of events during the wars in France. Having received their information, often repeated, and putting aside all doubtful reports, and those disproved by later accounts, I spent a considerable time in weighing them up and counterchecking them for truth.

Chastellain, too, was a conscientious memorialist, while Le Fevre and Waurin drew extensively on both their own knowledge and experience and the earlier work of Monstrelet.

Certainly, as far as Henry V is concerned, Enguerrand de Monstrelet is much the most important of the fifteenth-century Burgundian court chroniclers. Born in the early 1390s, he probably experienced military campaigning in the 1420s, served Philip the Good Duke of Burgundy from the mid-1430s, compiled his chronicle in the 1440s, and died in 1453. Although very much a Burgundian by loyalty (formally presenting his chronicle to Philip the Good in 1447, indeed), when writing of Henry V and his times Monstrelet's account is clearly coloured, too, by his dislike of the Armagnacs and admiration for the English king's single-mindedness and ruthless determination. From the very beginning, he tells us, Henry V made it plain that, if his just demands were not met, he would not only invade France but 'despoil the whole of that kingdom' and, by the sword, deprive Charles VI of his crown; once embarked on the conquest of Normandy, he 'conquered towns and castles at his pleasure, for scarcely any resistance was made against him, owing to the intestine divisions of France' (as well as sheer 'fear of King Henry'); and, following the Treaty of Troyes, he controlled the Valois king just as he pleased, thereby causing 'much sorrow in the hearts of all Frenchmen'. As for the English king himself, he was 'very wise and capable in everything he undertook', possessed 'an iron will' and 'made greater conquests' in France 'than any before him for many years past'. Yet this same ruler would not allow his subjects to look him full in the face when addressing him and, indeed, was:

...so feared by his princes and knights, captains and all kinds of people, that there was no one, however close or dear to him, who was not afraid to go against his orders, especially those of his own kingdom of England. Everyone under his rule, in France and England alike, whatever his rank, was reduced to this same state of obedience.

And the chief reason for this, Monstrelet added, was that 'anyone who thwarted his will and disobeyed his orders was most cruelly punished and received no mercy'.[24]

Georges Chastellain, official chronicler and staunch defender of Burgundy and its court, campaigned with Philip the Good as a young man, served as a ducal councillor and met many of the famous people of his day. Notably well-informed on both political and military matters, his chronicle (covering the years 1419-75) provides an independent-minded if clearly pro-Burgundian judgement on Henry V and his conquests. Although one of the English king's fiercest critics, he nevertheless declared it was not his intention 'to detract from or diminish in my writings either the honour or glory of that valiant prince' in whom 'valour and courage shone forth as befitted a mighty conqueror'. Indeed, he assures us, Henry V was a 'prince of justice' who 'gave support to none out of favour, nor did he suffer wrong to go unpunished out of regard of kinship'. Yet, for Chastellain, the king was also a 'cruel man', a 'hard persecutor' and a 'tyrant'; by his hand, 'as though beneath the scourge of God', the 'noble blood of France was so piteously slain at Agincourt'; and, in 1422, despite promising to honour his father-in-law Charles VI as long as he lived, he had made 'a figurehead of him, a cipher who could do nothing'. Indeed, Henry V had become:

> ...a foe to every brave and valiant man in the realm, and would have liked to exterminate them all, whether in battle or by some other cunning means under a pretext of justice. Even those who were now fighting by his side and through whom he ruled and controlled France, the Burgundians, he wished to supplant and keep down in subjection: he wanted the very name and race to be extinguished in order that he might live there alone with his Englishmen.[25]

Although Chastellain covers much the same ground as Monstrelet when recounting the events of Henry V's time, he was no plagiarist. Jean Le Fevre of St Remy and Jean Waurin, by contrast, were deeply influenced by him: indeed, arguably, they merely supplemented what he had already written. Le Fevre, it is true, seems to have accompanied the English army (probably in a heraldic capacity) on its march from Harfleur to Agincourt in 1415; he may have visited England in 1416;

and, in 1431, he was appointed king of arms to Philip the Good's recently established chivalric Order of the Golden Fleece. Unfortunately, he only began to compile his chronicle some thirty years later, and then mainly, so he tells us, 'to escape laziness'. On Henry V he adds little to Monstrelet's narrative although, interestingly, does remark approvingly, when describing the king's siege of Meaux in 1421/2, that 'it was a pretty thing to see'. Jean Waurin, too, drew heavily on Monstrelet and, also like Le Fevre, had seen military action at first hand: indeed, he was probably a page in the French army at the time of Agincourt, fought with the English in the 1420s and, later, against them as a firm Burgundian partisan. Thereafter, he served at the Burgundian court and on various ducal embassies; he visited England in 1467; and, clearly, he had a particular interest in English affairs. Unfortunately, he probably did not put pen to paper on Henry V until more than forty years after the king's death, but, when he did, he certainly presented an interestingly mixed picture. Closely following Monstrelet, he reported that Henry V was 'much feared and dreaded by his nobles, knights and captains, and people of every degree' because 'all those who disobeyed his orders or infringed his edicts' were 'put to death without mercy', and he clearly disapproved of the king's massacre of French prisoners 'in cold blood' at Agincourt. However, he also judged Henry 'a most clever man' who was 'expert in everything he undertook'; he believed the French wars occupied his mind both night and day; he praised his rigorous military discipline; and he concluded that, in the end, his territorial conquests were greater than those achieved by any of his predecessors. 'Even now', he declared in the 1460s, 'as much honour and reverence is paid at his tomb as if it were certain he had become a saint in heaven'.[26]

4

TUDOR JUDGEMENTS

When Henry V suddenly succumbed to disease and death in 1422, his reputation was high and his infant son Henry VI, under the terms of the Treaty of Troyes, soon became king of both England and France. Yet, by the mid-1450s, not only had the Lancastrian empire across the Channel been lost but England itself had been plunged into civil war. During the Wars of the Roses, moreover, Lancastrian and Yorkist dynastic rivalry had dire consequences indeed: Henry VI was deposed in 1461 and Edward IV seized the throne; less than a decade later, in 1470, Edward IV was deprived of his crown and Henry VI restored; just six months after that, in the spring of 1471, Edward IV regained control of the kingdom and Henry VI met a mysterious death in the Tower of London; following the Yorkist king's own demise in 1483, his brother usurped the throne as Richard III and, probably, engineered the murder of his young nephews Edward V and Richard Duke of York soon after; and, in August 1485, Richard III himself bit the dust on the battlefield at Bosworth and the Tudor dynasty triumphed in the person of Henry VII. By then over a dozen battles had been fought, many eminent men had perished either in the field or by execution, and large numbers of ordinary folk, too, had lost their lives. Not surprisingly, all this was seized upon by early Tudor propagandists anxious, as they were, to justify the *new* dynasty's rightful possession of the crown. Indeed, there soon developed a powerful tradition of the Tudors as saviours of England from the chaos and confusion of the Wars of the Roses; Henry VII, as the agent of divine retribution who put an end to decades of bloodshed, deliberately promoted dynastic harmony by marrying Edward IV's eldest daughter Elizabeth of York; and Henry VIII, a product of that match, became the veritable symbol of nationhood and national unity. Fifteenth-century kings, by contrast, were fair game for vigorous denigration: Henry IV as the usurper who unjustly deposed and murdered Richard II; Henry VI as the pious but politically naïve ruler who not only failed in France but plunged his country into civil war; and Richard III as a physically deformed and mentally warped tyrant who fully deserved his bloody end at Bosworth. Edward IV, as Elizabeth of York's father and, in some respects, a worthy precursor of Henry VII, got a more positive write-up, but only Henry V attracted out-and-out praise and admiration.

Sixteenth-century chroniclers and historians, in fact, tended to portray Henry V as the very embodiment of heroism, patriotism and nationalism. As a king who not only revelled in chivalry and feats of arms but also led his people to honourable victory over England's traditional enemy, he provided an irresistible role model of past greatness from whose behaviour the Tudor present could clearly benefit enormously: indeed, he became a veritable stereotype of royal purity, prowess and perspicacity. The Warwickshire antiquarian John Rous, who compiled a *History of the Kings of England* shortly before his death in 1491, certainly believed Henry V deserved perpetual praise for his valour, wisdom and resolution in conquering Normandy, marrying Catherine of Valois and becoming *de facto* ruler of France. A prominent London draper, Robert Fabian, who put together his *New Chronicles of England and of France* during the early years of the sixteenth century, particularly latched on to the notion of Henry V's dramatic transformation once he became king:

> This man, before the death of his father, gave himself over to vice and insolency, and drew to him riotous and wildly inclined people; but, after he was admitted to the rule of the land, he suddenly became a new man and turned all that wildness to sobriety and seriousness, and vice into constant virtue.

As for the Italian humanist historian Polydore Vergil, commissioned by Henry VII to write a comprehensive narrative survey of England's history from ancient times to the present in 1507, he firmly believed history 'displays eternally to the living those events which should be an example and those which should be a warning'. Not surprisingly, then, he portrayed Henry V as a paragon of piety and patriotism, fully convinced of his God-justified right to the French throne, while the 'glorious battle of Agincourt' was rightly regarded by the English people as 'amongst their foremost victories'.[27]

Henry VIII's accession to the English throne in 1509 proved seminal for Henry V's future reputation. Not only was the new Tudor king captivated by his ancestor's self-proclaimed image of heroic kingship, he himself clearly aspired to be seen, and remembered, in similar terms. Throughout his reign he styled himself king of France and, at any rate in his early years, dreamed of recovering England's French inheritance and, in the process, covering himself in glory and emulating the military achievements of his Lancastrian predecessor. In the summer of 1513, indeed, he invaded north-eastern France with a force of over 30,000 men, won a minor cavalry engagement (the so-called battle of the Spurs), and even captured Therouanne and Tournai. Although a pale shadow of the Agincourt campaign, and never consolidated by further warfare and conquest, this expedition certainly boosted Henry VIII's ego and, more importantly, stimulated the compilation of a *First English Life of Henry V.*

The anonymous author of the *Life* commenced writing early in the summer of 1513 and completed his work by the autumn of 1514; most of the narrative is a free translation of Tito Livio's *Vita Henrici Quinti*, although the translator also drew on Monstrelet, a version of the *Brut* and now lost reminiscences of James Butler fourth Earl of Ormonde; and, not only did he dedicate the manuscript to Henry VIII, he had a clear didactic purpose in mind as well. Specifically, he tells us in a prologue, he is writing so that the Tudor king, on the eve of invading France himself, might 'by the knowledge and sight' of this work be 'provoked in his war' to emulate 'the noble and chivalrous acts of this so noble, so virtuous and so excellent a prince' Henry V and, by so doing, achieve 'like honour, fame and victory'. He particularly commends:

> ...the virtuous manners, victorious conquests and excellent maxims
> of that most renowned prince in his days, King Henry the Fifth, of
> whose superior in all nobleness, manhood, and virtue, to my knowl-
> edge, it is not read nor heard amongst princes of England since

William of Normandy obtained the government of the realm by conquest.

Moreover, 'pride and glory had no place' in his heart; from the time of his father's death until his own marriage 'he never had carnal knowledge of women'; and, when pursuing his desire for justice in France, 'the hand of God was ever with him'. All in all, Henry V was:

> ...marvellously wise and circumspect, strong, hardy and of high courage: for the little time he reigned he achieved many and great conquests in France, and more than any of his ancestors for a long time past.

Perhaps the most original and interesting, if also the most problematic, passages in the *First English Life* are those deriving, so its compiler tells us, from 'the report of a certain and honourable ancient person the Earl of Ormonde'. James Butler fourth Earl of Ormonde, who died in 1452, had certainly known and campaigned with Henry V and may have left a written record of personal memories directly consulted by the translator; alternatively, his source may have been the fourth earl's youngest son (the seventh earl) who was still alive in 1513. What he learned was clearly anecdotal and needs to be treated with great caution, but the Ormonde stories – not least the additional material they provide about Henry V's wild youth, his conversion to sobriety and chastity on becoming king and his behaviour when campaigning – are certainly vivid and cannot simply be ignored.[28]

Edward Hall, who died in 1547, was very much a man of his times and his *Union of the Two Noble and Illustrious Families of Lancaster and York* was clearly intended to glorify the house of Tudor, especially Henry VIII. In a chapter entitled 'The Victorious Acts of King Henry the Fifth' he concluded that, since the second Lancastrian king deliberately sought to extirpate his father's sin of usurpation in 1399 by having Richard II's remains reburied at Westminster and thereafter proved the very model of chivalric kingship, God's full vengeance on the Lancastrian dynasty was postponed for a generation. Indeed, Edward Hall's Henry V, once he has turned his back on a riotous youth and banished his evil companions from the court, becomes the 'mirror of Christendom and glory of his country', the 'flower of kings past and a glass to them that should succeed'. On the eve of Agincourt he assured his troops that 'England shall never pay ransom, nor Frenchmen triumph over me, for this day by famous death or glorious victory I will honour and obtain fame'; as for the battle itself, since the king put in God his 'whole confidence, hope and trust', the Almighty did indeed reward him with just such a glorious victory. Moreover, declared Hall enthusiastically, 'in strength and ability of body, from his youth few were comparable to him'; he abstained from 'lascivious living and blind avarice' and 'no man could be found more temperate in eating and drinking'; and, as for his courage, it was 'so constant and his heart so immutable that he cast away all fear'. All in all, Henry V was:

> ...a king whose life was immaculate and his living without spot. This king was a prince whom all men loved and none disdained. This prince was a shepherd whom his flock loved and lovingly obeyed. This shepherd was such a justiciary that no offence was unpunished nor friendship unrewarded. This justiciary was so feared that all rebellion was banished and sedition suppressed.[29]

During Elizabeth I's reign Henry V's reputation as a great English patriot, a powerful and popular ruler and, indeed, a veritable national hero was further consolidated. Soon after the queen's accession the chronicler Richard Grafton described him as 'the noblest king that ever reigned over the realm of England' while, probably in the mid-1570s, yet another Latin life of the king was penned by the Elizabethan lawyer Robert Redman. In the prologue to a work heavily dependent on Edward Hall, Redman declared, rather disingenuously, that in recent years the memory of Henry V had increasingly passed into oblivion and consciously set himself the task of remedying this, not least since Henry V's strength of character and outstanding achievements put him in strong contention for similar treatment to that enjoyed by great Roman leaders of the past. Raphael Holinshed, whose chronicle first appeared in 1578, also drew substantially on Edward Hall in a work specifically designed 'to put men in mind not to forget their country's praise'. Henry V, Holinshed and his co-authors concluded, was:

...a majesty that both lived and died a pattern in princehood, a lode-
star in honour, and a mirror of magnificence; the more deeply
lamented at his death, and famous to the world always.

John Stow, whose *Annals of England* were published in 1592, similarly
emphasised the 'exploits worthy of great renown' performed by a king
who, at Agincourt, 'never failed his men' but 'fought with his enemies
with an ardent heart, as a famished lion for his prey, receiving on his
helmet and the rest of his armour many and great strokes'.[30] And, just a
few years later, the Elizabethan picture of Henry V was to be immortalised by William Shakespeare.

5

WILLIAM SHAKESPEARE'S
HENRY V

Historical plays were clearly very popular in Elizabethan times and, as the contemporary satirist Thomas Nashe put it, they were mainly 'borrowed out of English Chronicles, wherein our forefathers' valiant acts, that have been long buried in rusty brass and worm-eaten books, are revived'. The defeat of the Spanish Armada in 1588 and the powerful patriotic sentiments unleashed by so dramatic an event permeated chronicle plays performed in the 1590s and ensured enthusiastic London audiences. Since this nevertheless proved a turbulent war-torn decade, Henry V, in particular, seemed to provide an admirable role model for the times, not least given the dramatic potential of semi-legendary tales of his transformation from reckless and dissolute prince to heroic, chivalric and militarily invincible king. Indeed, several plays about the second Lancastrian appear to have been staged during these years, most notably *The Famous Victories of Henry V: Containing the Honourable Battle of Agincourt*. Printed in 1598 but probably first staged a decade or more earlier, the *Famous Victories* has little to recommend it beyond the fact that the play conveniently brought together material (particularly from Holinshed's *Chronicle*) subsequently drawn on far more compellingly by William Shakespeare. Early scenes very much focus on the wild and irresponsible behaviour of Prince Hal and his worthless drinking companions, even the prince's commitment to prison following a riot in Eastcheap, until, rebuked by the sick Henry IV for 'doings that will end thy father's days', he vows that 'this day I am born new again'. Following his accession he orders his former cronies 'upon pain of death' not 'to approach my presence by ten miles space' and, for the rest of the play, devotes himself to the invasion of France, rallying his troops on the eve of Agincourt by declaring (in striking anticipation of Shakespeare):

> My Lords and loving Countrymen,
> Though we be few and they many,
> Fear not, your general is good, and God will defend you:
> Pluck up your hearts, for this day we shall either have
> A valiant victory, or an honourable death.[31]

Three Shakespearean plays cover the life and career of England's second Lancastrian king: *Henry IV Part 1*, *Henry IV Part 2* and *Henry V*. *1 Henry IV* and *2 Henry IV* were probably written, and first performed, in 1597/8, while *Henry V* was staged, as likely as not, at the newly built Globe Theatre between March and September 1599:

> Can this cockpit hold
> The vasty fields of France? Or may we cram
> Within this wooden O the very casques
> That did affright the air at Agincourt?

Although clearly familiar with *The Famous Victories of Henry V*, Shakespeare's most important source was Holinshed's *Chronicle*, available to him in its second edition (published in 1587), supplemented, in particular, by Edward Hall. Since he was writing dramas not histories, though, he was perfectly willing to take liberties with what he found in his sources. Chronology was certainly not sacrosanct nor was the telescoping of events to facilitate narrative development or heighten dramatic tension in any way out of order. In *1 Henry IV* the historical action very much revolves around rebellion culminating in the battle of Shrewsbury (1403), regardless of the complexity of events in the early part of the king's reign (although almost half the play, in fact, is given over to the reckless and dissolute behaviour of Prince Hal and his disreputable companions). The Prince of Wales and Henry Percy Earl of Northumberland's son Hotspur are portrayed as rivals of about the same age; when news of Percy's success at the battle of Homildon Hill (1402) is brought to him, Henry IV pointedly contrasts Hotspur's virtues with the prince's shortcomings; and, at Shrewsbury, Prince

Henry slays his rival in single combat: yet, in reality, Hotspur was at least twenty years older than the prince and, if he really had been slain in battle by his rival, surely this would have been specifically recorded in contemporary and near-contemporary sources. In *2 Henry IV* history is even more seriously distorted for dramatic purposes: again, a great deal of attention is devoted to Prince Harry and his Boar's Head Tavern cronies, while the last few years of the king's reign virtually disappear as Shakespeare leaps from Archbishop Scrope's rebellion in 1405 to Henry IV's last illness and death in 1413. Much of the early part of *Henry V* lacks historical authenticity too, and even more misleading is the strong impression conveyed that, as a result of the king's great victory at Agincourt, the whole of France now fell under his control. In all three plays Shakespeare certainly made the most of legendary and semi-legendary material, particularly the rich vein of stories concerning the life and behaviour of Prince Hal. Towards the end of *2 Henry IV*, for instance, there is the dramatic scene where the prince, believing his father to be dead, removes the crown from his bedside and takes it away, only to be recalled by the still living king: splendidly related by the early fifteenth-century Burgundian chronicler Enguerrand de Monstrelet, it came to Shakespeare via Hall and Holinshed. Even more famously, there is the tale in *Henry V* of how the French dauphin, during negotiations preceding the Agincourt campaign, scornfully sent the English king a present of tennis balls (with the clear inference that he is capable only of trivial pursuits). And then, of course, there are Sir John Falstaff, Bardolph and the rest of Prince Harry's drinking companions. The bibulous, red-nosed Bardolph is entirely unknown to history. Falstaff is more problematical. In *The Famous Victories of Henry V* there is a character called Sir John Oldcastle and such, initially, was Falstaff's name in *1 Henry IV*. A Sir John Oldcastle certainly was a companion-in-arms of Henry V before his accession but he bore no resemblance to the Shakespearean figure; however, when Elizabethan descendants of the real Oldcastle protested at Shakespeare's fat, cowardly and dishonourable creation, he changed the hard-drinking knight's name to Sir John Falstaff. Again, there was indeed a genuine Sir John Falstaff (or, rather, Fastolfe) but he was a retainer not of Prince Henry but of his brother Thomas Duke of Clarence. In fact, the Sir John of *1 Henry IV* and *2 Henry IV* is very much a product of William Shakespeare's own vivid imagination.

The Prince Hal of *1 Henry IV* certainly revels in the degenerate company of the Boar's Head Tavern, enjoys horseplay and delights in practical jokes. Yet he is also a young man rather aloof from his sack-soaked cronies, frequently treating them with an ironic disdain, and always well aware of the very different destiny awaiting him:

> I know you all, and will a while uphold
> The unyok'd humour of your idleness,
> Yet herein will I imitate the sun,
> Who doth permit the base contagious clouds
> To smother up his beauty from the world,
> That, when he please again to be himself,
> Being wanted, he may be more wond'red at
> By breaking through the foul and ugly mists
> Of vapours that did seem to strangle him.

Moreover, when rebellion against his father forces him to choose between vanity and sloth (to which he is drawn by Sir John Falstaff and his other Eastcheap chums) or military and chivalric virtues (already evident in his younger brother John of Lancaster), he firmly opts for the latter and, indeed, plays a pivotal role at the battle of Shrewsbury. In *2 Henry IV*, too, when he has to choose between lawlessness and misrule, or order and justice, he eventually opts for the paths of righteousness. And, once he has become king himself, he wastes no time in rejecting his former companions and blocking their hopes of advancement:

> Presume not that I am the thing I was,
> For God doth know, so shall the world perceive,
> That I have turned away my former self;
> So will I those who kept me company.

Throughout, in fact, while clearly making the most of traditional stories of Prince Hal's wild and irresponsible youth, Shakespeare was also establishing palpable foundations for the grave, dutiful and courageous ruler and military commander he was to portray in *Henry V*.

'This mirror of all Christian kings', this 'true lover of the holy Church', this 'star of England' indeed, seems to blossom before our eyes in *Henry V* into the familiar Lancastrian hero-king of English mythology. 'The breath no sooner left his father's body', declares the archbishop of Canterbury at the very beginning of the play:

> But that his wildness, mortified in him,
> Seem'd to die too; yea, at that very moment
> Consideration like an angel came
> And whipp'd th'offending Adam out of him,
> Leaving his body as a paradise
> T'envelop and contain celestial spirits...
> Nor never Hydra-headed wilfulness
> So soon did lose his seat, and all at once,
> As in this king.

At the siege of Harfleur Henry V certainly seeks to present himself as the inspirational military leader and archetypal man of action:

> Once more unto the breach, dear friends, once more;
> Or close the walls up with our English dead...
> Stiffen the sinews, summon up the blood,
> Disguise fair nature with hard-favour'd rage...
> Now set the teeth and stretch the nostril wide;
> Hold hard the breath, and bend up every spirit
> To his full heart. On, on, you noblest English...

'And you, good yeomen', he continues as the oration reaches its climax:

> Whose limbs were made in England, show us here
> The mettle of your pasture: let us swear
> That you are worth your breeding – which I doubt not;
> For there is none of you so mean and base
> That hath not noble lustre in your eyes.
> I see you stand like greyhounds in the slips,
> Straining upon the start. The game's afoot:
> Follow your spirit; and upon this charge
> Cry 'God for Harry, England and St George.'

Similarly, before the commencement of the battle of Agincourt, the king declares:

This day is call'd the feast of Crispian.
He that outlives this day; and comes safe home,
Will stand a tip-toe when this day is nam'd,
And rouse him at the name of Crispian...
This story shall the good man teach his son,
And Crispin Crispian shall ne're go by,
From this day to the ending of the world,
But we in it shall be remembered –
We few, we happy few, we band of brothers;
For he today that sheds his blood with me
Shall be my brother; be he ne're so vile,
And gentlemen in England now a-bed
Shall think themselves accurs'd they were not here,
And hold their manhoods cheap whiles any speaks
That fought with us upon Saint Crispin's day.

Stirring stuff indeed! Yet beneath such seemingly transparent expressions of inspirational warrior kingship (and probably lost on most of Shakespeare's audience in 1599 and ever since) lies an altogether more sophisticated, and perhaps far less admirable, portrait of Henry V. Superficially, Shakespeare's king certainly is the embodiment of purist patriotism, a paragon of honour and bravery, and also a humane man anxious to empathise with, and boost the morale of, his troops. Yet this is no mere glorification of heroic kingship. Arguably, even the most famous passages of military exhortation display a degree of qualifying irony. The opening scene of the play, where leading churchmen cynically, successfully and unhistorically persuade the king to embark on foreign adventures so as to prevent his planned confiscation of ecclesiastical property at home, surely calls into question the high-mindedness of Henry V's motives for invading France. When the king disguises himself as a common soldier the night before Agincourt he meets an infantryman who is recalcitrantly resistant to any notion he should be content to die in battle and chooses to emphasise, rather, how bloody and destructive war can be; Henry fails to get the better of the argument; and, after the battle is duly won, he laboriously organises a ruse (shades of Prince Hal) that results in the soldier being beaten up. And, interestingly, this seriously unheroic episode occupies a considerable amount of stage time in the play. Nor does Shakespeare duck the sheer callousness of the king on occasion. At the gates of Harfleur, for instance, his address to the town's governor and citizens is chilling to say the least:

> What is it then to me if impious war,
> Array'd in flames, like to the prince of fiends,
> Do, with his smirch'd complexion, all fell feats
> Enlink'd to waste and desolation?
> What is't to me where you yourselves are cause,
> If your pure maidens fall into the hand
> Of hot and forcing violation?
> What rein can hold licentious wickedness
> When down the hill he holds his fierce career?
> We may as bootless spend our vain command
> Upon th'enraged soldiers in their spoil,
> As send precepts to the Leviathan
> To come ashore.[32]

Yet the king's romantic wooing of Catherine of Valois towards the end of the play suggests an altogether softer side to the king's nature. Most famously, and most controversially, there is Henry V's stark order, in the heat of battle at Agincourt, to slaughter all French prisoners: indeed, he repeats the command twice and a common soldier also reports that the king 'has caused every soldier to cut his prisoner's throat'. Moreover, in the epilogue to *Henry V*, Shakespeare makes it clear that, splendid though the king's achievements may have been (and certainly a salutary lesson for his own time), they were soon to be squandered when 'so many had the managing' of his son and successor Henry VI that 'they lost France and made England bleed'.

6

FROM WILLIAM SHAKESPEARE
TO C.L. KINGSFORD

Since 1599 William Shakespeare's portrayal of Henry V has clearly exercised enormous influence not only on popular perceptions of the king but even on historians; so, too, both via Shakespeare and in their own right, have the sixteenth-century sources on which the playwright drew; and, as more and more of them found their way into print, contemporary and near-contemporary lives and chronicles also became ever more familiar to, and extensively quoted by, authors of widely read narrative histories of England. In 1611, for instance, John Speed's *History of Great Britain* made extensive use of Raphael Holinshed and John Stow; in 1627 Michael Drayton composed a poem of over 2,500 lines on the battle of Agincourt, firmly echoing Tudor sources in its stress on the good fortune England always enjoyed when united in war against a foreign enemy; and, in the early eighteenth century, Thomas Hearne published editions of both Tito Livio's *Vita Henrici Quinti* and the Pseudo-Elmham text *Vita et Gesta Henrici Quinti*. Early fifteenth-century records and papers, too, began to be systematically collected and preserved by seventeenth-century antiquarians such as Sir Robert Cotton and their value increasingly recognised. Indeed, in 1693, Thomas Rymer was specifically commissioned by the government to search out and publish surviving records of English foreign and diplomatic relations from the Middle Ages to his own time. The multi-volumed *Foedera, conventiones, literae, et cujuscunque generis acta publica* that resulted was a remarkable achievement by any standards. The ninth volume, covering Henry V's reign, appeared in 1709 and, in an 'epistle dedicatory' to Queen Anne, Rymer certainly praised 'the acts and achievements of that most glorious prince, your royal progenitor, King Henry the Fifth', whose reign is 'for ever renowned' for his victory at Agincourt. Long before his own volume of early fifteenth-century documents appeared, however, Rymer had made relevant material available to Thomas Goodwin, a nonconformist cleric who published the first major secondary study of *The History of the Reign of Henry the Fifth* in 1704. Even so, Goodwin continued to rely heavily on Tudor historians and, when he did draw on earlier English and French chroniclers, he tended to value them no more highly than later derivative accounts. Nor was he any less didactic than they, happily interpolating moral judgements all over the place and primarily concerned to present Henry V as a universal exemplar of heroic virtue whose 'excess of courage' on occasion even led him to 'hazard a life on which alone depended the safety of his whole army'.[33]

Despite the pioneering biography of Thomas Goodwin, Henry V did not attract a great deal of attention in the eighteenth and early nineteenth centuries beyond the coverage contained in multi-volumed histories of England. Interestingly, though, he did not escape criticism. The French lawyer and Huguenot refugee Paul Rapin de Thoyras in the 1720s, for instance, emphasised the king's ambitious and avaricious nature, noted the extent to which he was assisted by internal political divisions in France and warned against exaggerating his achievements. The Scottish philosopher-cum-historian David Hume, in 1762, also emphasised the importance of on-going French civil war in explaining Henry V's successful campaigns, as well as expressing scepticism about the low number of English fatalities at Agincourt reported by so many chroniclers and criticising the king's failure to cash in on his great victory. For the eminent man of letters William Hazlitt in 1817, Henry V may indeed have been a hero by virtue of his readiness 'to sacrifice his own life for the pleasure of destroying thousands of others' and a king of England even if 'not a constitutional one', but 'we feel little love or admiration' for a ruler who, 'because he did not know how to govern his own kingdom, determined to make war on his neighbours'! The antiquarian Sir Harriss Nicolas, in his richly documented narrative *History of the Battle of Agincourt* (1827), judged Henry V's invasion of France in 1415 an unjustified war of aggression. J.R. Green, in his popular *Short History of the English People* (1874), also considered the king's war against France, fought in pursuit of an 'utterly baseless' claim to the French crown, 'a wanton act of aggression on the part of a nation tempted by the helplessness of its opponent, and galled by the memory of former defeat'; as for Henry V himself, although personally courageous and 'a great conqueror', he perpetrated terrible carnage at Agincourt and failed to capitalise on its result. And, as late as 1892, Sir James Ramsay, while admitting Henry V's ability, nevertheless remarked as well on his grasping nature and unscrupulous behaviour, and believed that, by the time of his death, he had in effect sealed the fate of the Lancastrian dynasty.[34]

For the most influential of all Victorian historians of the Middle Ages, however, Henry was 'by far the greatest king in Christendom' at the time and fully merited the admiration of his contemporaries. In the final volume of his *Constitutional History of England* (published in 1878), in fact, William Stubbs particularly stressed the importance of judging Henry V by the standards of his own age, arguing that, if we do so, we can confidently 'set aside the charges of sacrificing his country to an unjustifiable war of aggression and of being a religious persecutor'. According to Stubbs the king was, on the contrary, 'one of the greatest and purist characters in English history', a devout Christian, truthful, honourable, temperate, liberal, merciful, cultivated and, above all, 'a brilliant soldier, a sound diplomatist and an able organiser of all forces at his command'. Indeed, he concluded enthusiastically, Henry V was:

> ...a leader in heart and soul worthy of England, [who] crowned his leadership with ample signal successes [and] made England the first power in Europe... A true Englishman, with all the greatness and none of the glaring faults of his Plantagenet ancestors, he stands forth as the typical medieval hero.[35]

William Stubbs was an Anglican clergyman who eventually became a bishop: yet he excused even Henry V's harsh treatment of the proto-Protestant Lollards because, by the early fifteenth century, they had clearly become a focus for subversion and sedition in English society. A.J. Church, author of a short biography of the king published in 1889, was also a cleric and he, too, was impressed by Henry V and his achievements. Aptly, in a series devoted to 'English Men of Action', he concluded that 'it is impossible to speak too highly' of the king's credentials as a military leader: indeed, his career after Agincourt was 'one of unbroken success – success earned by courage, foresight, tactical skill, fertility of resource, economy of strength, in short, all the qualities of a great captain'. Sincerely pious, temperate, chaste, and profoundly convinced he was an agent of the Almighty, Henry V found time even in the midst of his campaigns:

> ...for the cares of civil government. England never had a more popular sovereign... [Even] in the country which he ruled as a stranger he won a general admiration and respect. It should not affect our estimate of his greatness that we now see his schemes of conquest to have been chimerical, his purpose of uniting the crowns of England and France an impossible dream, [since] he had come nearer than any who had come before him to the accomplishment of the great hopes of his predecessors.[36]

Not until 1901 did the first full-length scholarly biography of the king appear when, in a 'Heroes of the Nation' series designed to ensure that great 'deeds and hard-won fame shall live', C.L. Kingsford published his *Henry V: The Typical Medieval Hero*. 'To his contemporaries', declared Kingsford in a narrative based firmly on the study of original sources, Henry V was:

> ...the flower of Christian chivalry, the most virtuous of all princes of his time. He stands in history as the true type of the medieval hero-king: stately in bearing and prudent in speech, valiant in arms and prudent in counsel, a lover of religion and a great justiciar.

Even as Prince of Wales, he was 'the most English of our Plantagenet kings, heart and soul in sympathy with his subjects, marked out by nature to be the leader of a united nation'. When he became king in 1413, he did so in a spirit of calm self-confidence, fully convinced of his right to rule; he soon proved both his capacity to govern and his ability to win, and retain, the trust and confidence of his subjects; and, so firm was his belief in the justice of his cause, Henry V's 'assertion of his claim to the throne of France must have appeared almost in the light of a duty'. Even as early as 1415, he 'may have dreamt that, when Western Europe had been united under his sway, he would restore the unity of the Church and become the leader of Christendom in a new Crusade';

while, as a result of his victory at Agincourt, he did indeed become 'the arbiter of European politics'. C.L. Kingsford's admiration for Henry V is most graphically illustrated by the long list of superlatives he showered on the king: courteous, charming, courageous, and cultivated, for instance, as well as zealous for justice, entirely free of vindictiveness and malice, and genuinely interested in the well-being even of the poor and weak. Throughout his reign, moreover, he vigorously directed policy and administration in England, personally supervised every aspect of his great expeditions to France and, when on campaign, not only demonstrated real concern for the welfare of his soldiers but willingly shared their hardships. Yet this splendid biography is no mere modern eulogy of a medieval hero, nor is Kingsford slavishly uncritical of the contemporary and near-contemporary lives and chronicles he knew so well. And, although enthusiastically endorsing William Stubbs' verdict that Henry V was a 'typical medieval hero' and never seriously questioning his belief that the king was also a 'constitutional' monarch who very much reflected the will of the English people in all his undertakings, Kingsford clearly did have reservations about the justice of the second Lancastrian's claims to France and, even more, the sheer cost of waging war there for so long. Significantly, too he did believe that Henry V, 'perfect pattern of the *medieval* hero' that he was, had had the sad misfortune to be born 'out of due time' and, as a result, condemned to be 'champion of a lost cause'. Nevertheless, he concluded:

> ...nothing can rob him of the fame due to those who have spent their lives in the quest of a great ideal. A special charm and pathos must always attach to the memory of that princely hero who, through the splendour of his achievements, illumined with the rays of his glory the decline of the medieval world.[37]

7

TWENTIETH-CENTURY
INTERPRETATIONS

During the twentieth century Henry V attracted more attention than ever before and not just from historians. Laurence Olivier's heroic portrayal of William Shakespeare's king in his propaganda-orientated wartime film of 1944 (dedicated, on-screen, 'To the Commandos of England') received, as Olivier himself acknowledged, 'beyond-wildest-dreams acclaim', and regular theatrical productions since of *1 Henry IV*, *2 Henry IV* and *Henry V* have certainly attracted enthusiastic audiences. Most notably, Kenneth Branagh won many plaudits for his less-than-heroic interpretation of Henry V and the harsh realities of war for both stage and screen in the 1980s (although Branagh, like Olivier, chose to omit the king's order, twice repeated in *Henry V*, that French prisoners be cold-bloodedly massacred at Agincourt). Modern literary scholars, too, have been reluctant to accept that Shakespeare's Henry V is the straight-forward epic embodiment of military heroism immortalised by Laurence Olivier. E.M.W. Tillyard, in the very year Olivier's film was released, suggested that, while the playwright made Prince Hal in *1* and *2 Henry IV* 'the true kingly type' even if not 'the ideal reigning king', he failed, in *Henry V*, 'to make interesting or consistent what should have been the perfect king in action'; L.C. Knights, in 1962, detected much irony in *Henry V*, even in the famous passages of military exhortation, and found it 'hard to regard the play as a simple glorification of heroic leadership'; and, in 2000, John Sutherland powerfully put the case for regarding the king as a veritable war criminal.[38]

From the 1960s burgeoning numbers of professional university-based historians set in motion an explosion of research into unpublished fifteenth-century records, not least the rich documentary sources for Henry V and his times; the growing reading public for history inspired a series of biographies of the king aimed at a more popular market; and, as a result, an increasingly well-informed debate about the second Lancastrian's personality, achievements and legacy got under way. As early as 1948 John Harvey, in an entertaining series of vignettes of England's Plantagenet kings, detected 'in the prominent nose, lantern jaw and compressed lips' of early portraits of Henry V 'the lineaments of the determined fanatic' and remarked on 'the dark and horrifying aspect of his character', as well as noting his courage as a soldier and brilliance as a general. A politician of outstanding ability and a military commander of considerable capacity who displayed all the qualities of a great leader, declared David Douglas in 1951, but 'revoltingly cruel' on occasion and 'at once calculating and courageous, superstitious and sincere'. For Richard Vaughan, in a biography of John the Fearless Duke of Burgundy published in 1966, he was not only 'the perfidious Henry' but also 'one of the most aggressive and shifty products of an age of violence and duplicity'. Kenneth Fowler, the following year, judged the king a good soldier and a sound administrator, clear and firm in his decisions, yet both a deceitful diplomat and a fortunate beneficiary of the prevailing political situation in early fifteenth-century France; John Palmer, in 1971, considered him 'a realist and opportunist of genius'; and, according to Maurice Keen in 1973, although an enormously ambitious man, ruthless and single-minded in pursuit of his perceived rights, and 'not a character that can command wide sympathy with the present generation', Henry V was nevertheless probably the ablest, and certainly the most successful, of all England's later medieval kings. For Charles Ross in 1974, too, the king was an outstandingly able ruler, a pious, brave and just man, but also ruthless, cruel and intolerant of opposition: 'the tragedy of his reign', moreover, was that 'he used his great gifts not for constructive reform at home but to commit his country to dubious foreign war'. More recently, in 1998, C.S.L. Davies concluded that, while Henry V was indeed 'a wholly exceptional commander, meticulous in planning and inspiring in the field', he also took 'immense if calculated risks' (not least at Agincourt, 'a gamble against extraordinarily high odds'); A.J. Pollard, a couple of years later, found him a charismatic leader who inspired confidence and managed to create a real sense of unity in the English political nation, yet at the same time a high-handed and increasingly rapacious ruler, intolerant of criticism, ever more obsessed by his French ambitions and, by the end, fortunate to die before his reputation could become tarnished; and Michael Hicks, in 2002, judged the king a vigorous and decisive man, an able administrator and champion of justice and, above all, a first-rate military commander – but also priggish, ruthless, coercive and relentless in pursuit of his chosen objectives.[39]

Much the fullest twentieth-century treatment of the life and career of Henry V is to be found in a three-volume narrative history of *The Reign of Henry the Fifth* published between 1914 and 1929. J.H. Wylie, author of Volume 1 and most of Volume 2, had scarcely got beyond 1416 by the time of his death in 1914; W.T. Waugh, drawing heavily on Wylie's early drafts and notes for 1415–1420 but himself entirely responsible for 1420–1422, finally completed and secured publication of Volume 3 in 1929. James Hamilton Wylie, who had already written a four-volume *History of England under Henry the Fourth* between 1884 and 1898, was immensely knowledgeable but also rambling, obsessively addicted to minute detail (as his elephantine footnotes amply demonstrate) and lacking in discrimination when handling the vast amount of source material he so avidly accumulated. Nevertheless, it is possible to discern Wylie's impressions of Henry V and, clearly, he was no great admirer of the king, regarding him as driven by ambition to deceit and untruthfulness and owing his success in France in 1415 more to good fortune than anything else. R.B. Mowat, who published a short biography of Henry V shortly (and perhaps significantly) after the end of the First World War, had no such reservations, commenting warmly on the king's piety, good fellowship, bravery, determination, judgement, sense of justice and, above all, unremitting industry. His campaigning plans were original and comprehensive, he was a master of strategy and tactics, his 'astonishing victory' at Agincourt 'permanently established his reputation as a general and made him the most famous soldier in Europe', and his 1417 French campaign 'distinguished him above all other medieval generals'. All in all, his short life was 'brilliant in the extreme' and his work 'a wonderful achievement'; indeed, declared Mowat, Henry V:

...educated the whole nation, and enthused it with the spirit of his own youth and energy. Like Alexander of Macedon he died young, having astonished the world. He left an empire that would crumble but he left an ideal that would never die.

W.T. Waugh, in the third volume of the narrative he had taken over from J.H. Wylie, also ended up rating Henry V highly. Hard, domineering, over-ambitious, bigoted, sanctimonious and priggish the king may have been, and his mind set on purposes 'unworthy of a great or good man'; nevertheless, concluded Waugh in 1929, he was:

> ...indisputably the greatest Englishman of his day; and placed beside the fleshy Sigismund, the afflicted Charles VI, the sluggish dauphin, the treacherous John the Fearless, the unstable Duke Philip, he towers above them all – more forceful in arms, more discreet in council, more steadfast in purpose, and, with all his imperfections, more honourable in life.[40]

Twentieth-century French historians, not surprisingly, proved altogether less inclined to admire Henry V and among the most distinguished of them was Edouard Perroy. In *La Guerre de Cent Ans*, first published in 1945, he declared that the king's military success and premature death 'at the peak of an unprecedented fame have raised him very high, perhaps too high, in the esteem of posterity'. Thus, while admitting that Henry V was a good soldier, a sound administrator and a formidable adversary, Perroy also emphasised that France at the time was 'full of faction' and Europe 'ruled by puppets' and, as for the king's so-called policy of conciliation following the conquest of Normandy and Treaty of Troyes, it merely camouflaged a veritable 'reign of terror'. A prince entirely sure of himself, his strengths and the justice of his cause, he was:

> ...all the more formidable because his talents were coupled with a character with unpleasant features. His hypocritical devoutness, the duplicity of his conduct, his pretence of defending right and redressing wrongs when he sought solely to satisfy his ambition, the cruelty of his revenge – all this heralded a new era, [a] world far removed from the knightly kings whose inheritance he received and whose plans he took up again.[41]

In 1936 the eminent English historian K.B. McFarlane concluded that, by leading his people 'in pursuit of the chimera of foreign conquest', Henry V 'gave a wrong direction to national aspirations' he himself did so much to stimulate. When lecturing to a non-specialist Oxford audience in 1954, however, even this most cautious of scholars found it impossible to contain his admiration for the king. Henry V, he declared, was pious and orthodox (but neither bigoted nor a prig), a strict disciplinarian (but not cruel), single-minded and, on occasion, ruthless (but also merciful). Even as Prince of Wales he proved himself 'a man of terrific vitality and driving force'. As king he was far-sighted, a resourceful diplomat and a military genius who, in seeking glory through conquest and, hopefully, crowning it by war against the infidel, was also a faithful exponent of the chivalric ideal; his concern for justice was genuinely felt, as was his interest in religious reform; and, by 1422, he had not only 'transformed the spirit of his own people' but also became 'the arbiter of Christian Europe'. Indeed, concluded McFarlane, 'by whatever standard he is judged', Henry V was 'superlatively gifted', 'born to rule and conquer' and, probably, 'the greatest man that ever ruled England'. E.F. Jacob, in 1947, also brought in a largely favourable verdict on the king. The picture of Henry V's personality drawn by the anonymous contemporary author of the *Gesta Henrici Quinti*, he thought, was well grounded as, indeed, was William Shakespeare's 'sound introduction' to the king. 'Powerful, magnetic and subtle he certainly was', a master of propaganda who 'knew how to use his own person to create an impression, to convince or to terrify', and a king who inspired great loyalty by both his 'serious and passionate purpose' and his 'irresistible grace and energy'. Ruthless he could be but 'there was no streak of cruelty or sadism in his nature' and, even if his sense of justice had 'an Old Testament quality', it was justice all the same. As for his conquest of France, it should rightly occupy centre stage in any narrative of the reign, not least since it is as a soldier that Henry V can be seen at his best, determined to win his just rights and fully confident of his ability to do so. By 1961, however, Jacob's estimate of the king had become noticeably less favourable than it had been in 1947. Henry V, he now declared, certainly did make:

...a deep impression on his contemporaries by his character, his sense of discipline and his love of justice. He was unquestionably formidable, for he could diagnose the weak points of his opponents and had the gift of severity and the power to coerce with a passionate dialectic of his own.

Yet he relied too much on John the Fearless Duke of Burgundy's not opposing him; his victory at Agincourt did not merit the praise lavished on it both at the time and since; and even the Treaty of Troyes was, at best, a hollow triumph. In the last analysis, Jacob concluded, Henry V was 'an adventurer not a statesman: the risk he took in the creation of a dual monarchy was too great, depended on too many uncertainties and fundamentally misread the nature of France.'[42]

Between 1967 and 1975 Henry V attracted no fewer than three biographers, all catering for the wider historical market in evenly-balanced and readable accounts of the king's character, life and reign. Harold F. Hutchison, in 1967, clearly admired Henry V as a masterly campaigner particularly adept at the tricky craft of siege warfare; his personal bravery and concern for the welfare of his troops is beyond question; and his passion for justice, too, cannot seriously be doubted. The king's catalogue of achievements was certainly formidable but, Hutchison suggested, it is 'legitimate to enquire whether all this achievement was really worthwhile or truly a success'. Henry's victory at Agincourt owed more to French folly than the king's generalship; his acts of cruelty on campaign were 'unworthy of any great general in any age'; and, as for his final campaign in 1421/2, it was futile to say the least. Nor is this Henry V a likeable man: indeed, 'his character seems as chilly as his face'. There is no doubt that in Henry of Monmouth 'England found its own patron saint of national glory', Hutchison concluded, but 'like most idols it has feet of clay' and history must also record 'the cold, priggish, ruthless efficiency' of the king, 'the barrenness of his glory and the futility of his achievement': even so, 'it cannot forbear tribute to an organising genius who was a hero to his own day, an upholder of the hard logic of implacable justice, and a heroic myth for generations to come'. Peter Earle, in a short but lively narrative history of the 'most celebrated of England's late medieval kings' first published in 1972, put much stress on the early life of this 'man brought up to fight' and his later out-dated 'pursuit of dynastic knight-errantry' in France. Henry V, he concluded, was nevertheless very much:

...the product of his times, and in his times warfare was endemic. That he was loyal, just and merciful as well as a soldier of genius meant that the men of his time admired and respected him. We may suspect that he was a successful showman as well as a successful soldier, but how can we ever be sure? If he was a hypocrite he was a very successful one, for he has succeeded in fooling not only his contemporaries but also our greatest playwright and many modern historians. So, as the dead march plays, let us join his brother Bedford in praising 'King Henry the Fifth, too famous to live long'.

Just three years after the appearance of Earle's succinct sketch, the American/Canadian historian Margaret Wade Labarge published *Henry V: The Cautious Conqueror*. Her Henry V, 'a typical, although unusually competent, representative of the fifteenth-century ruling class', was 'an intensely private and complex man' but also a man entirely bereft of glamour: a 'secretive king', a 'strong and forceful leader' and an 'enigmatic and fascinating figure', he 'inspired awed respect even among his closest advisers', believed the king 'held a quasi-religious position' in society, and would not even tolerate 'the breath of criticism' let alone any opposition to his plans. Utterly convinced of the justice of his claims in France, as well as his rightful title to the English throne, he clearly saw, in a French kingdom racked by faction and civil war, an ideal opportunity to realise chimerical dreams of uniting the two crowns. Yet he was perhaps fortunate to die while his reputation as a brilliant commander and tactician was still intact. Henry V, Labarge concluded, had none of the attractive virtues:

> ...he had little charm, although a real concern for his soldiers; no sense of humour; and a truly terrifying conviction of his own position as the instrument of God. But, in the light of his own day, he was an outstandingly efficient, able and above all just king. He provided strength and good government for England during his short reign and achieved a position in France never equalled by any other English king.[43]

G.L. Harriss, who edited a series of essays on *Henry V: The Practice of Kingship* in 1985, had once been a pupil of K.B. McFarlane and, clearly, very much shared his former mentor's positive impressions of the king. Henry V, he believed, was a man of great personal magnetism, mental stamina and physical energy, pious, orthodox, chaste, abstemious in food and drink, magnanimous and of good faith. The epitomé of chivalry and knighthood, he 'perfectly exemplified the chivalric ideal' in 'the prowess, fortitude, inspiration, coolness and discipline' he consistently displayed. From the very beginning of his reign he projected himself as the perfect king, the exemplar of kingship, the saviour of his realm and people, and the liberator of English national spirit. A visionary rather than an adventurer, and a man of some originality as well as a military genius when pursuing the crown's traditional rights in France, he also demonstrated, at home, how the system of medieval government could be made to work effectively and in the interests of both king and country. Henry V, in fact, became:

> ...the symbol of national identity to a degree only later equalled by Elizabeth I... In providing his subjects with order, efficient administration and military glory, the king met their deepest yearnings and won their abiding loyalty... The simple record of Henry V's achievement is sufficient to establish him as a great king... His ambitions in France were inspired by a new vision and new methods [and], given the years, energy and luck he might have reshaped the development of both nations.

Even as it was, he 'left to his infant son a secure throne, a united political class, an efficient administration, and a people orthodox in belief, with a new pride in their achievement and destiny'. Edward Powell, also in the later 1980s, very much shared Harriss's enthusiasm for the second Lancastrian king. Concentrating his attention on Henry V's domestic record, he judged him a particularly well-educated prince, a king of extraordinary ability and a dynamic and powerful monarch who ruled with remarkable vigour and sense of purpose, and achieved unprecedented success. Presenting himself as the soldier of Christ, fighting to defend the Church and Christian faith against heresy, this powerful sense of mission also convinced him of the justice of his claims in France and he was at his most God-like in the dispensation of justice. Indeed, concluded Powell:

No king came closer to embodying the contemporary ideal of the just king than Henry V. His success in the administration of justice must rank with his greatest achievements, alongside the battle of Agincourt, the conquest of Normandy and the Treaty of Troyes, which established the union of the crowns of England and France.[44]

G.L. Harriss and Edward Powell placed themselves firmly in the pro-Henry V camp; Desmond Seward and T.B. Pugh, by contrast, no less forcefully joined the ranks of the king's critics. Seward, a perceptive, well-informed and experienced historical biographer particularly at home with English and French narrative sources, very much concentrated (in 1987) on Henry V as a warlord. The king, he believed, never had any intention of securing his inheritance across the Channel by *peaceful* means: whatever the cost, he wanted war. Moreover, although 'no one can deny that Henry V was a very great soldier', his military record was far from unblemished: the siege of Harfleur in 1415 provided a 'disastrous start' to the king's first French campaign; his subsequent march from Harfleur to Calais was 'a foolhardy adventure'; his massacre of 'captive, unarmed noblemen' at Agincourt was deplorable; his conquest and settlement of Normandy, 'as much about loot as dynastic succession', was characterised by ruthlessness and lack of compassion; and, in the end, Henry V obtained control of no more than a third of France and even that success was achieved only because the kingdom was temporarily divided between two powerful armed factions. The king's reputation, Seward declared, is:

> ... based on admiration and not on affection. He was ruthless in subordinating his feelings to his ambitions, [and the] man always gave place to the warlord – there was something a little inhuman in him... the horrors unleashed by him [in France] were unforgivable, and also unforgettable... He was incapable of seeing where his wonderful gifts as a soldier and a diplomatist were leading him, [and] the king was basically an opportunist, albeit an opportunist of genius.

'For all his brilliance', in fact, 'Henry V's ambition ended by bankrupting and discrediting his son, and by ruining his dynasty'. T.B. Pugh in 1988 was, if anything, even more damning in his verdict. The king's personal character, he believed, was cold and singularly lacking in generosity; he could be hard, grasping and unscrupulous; and his 'wilful acts of injustice were ignoble and unworthy of a great ruler'. Renewing the French war in 1415 was 'a fatal error of judgement because an imperialist war on French soil was contrary to England's real interest' and, anyway, 'obsolete schemes of conquest were inevitably bound to end in failure and disillusionment'. Although more talented than any of his predecessors on the English throne since Henry II (in the twelfth century) and rightly credited with making England a major power in European affairs, Henry V was nevertheless 'a man of limited vision and outlook' who, 'by dying when his fortunes were at their zenith, avoided the inevitable bitter harvest of defeat'.[45]

Perhaps the most eminent later twentieth-century historian of Henry V and his times, and author of the most recent academic biography of the king (published in 1992), is Christopher Allmand. Rightly emphasising, in a largely sympathetic treatment of his subject, that Henry V was a complex character, not at all easy to fathom, Allmand was particularly struck by how very English an Englishman the king was and his crucial role in helping to create an increasingly conscious and successful English nation. Personally, Henry V was a man of great mental and physical energy, a staunch exponent and defender of religious orthodoxy, a powerful advocate of justice and, above all, a military-minded and military-orientated king who probably felt most at ease in the company of fellow soldiers and for whom generalship became virtually a way of life. Acutely conscious of his own ability and determined to make the most of it, he had an 'exalted sense of his high responsibility to God', a clear vision of what he wanted to do, and the sheer drive and single-mindedness needed to pursue his chosen objectives at whatever cost to himself. At home, he sought to become master of every aspect of government, understood well what his people wanted of him, and devoted much attention to winning and retaining the support of both the nobility and parliament, securing effective financial administration and promoting law and order in a country that had seen all too much disturbance in recent years. The invasion of France in pursuit of his just rights he saw 'as part of an obligation incumbent upon him as king' and, when on campaign, proved:

> ...a natural commander of men, confident in himself, able to inspire
> others, a firm believer in the virtue of order and the need for

discipline among all ranks of the army. His moral authority lay at the root of his success [and as] a leader, as a strategist bent on conquest, as an organiser of military power, Henry was highly successful.

Even if Troyes was but a hollow triumph, and the concept of dual monarchy envisaged by the treaty unrealistic in the long term, Allmand concluded:

> … a careful consideration of his whole achievement reveals much regarding Henry's stature both as man and king. From it emerges a ruler whose already high reputation is not only maintained but enhanced.[46]

Since the publication of Christopher Allmand's biography of the king in 1992, the most important new work on Henry V – especially his victory at Agincourt and its significance – has come from the pen of Anne Curry and she, too, has a high opinion of the second Lancastrian and his achievements. Henry V, she believes, was an impressive – indeed exemplary – ruler who possessed all the characteristics expected of a medieval king. Intelligent, pious, energetic, courageous and renowned for his encouragement of justice and good governance, he proved himself both a very competent man-manager and capable of a high degree of personal involvement in government. A military hero in his own lifetime, he enjoyed campaigning, led from the front, masterminded strategy and, although ruthless on occasion and unflagging in his enforcement of strict military discipline, he was also notably fair and impartial. For Curry, moreover, the Treaty of Troyes was no transitory testament to Henry V's ambition but a realistic settlement and a monument to his belief in justice and reconciliation. He was praised and appreciated not only by his own people but even by the French. As for his legacy, before blaming him for the disasters of his son Henry VI's reign, historians should remember that it took the French more than twenty-seven years to recover what Henry V had conquered in less than seven.[47]

II

LIFE AND REIGN
OF HENRY V

8

FORMATIVE YEARS

Henry V, grandson of John of Gaunt Duke of Lancaster (the most powerful magnate in England at the time), eldest son and heir of Henry Bolingbroke Earl of Derby and his first wife Mary Bohun, and first cousin once removed of the reigning king Richard II, was born at Monmouth, probably on 16 September 1387. Legend has it he was puny at birth, delicate throughout his early years and even suffered a bout of serious illness at the age of eight but, in fact, his boyhood in the 1390s seems to have been both conventionally aristocratic and physically bracing. Indeed, according to the *Versus Rythmici* composed by an anonymous monk of Westminster who seems to have been close to young Henry of Monmouth, not only was he, most appropriately, born of native English parents, he enjoyed all manner of outdoor pursuits, especially fishing, falconry and hunting, as well as exploring the English countryside both on foot and on horseback. An early introduction to swordmanship, too, is suggested by the purchase of a new scabbard for him in the mid-1390s. His father, however, was unusually well educated for a great magnate, genuinely interested in literature and fond both of listening to music and participating in its performance, and this may help explain why his eldest son received such a firm grounding in languages, literature and music. By the age of seven, when several grammar books were bought for him in London, he was learning Latin; by the time he grew to manhood he could both read and write Latin, French and English; and, so the monk of Westminster tells us, 'he often read his books', particularly legal and theological texts. There is even a tradition that he resided for a time at Queen's

College, Oxford, under the tutelage of his uncle Henry Beaufort (chancellor of the university in 1397/8) but, since he was only ten years old at the time and there is no contemporary record of his living in the city, the story is almost certainly apocryphal. The suggestion, in the *First English Life* of 1513/4, that he 'delighted in song and musical instruments', by contrast, is convincing: indeed, there is specific evidence of the purchase of harp strings for 'the young Lord Henry' in 1397.

In 1398 Henry of Monmouth's life was thrown into turmoil when his father was exiled and his young son found himself a virtual hostage in Richard II's household. Moreover, when the king departed for Ireland at the end of May 1399 he took Henry with him. While there, according to a French chronicler, Jean Creton, who was himself in Richard II's entourage at the time, the king 'out of pure and entire affection' for this 'fair young bachelor and handsome' twelve-year-old lad dubbed him a knight, declaring as he did so:

> 'My fair cousin, henceforth be gallant and brave, for unless you conquer you will have little name for valour'.

Soon afterwards news reached Ireland that Henry's father who, on the death of his own father John of Gaunt Duke of Lancaster earlier in the year had been deprived of his ducal inheritance, had launched an invasion of England. Richard II's response, at any rate as reconstructed by the early fifteenth-century chronicler Thomas Otterbourne, was to summon young Henry to his presence and dramatically reproach him with his father's treason:

> 'Henry, my boy, see what your father has done to me! He has invaded my land and put my subjects to death without mercy, [and] through these unhappy doings you will perhaps lose your inheritance'.

Although 'but a boy', the youth is said to have replied robustly and 'in a manner beyond his years':

> 'In truth, my gracious lord and king, I am greatly grieved by these tidings but I believe your lordship understands that I am innocent of my father's deeds'.

'I know that you have no part in your father's crime', the king is then supposed to have reassured him, 'and therefore I excuse you of it'. By the time Richard II arrived back in England, however, Henry of Monmouth's father had not only won powerful aristocratic backing for his claim to the duchy of Lancaster but also set his sights on the crown itself. Soon after young Henry returned from Ireland, apparently, he joined Richard II at Chester and, according to a pro-Richard *Brut* chronicler, when ordered by his father to quit the king's presence *only* did so when reminded of his filial duty by Richard II himself:

> 'Good son Henry, I grant you leave to obey your father's commandment. I know well there is one Henry who will do me much harm but suppose it is not you. Wherefore I pray you to be my friend, for I know how it will go'. And so, on the following day, Henry took leave of the king his godfather with a heavy heart and went to his father. And after that the king was arrested...

Richard II's deposition, and Henry Bolingbroke's seizure of the throne as Henry IV, rapidly followed and, a few months later, Richard was probably murdered in Pontefract castle on the new king's orders.[1]

Did Henry of Monmouth perhaps feel more affection for Richard II than his own father and might the later fraught relationship between Henry IV and his son have its origins in the events of 1399? It is impossible to answer these questions but, certainly, within a few months of his own accession Henry V did arrange the reburial of Richard II's corpse with full royal ritual in Westminster Abbey: the second Lancastrian, reported the well-informed St Albans' chronicler Thomas Walsingham, felt he owed as much veneration to the deposed king as his own father, and so 'raised and transported' his body (buried by his father, without ceremony, at King's Langley) to be 'regally entombed at Westminster'; in similar vein, a fifteenth-century *Brut* tells us that, 'for the great and tender love that he had for King Richard, he translated his body from Langley to Westminster, and buried him beside Queen Anne his first wife, as his desire was'. Indeed, according to Henry V's anonymous biographer Pseudo-Elmham (probably writing in the early 1440s), on first encountering the young Henry of Monmouth Richard II had even declared:

Here shewes howe dan Jane Duches of Breteyn doughter of the kyng of
Naveru. and nowe wedded wif to Henry the iiijth kyng of Englond was
Crowned Quene of this noble Reame of Englond

Coronation of Henry IV's second queen Joan of Navarre in Westminster Abbey, February 1403.
Although Henry V and his stepmother enjoyed a cordial relationship for years, this did not prevent
the queen dowager's sudden arrest and imprisonment in the autumn of 1419, a ruthless and wilful act
of injustice occasioned by sheer royal greed.

We have heard that our England should foster a certain Prince Henry who, with respect to the nobility of his manners, the exceeding greatness of his deeds, his immense soldierly industry, the high reward of his deserved fame, will shine forth abundantly through the whole world, and that according to what an occult book that he has frequently consulted has said, he is certain this is the very Henry.

Obviously this partisan and relatively late source needs to be treated with great caution but, at the very least, Pseudo-Elmham might well reflect a powerful early fifteenth-century legend.[2]

The events of 1399 changed the status and future prospects of Henry of Monmouth even more dramatically than his father's exile the previous year. As the new king Henry IV's eldest son he now became heir to the kingdom and, within weeks, Prince of Wales, Duke of Cornwall, Earl of Chester, Duke of Aquitaine and Duke of Lancaster. Lack of enthusiasm for Richard II in 1399, however, did not necessarily add up to positive commitment to Henry IV and the king had to make an all-out effort to widen the basis of his support during the early years of the reign, not least by frequently consulting the nobility and generous political patronage. Financial problems also made for difficulties with parliament: the Commons proved reluctant to sanction even much needed taxation and, in return for grants, pressed hard for reforms of government; Henry IV received several humiliating reverses at their hands; and, on more than one occasion (most notably in 1406) had no choice but to make concessions potentially threatening to the crown's power and freedom of action. Most seriously, Henry IV had to face a string of rebellions in England during his early years and a prolonged revolt in Wales led by Owen Glendower, as well as the very real possibility of a French invasion. The Scots, too, were notably aggressive: indeed, if we are to believe Tito Livio and Enguerrand de Monstrelet, young Henry of Monmouth may have had his first serious experience of military campaigning (at the age of thirteen!) when he accompanied his father on a short expedition to Scotland in the summer of 1400. Only when a Scottish army was defeated by Henry Percy Earl of Northumberland and his son Hotspur at the battle of Homildon Hill in 1402 and James I of Scotland became a captive of the English in 1406 was this danger at last neutralised if not entirely removed. In England itself, moreover, Henry IV had to face no fewer than three

The battle of Shrewsbury, 21 July 1403. Although only sixteen years old, Henry V (as Prince of Wales) fought bravely and received a severe wound in the face at Shrewsbury: indeed, he was probably lucky to survive the action.

Percy-inspired rebellions. Both Henry Percy Earl of Northumberland and his eldest son had been prominent supporters of the successful Lancastrian challenge to Richard II in 1399 but, by 1403, such were their ambitions, and grievances against the new regime, that they came out in open rebellion. Fortunately for Henry IV the rebels were defeated at the battle of Shrewsbury on 21 July 1403; Hotspur, who may have provided an early military role model for the king's son, was killed; and Henry of Monmouth himself, now sixteen years of age, won his spurs. Although but a boy, reported Thomas Walsingham, the Prince of Wales displayed conspicuous bravery in the field; Pseudo-Elmham learned that, although wounded in the face by an arrow, he declared he would rather die than stain his newly won soldierly reputation by flight; and, according to Tito Livio, he even angrily demanded: 'Lead me, thus wounded, to the front line so that I may, as a prince should, kindle our fighting men with deeds not words'. It is also worth noting, though, that the young prince was lucky to survive Shrewsbury and that, at this stage, there were men from his own retinue and earldom of Chester fighting against him. Moreover despite, or perhaps because of, his son's death at Shrewsbury, Henry Percy Earl of Northumberland backed a further rebellion against the crown in 1405; Richard Scrope Archbishop of York, another of its leaders, was executed; and, again, Henry of Monmouth probably played a significant role in the revolt's suppression. Not until 1408, when Northumberland himself was killed in a further rebellion, did the Percy menace to Henry IV's throne at last disappear.

Perhaps Wales, galvanised into real nationalistic fervour by the charismatic and dynamic Owen Glendower, provided the most potent challenge of all to the new Lancastrian dynasty and it was here, too, that Henry of Monmouth spent much of his teenage years. The Welsh revolt broke out in 1400 and, from the autumn of that year, the Prince of Wales was nominally in charge of both the country's administration and the task of regaining control of his own newly granted principality. Early in 1403 he was appointed king's lieutenant in Wales, and clearly, from then until the fall of Harlech castle in February 1409 (which finally ended Welsh resistance) he played an active role in the long process of defeating Owen Glendower's challenge to English rule: indeed, the Lancastrian reconquest of Wales firmly established his military reputation. Henry IV himself affirmed that he had consciously sent his 'first-born son into Wales for the chastisement of the rebels' and the letters exchanged between father and son during these years suggest that, at this time, there existed real trust and respect – perhaps even affection – between the two. Parliament, too, expressed its confidence in the prince's endeavours on several occasions: in 1405, for instance, it praised him as a courageous young man, obedient to his father's will, whose achievements against the Welsh rebels were commendable and, in April 1406, again thanked him for his services in Wales. Yet, also in April 1406, the speaker of the Commons requested that the Prince of Wales (whose commission as king's lieutenant had been renewed a year earlier) should henceforth reside *continuously* in Wales, and, in June 1406, further concern was voiced about Prince Henry's continued failure to take up his command in person. Such criticisms, moreover, were not without justification: the recovery of Anglesey in 1406, for instance, seems to have owed little to the prince, nor did he play any significant role in the final capitulation of Harlech in 1409. Even so, Henry of Monmouth's participation in the Welsh campaigns of 1403–1409, patchy though it may have been, clearly did have real significance, not least for himself and his future reputation. In a nutshell, it was in Wales that he learned the craft of warfare, and gained the knowledge and experience of campaigning in a difficult terrain that he was eventually to deploy so successfully in the conquest of Normandy. Here, for the first time, he confronted the problems of military command, man-management and war finance; the organisation of siege-warfare and the significance of controlling fortified towns and castles; the need for effective supply lines; and the importance of regular victualling, and maintenance, of garrisons. Above all, he learned the qualities of imagination, determination and sheer persistence required of a general if he were to succeed against guerrilla forces reluctant to engage in the field. During his Welsh campaigns, too, Henry of Monmouth built up a strong and durable affinity of young noblemen (such as Thomas Fitzalan Earl of Arundel and Richard Beauchamp Earl of Warwick) and first encountered many of the lieutenants he was later to rely upon in France.

Once he had 'crushed those who rebelled against him', reported the chronicler Adam Usk, Henry IV 'fell sick' and thereafter, until his death, he was tormented 'by a rotting of the flesh, a drying up of the eyes and a rupture of the intestines'. In fact, the king first began to suffer serious ill health in 1406 and it is surely no coincidence that, by 6 December at the latest, his eldest son had become a member of the royal council and henceforth regularly attended its meetings. Initially, Thomas Arundel Archbishop of Canterbury (one of Henry IV's very earliest supporters) seems to have taken the political lead, becoming chancellor at the end of January 1407, but, despite his continuing responsibilities in Wales, the twenty-year-old Henry of Monmouth became more and more a force to be reckoned with in London. In 1407, indeed, he was present at almost two-thirds of known council meetings and, together, he and Arundel came very much to dominate its proceedings. When Henry IV's physical condition became even more grave in the winter of 1408/9, virtually all policy and decision-making power fell into the council's hands. Before long, however, the Prince of Wales and his growing faction, headed by his uncle and long-time political mentor Henry Beaufort Bishop of Winchester, not only began to question the wisdom of Arundel's cautious hand-to-mouth leadership but also became ever more overtly sympathetic towards parliament's so frequently reiterated demands for improved defences, tighter financial management and conciliar reform. Nor did Prince Henry find it easy to tolerate the increasing favour being shown to his own younger brother Thomas. Eventually, after several months of ever more bitter wrangling, Arundel was forced to resign the chancellorship in December 1409; the Prince of Wales seized power for himself; and, early in 1410, a new council was constituted very much dominated by his own close associates.

No doubt Henry IV's serious ill health provides the main explanation for his sanctioning rule by a council consisting largely of Prince Henry and his faction from January 1410 until November 1411. Particularly prominent were Henry Beaufort Bishop of Winchester and his brother Sir Thomas, together with members of the younger generation of nobility who had fought with Henry of Monmouth in Wales. The king himself seems largely to have withdrawn from the political arena, leaving his eldest son free to exercise royal authority as he saw fit and pursue policies of his own. During the period of his ascendancy, moreover, the prince proved himself an energetic and responsible ruler; the council, largely united in loyalty to him as it was, functioned far more effectively as an administrative organ than its predecessor; and, at home, all demonstrated a real commitment to the restoration of good governance. Their aspirations were probably greater than their achievements (particularly when it came to the restoration of law and order) but progress certainly was made in reforming English government finance (much needed) and, partly as a result no doubt, relations between crown, council and parliament became more amicable than they had been for years. Closest to the prince's heart, almost certainly, was the conduct of foreign policy, particularly his dealings with France, England's traditional enemy and, before the end of 1410, plunged into civil war as Armagnac and Burgundian factions struggled for control of the mentally afflicted king Charles VI and the French realm. For over three hundred years English possessions in France had resulted in intermittent Anglo-French warfare and, since the Treaty of Bretigny in 1360, the precise nature of English claims to Aquitaine had been a matter of particular dispute. When both Burgundians and Armagnacs appealed to England for support in 1411, French concessions on the vexed issue of English sovereignty there inevitably became the price for military assistance. Already, Henry IV himself may well have been inclined towards the Armagnac faction but it was his son's pro-Burgundian leanings that prevailed. Indeed, in October 1411, a small English force under the command of Thomas Fitzalan Earl of Arundel (former companion-in-arms of the Prince of Wales) was despatched to France, possibly in return for a Burgundian promise not only to recognise Lancastrian sovereignty in Aquitaine but even assist England's recovery of Normandy (lost by King John two centuries earlier). Perhaps intended as a mere advance guard for a larger expeditionary force to be led by Prince Henry himself, it nevertheless distinguished itself in helping defeat the Armagnacs at the battle of St Cloud and enabling John the Fearless Duke of Burgundy to enter Paris in triumph. By the time a Burgundian embassy arrived in England early in 1412 to secure further English assistance, however, Henry IV had taken power back into his own hands and Lancastrian policy towards France was about to change dramatically.

The Prince of Wales had probably sanctioned Arundel's expedition to France in clear defiance of his father's wishes and, despite continued ill health, Henry IV may well have been galvanised into action against his son as a result. Perhaps relations between the two, never close, had now become so severely strained that an out-and-out confrontation was inevitable anyway. And the king's reassertion of his royal authority in November 1411 may well have stemmed, too, from rumours that the prince, now bent on securing permanent power for himself, had embarked on the more sinister stratagem of forcing his father to abdicate the throne. According to the *First English Life* of 1513/4, Prince Henry's court since early 1410 had always been 'more abundant than his father's' and, among his entourage, none exercised more influence than Henry Beaufort Bishop of Winchester. Perhaps, indeed, the notion of young Henry's now taking the crown for himself was Beaufort's brainchild. Certainly, at least one anonymous chronicler reported the making of an agreement 'between Prince Henry, first-born son of the king, Henry Bishop of Winchester, and almost all the lords of England, that they should ask the king to give up the crown of England, and permit his first-born son to be crowned'; another specifically represents Prince Henry as counselling his father to relinquish his throne; and, interestingly, Beaufort himself felt the need, early in Henry VI's reign, to repudiate in parliament reports that he had 'stirred the king that last died, the time also that he was prince, to have taken the governance of this realm and crown upon him' during his father's lifetime. Whatever the truth of the matter, the Prince of Wales certainly paid the price of even seeming to threaten the king's position. By the end of November 1411 he had been peremptorily deprived of all power and, before long, supplanted by his younger brother Thomas; his supporters on the council, including the Beauforts, also found themselves out of office; and Henry IV, at any rate to all outward appearances, had fully resumed personal control of national affairs. For the rest of the reign, indeed, Prince Henry ceased either to attend the council or play any role in government.

As the chronicler John Harding graphically put it, Henry IV 'discharged the prince from his council' and 'set my lord Sir Thomas in his stead'; his second son (who had himself suffered at the hands of his elder brother, his council and, especially, Henry Beaufort) no doubt seemed, in the circumstances, a natural ally; and Thomas's priorities, almost certainly, explain the abandonment of Henry of Monmouth's pro-Burgundian stance in favour of an alliance with the Armagnac faction in France. Under the terms of the Treaty of Bourges, ratified in London in May 1412, the Armagnacs undertook to recognise England's just title to the duchy of Aquitaine (with no mention of French sovereignty) and offered to assist Henry IV in regaining control of it; in return, the king pledged himself to back the Armagnacs against the Burgundians. All four of Henry IV's sons, including the Prince of Wales, swore to observe the treaty but, clearly, it marked a complete reversal of the prince's earlier pro-Burgundian policy and he can hardly have been overjoyed by it; moreover, as he may well have realised, the chances of the Armagnacs fully honouring its terms if it ever came to the crunch were remote to say the least. Even so, Henry IV soon moved to meet his own obligations and the result was the first major Lancastrian expedition to France. Not surprisingly, leadership was entrusted not to Prince Henry but to his brother Thomas (now Duke of Clarence) and, in August 1412, he crossed the Channel with a substantial force resolved, no doubt, not only to aid the Armagnacs but also win back his father's rightful inheritance in Aquitaine. The result could hardly have been more humiliating. By the time Clarence arrived in France hostility between the warring factions had temporarily ceased and, met by a now uniformly hostile (if fragile) front, he tamely allowed himself to be bought off before returning home, after a good deal of plundering, from Bordeaux (ironically, the chief city and port of the very Aquitaine he had hoped to make his own). No wonder English chroniclers chose to play down the scale and significance of this so much heralded yet, in the end, so entirely futile a campaign.

None of this did anything to help foster more cordial relations within the royal family: quite the contrary, in fact. Indeed, as early as mid-June 1412, the Prince of Wales had felt the need to issue a public statement defending himself against malicious rumours and vigorously justifying his recent behaviour. In particular, so Thomas Walsingham tells us, he wished to challenge the king's *familiares* 'who, as it is said, sowed trouble between father and son', and rebut those 'sons of iniquity' who had not only accused him of trying to thwart his brother's proposed expedition to Aquitaine but also of plotting to seize the crown. Significantly, too, he complained of 'sowers of wrath and instigators of discord who, with something like the guile of the serpent', were determined 'to disturb the line of succession' (presumably a reference to reports that the king might be about to declare his brother Thomas, rather than himself, heir to the throne). A fortnight later the prince arrived in London, accompanied by 'much people of lords and gentles', secured an audience with his father, protested his loyalty and

demanded that those who had slandered him be dismissed and punished. In response, the king promised that, in the fullness of time, his
son's detractors might be judged by parliament, and with that he had to
be content. An uneasy reconciliation between the two followed but
nothing was done about Prince Henry's complaints; rather, new
rumours began to spread that, as captain of Calais, he had embezzled
the garrison's wages. Towards the end of September 1412 an enraged
prince once more entered London 'with a huge people'. Once there, if
we are to believe a tradition preserved in the *First English Life*, he
solemnly sought confession, received communion and then:

> ...disguised himself in a gown of blue satin or damask made full of
> eyelets or holes and at every eyelet the needle wherewith it was made
> hanging there by a thread of silk; and about his arm he wore a dog's
> collar set full of S's of gold and the rings for them also of fine gold.
> [Thus curiously attired] he came to the king his father who at that
> time lay at Westminster [Hall]. Then the king caused himself to be
> borne in his chair (because he was diseased and could not walk) into
> his secret chamber; where in the presence of three or four persons in
> whom the king had his most confidence he commanded the prince
> to show what was in his mind. Then the prince, kneeling down
> before his father, said to him: 'Most redoubted lord and father, I am
> this time come to your presence as your liegeman, and as your true
> son, in all things to obey your grace as my sovereign lord and father.
> And whereas I understand that you have me in suspicion of my
> behaviour against your grace, and that you fear I would usurp your
> crown against the pleasure of your highness, [how] much rather
> ought I to suffer death to bring your grace [from] that fear that you
> have of me, who am your true son and liegeman... And therefore
> most redoubted lord and father, I desire you in your honour of God,
> for the easing of your heart, here before your knees to slay me with
> this dagger'. And at that word with all reverence he delivered to the
> king his dagger, saying: 'My lord and father, my life is not so dear to
> me that I would live one day that I should be to your displeasure...
> And in your thus doing in the presence of those lords, and before
> God and the Day of Judgement, I clearly forgive you my death'. At
> these words of the prince the king, taken with compassion of heart,
> cast from him the dagger, and embraced the prince, and kissed him,

and with effusion of tears said to him: 'My right dear and heartily beloved son, it is true that I partly suspected you, and as I now perceive, undeservedly on your part; but seeing this your humility and faithfulness, I shall neither slay you nor henceforth any more have you in distrust for any report that shall be made to me. And therefore I raise you upon mine honour'.[3]

A month later the Prince of Wales was exonerated of all charges of malpractice as captain of Calais and, this time, the reconciliation between father and son seems to have been complete and lasting.

Clearly, by the autumn of 1412 the king was terminally ill, and perhaps recognisably so: hence, probably, why Henry of Monmouth and his friends were now content to await the inevitable without further dissent. Indeed, if we are to believe another tradition, preserved this time by Enguerrand de Monstrelet:

In the last few days of his illness the king was quite helpless. One day those who were looking after him, seeing that he had stopped breathing, thought he had indeed died and covered his face with a cloth. Now it is the custom in that country, when the king is ill, to place his crown on a couch near the bed so that his eldest son and heir can take it as soon as he is dead. This had been done and the eldest son readily took it when the attendants gave him to understand that his father was dead. But soon after this the king sighed deeply, uncovering his face, and his mind suddenly became clear. He looked to where the crown had been and, not seeing it, asked where it was. His attendants replied: 'Sir, my lord the prince your son has taken it away'. The king asked for him to be sent for, and he came. Then the king asked him why he had taken away the crown, and the prince replied: 'My lord, those here present had given me to understand that you had departed this life, and since I am your eldest son and your crown and kingdom will belong to me when you have gone from this world to the next, I took it'. Then with a sigh the king said to him: 'Fair son, what right have you to it? For I never had any as you well know'. 'My lord', replied the prince, 'as you won and kept it by the sword, so shall I keep and defend it all my days'. 'Do as seems good to you', said the king, 'I leave everything else to God and pray him to have mercy on my soul'. Soon afterwards, without speaking again, he died.[4]

This splendid tale may have at least an element of truth in it; so might the sermon on justice and mercy put into the dying king's mouth by the anonymous author of the *First English Life*. What probably is beyond question is that, by the time he finally died in the Jerusalem chamber at Westminster Abbey on 20 March 1413, Henry IV had indeed achieved peace and reconciliation between himself and all four of his sons.

9

ACCESSION, LOLLARDS
AND SOUTHAMPTON PLOT

Even as Henry IV lay dying, so the Italian humanist Tito Livio tells us, the Prince of Wales, 'reflecting that he was about to inherit his father's kingdom, summoned a monk of most exemplary purity to whom he confessed his past sins'. As elaborated by Pseudo-Elmham a few years later, on the very night of the old king's death his eldest son and heir specifically chose to visit a recluse who occupied a cell in the south transept of Westminster Abbey and, in long and secret conversation with him, threw himself on God's mercy and resolved henceforth to become a different man. Emerging next morning, on 21 March 1413, he was duly proclaimed king as Henry V and, less than a month later on 9 April, came his coronation. The weather was not clement! Indeed, declared Adam Usk colourfully, the day was:

> …marked by unprecedented storms, with driving snow which covered the country's mountains, burying men and animals and houses and, astonishingly, even inundating the valleys and fenlands, creating great danger and much loss of life.

Usk certainly revelled, too, in the unexpected on such great ceremonial occasions. When reporting Henry IV's coronation in October 1399, he had remarked that, after the king's anointing, 'there ensued such a growth of lice, especially on his head, that he neither grew hair nor could he have his head uncovered for many months'; Henry V, during his coronation mass, 'dropped one of his obligatory nobles on the floor, and both he himself and those who were present had to search carefully to find it before it could be offered up.[5] The possible symbolic significance of a coronation day marked by heavy snow and hail certainly did not escape the notice of contemporaries, although their interpretations varied. Most notably while, for John Strecche, such conditions were clearly indicative of both the new king's icy temperament and the prospect of severe rule to come, Thomas Walsingham declared enthusiastically that, just as winter is inevitably followed by spring, so the passing of the coronation storms heralded the end of hard times and the dawn of a new era of hope and prosperity. What early fifteenth-century biographers and chroniclers particularly focussed on, however, was the transformation of Henry of Monmouth himself once he became England's second Lancastrian king.

Once anointed and crowned in Westminster Abbey, so an anonymous English chronicler tells us, Henry V 'suddenly changed into a new man' and, henceforth, devoted himself single-mindedly 'to live virtuously in maintaining Holy Church, destroying heretics, keeping justice and defending his realm and subjects'; Thomas Walsingham, similarly, recorded his dramatic transformation into 'another man, zealous for honesty, modesty and gravity'; and Tito Livio, too, learned how he so 'reformed and amended his life and manners' that 'all his acts were suddenly changed into gravity and discretion'. Most remarkably, Livio also noted, from the time of his father's death until his marriage to Catherine of Valois in June 1420, 'he had no carnal knowledge of any women'. Perhaps, for both contemporary and near-contemporary writers and, indeed, the image-conscious Henry V himself, promulgating such a story of overnight conversion to serious-minded and duty-driven adulthood was part-and-parcel of the deliberate creation of a convincing hero-king tradition. Yet it cannot be rejected out of hand. Nor can complementary tales that, as the *Brut* put it, 'before he was king, when he was Prince of Wales, he fell and inclined greatly to riot and drew to wild company'.

By the early sixteenth century the anonymous author of the *First English Life*, drawing heavily on Tito Livio and, probably, the lost reminiscences of James Butler fourth Earl of Ormonde, could confidently record 'the common fame' that Henry of Monmouth:

> ...exercised immoderately the feats of Venus and Mars, and other pastimes of youth, for as long as the king his father lived [and],

accompanied by some of his young lords and gentlemen, would wait in disguise for his own receivers and rob them of their money.

Yet sometimes, the biographer added, when engaged in such reprehensible behaviour 'both he and his company were surely beaten'; moreover, when his receivers complained of such treatment:

> ...he would reimburse them of as much money as they had lost, and ensured they did not leave him without great rewards for their troubles and vexations. [Indeed], he that best and most bravely had resisted him and his company in their enterprise, and from whom he had received the greatest and most strokes, would be sure to receive from him the greatest and most bounteous rewards.[6]

Some twenty years later, in his *Book Named the Governor*, Sir Thomas Eliot recorded (for the first time) what was destined to become the most famous legend of Prince Hal's unruly behaviour and its consequences. During his father's lifetime the 'most renowned' Prince of Wales was 'noted to be fierce and of wanton courage', declared Eliot, so much so that when 'one of his servants, whom he favoured well, was arraigned at the King's Bench for committing felony', and 'incensed by light persons about him', in 'furious rage' he 'came hastily to the bar, where his servant stood as a prisoner, and commanded him to be set at liberty'. Chief Justice William Gascoigne, in response, 'exhorted the prince' to allow his servant to be judged by 'the ancient laws of the realm', at which Prince Henry:

> ...nothing appeased, but rather more inflamed, endeavoured himself to take away his servant. The judge, considering the perilous example and inconvenience that might thereby ensue, commanded the prince upon his allegiance to leave the prisoner and depart, at which command the prince, set all in a fury and in a terrible manner, came up to the place of judgement, men thinking that he would have slain the judge...

Gascoigne, 'with an assured and bold countenance', promptly ordered that for his 'contempt and disobedience' the prince be committed to King's Bench prison and he, 'laying his weapon aside', duly obeyed, much to the approval of his father.[7]

Such stories certainly provided rich veins of material for William Shakespeare's portrayal of Prince Hal (much enhanced by the introduction of the likes of Sir John Falstaff and Bardolph). But are they no more than legends? Interestingly, one of Henry V's very first acts as king was to dismiss William Gascoigne, who had served as chief justice of King's Bench throughout his father's reign, probably because he had fallen out with the judge when leader of the royal council in 1410/11. Such an act by an incoming king was certainly unusual but it hardly provides sufficient justification for accepting Sir Thomas Eliot's dramatic tale; more significant is the lack of any contemporary or near-contemporary report: in particular, there is no evidence of any such incident in either the King's Bench records or the legal Year Books of the time and, had it been authentic, there surely would have been. Nor is there any specific early fifteenth-century evidence to back up the story of the prince robbing his own receivers. Yet, since more generalised notions of Prince Henry's reckless and dissolute youth can be traced back to within twenty years of his death, they are probably not entirely without foundation. Even an heir to the throne as conscientious as he seems to have been most of the time may well have enjoyed occasional bouts of boisterous relaxation, as did his younger brothers: indeed, there are indications that they, at least, even became involved in a brawl between courtly factions at an Eastcheap tavern on one occasion! Tito Livio certainly tells us that Prince Henry indulged, from time to time, in such pleasures as 'the licence of a soldier's life' permits; soldiers, past and present, have always had a reputation for enjoying lively, heavy-drinking companionship when freed from the rigours of campaigning; and, maybe, Henry of Monmouth was no exception.

When it comes to Henry V's appearance and more reputable leisure pursuits we are on altogether firmer ground. The Benedictine monk of Westminster, who probably had ample opportunity to observe the new king, provides a particularly detailed description of Henry V's physical attributes at the time of his accession. Even if deliberately flattering, it has a clear ring of authenticity; Tito Livio and Pseudo-Elmham confirm the main points of the Benedictine's depiction; and the most familiar surviving portrait of the king, of later fifteenth or early sixteenth-century date but probably based on a more nearly contemporary likeness, highlights strikingly similar traits. Henry V, Tito Livio reported, was 'taller than most men, his face fair and set on a longish neck, his body graceful, his limbs slender but marvellously strong'. The monk of Westminster, similarly, drew attention to the king's above average height, well-proportioned face, long neck, and lean slender body; additionally, he tells us, Henry V had a round head, broad fore-head (indicative of wisdom and intelligence), thick brown hair, small ears, bright hazel eyes (dove-like when calm but fierce as a lion's in anger), straight nose, white even teeth, healthy red lips, and a smooth fresh complexion. Of his physical strength, too, there was now no question, as Tito Livio emphasised:

> ...he was marvellously fleet of foot, faster than any dog or arrow. Often he would run with two of his companions in pursuit of the swiftest of does and he himself would always be the one to catch the creature. He had a great liking for music and found enjoyment in hunting, military pursuits and the other pleasures that are customarily allowed to young knights.[8]

For the monk of Westminster, he was 'a bold archer' who avoided inac-tion, 'not fleshy nor burdened with corpulence but a handsome man, never weary, whether on horseback or on foot': indeed, the monk specifically recorded how the king, on one occasion, not only shot a great stag with an arrow but promptly presented it to his own religious community. No less admirably, he tells us, Henry V, whose mood tended to vary between elation and gravity, was fond of reading, dili-gent in the administration of justice, prompt to remedy abuses, not given to either vice or gluttony, liberal in alms-giving and, above all, regular in both his fasting and attendance at mass. As for Jean Fusoris, a French visitor to the king at Winchester in 1415, he gained the power-ful impression that, although Henry had the noble stature and fine manner of a lord, he was nevertheless, even on the eve of launching his first invasion of France, more suited temperamentally to enter the church than devote himself to the rigours of warfare and campaigning.

Yet, from the very beginning of his reign, Henry V probably had one overriding ambition: the assertion, whether by diplomacy or military action, of traditional English claims in France. Even so, this self-confident young man of twenty-five realised that, first of all, he must restore order and unity to his realm at home and, fortunately for him, not only the rul-ing elite but also the people at large seem to have been only too ready by

1413 to embrace their charismatic young king's vision for the future. Virtually his first act, if we are to believe the *Brut*, was to command:

> ...all his people who were parties to his misgovernance before that time, and all his household, to come before him. And when they heard that, they were full glad, for they supposed that he would have promoted them to great offices, that they would stand in great favour and trust with him, and be nearest of counsel.

Instead, although 'some of them winked at him', others smiled and many 'made foolish grimaces', he 'kept his countenance very serious' and declared:

> 'Sirs, you are the people that I have cherished and maintained in riot and wild governance [but] from this day forward you must forsake all misgovernance and live according to the laws of Almighty God and the laws of our land [or] be truly punished according to the law, without any favour or grace'.

And, after rewarding them 'richly with gold and silver, [he] charged them all to leave his household and never come any more into his presence': only the three former companions who had dared in the past to criticise his lifestyle now remained in favour.[9] Perhaps this helps explain why, according to another anonymous chronicler, Henry V was subsequently crowned 'with the agreement of the greater part of the lords of the realm': indeed, so Tito Livio tells us, at his coronation 'all noblemen of the realm swore an oath of loyalty to him', after which he 'appointed men whom he considered to be honest and fair to be judges throughout his kingdom and selected other necessary officials for posts in all his lands'. And at his coronation banquet, Adam Usk reported, 'the king had it proclaimed that all criminals, even those who had committed treason, would be pardoned'.

Clearly, not only did Henry V have every confidence in his God-given right and capacity to rule, he had every intention of living up to the heightened sense of expectation, optimism and hope for the future that greeted his accession by opening a brand new chapter in the history of the Lancastrian dynasty. Although he retained the services of many of his father's former advisers, he also rapidly promoted to high office men

Richard Beauchamp, an early companion-in-arms of Prince Henry of Monmouth, dubbed a knight
by Henry IV following the battle of Shrewsbury, 1403.

previously associated with himself as Prince of Wales, most notably Thomas Fitzalan Earl of Arundel, Richard Beauchamp Earl of Warwick and Henry Beaufort Bishop of Winchester (the new king's first chancellor). From the start of the reign, too, he demonstrated a willingness to be reconciled with men or the descendants of men who had opposed his father's usurpation or rebelled against him: the young Edmund Mortimer Earl of March, for instance, despite possessing a claim to the throne rivalling Henry V's own, was released from house arrest and restored to his hereditary estates, while even young Henry Percy Earl of Northumberland (whose grandfather had rebelled against Henry IV in 1403, 1405 and 1408) was eventually allowed to return home from his Scottish exile in 1416. In return, Henry V made it clear that he intended to be obeyed by all his subjects, great and small, not least the Welsh: by the time he invaded France in the summer of 1415, Wales – in rebellion against his father for more than half his reign – had not only been pacified but also largely reconciled to English rule, ensuring the maintenance of peace there even during extensive royal absences abroad. In England, too, the king was determined to put the problems of the past behind him. Popular versifiers in 1413 highlighted these graphically: in particular, they called for a vigorous application of the rule of law and a purge of those responsible for promoting disorder in the country. The new chancellor Henry Beaufort, in his opening address to the first parliament of the reign in May 1413, echoed such sentiments by committing the government to restoring law and order, sorting out royal financial weaknesses (long a major bone of contention between crown and parliament) and defending the country's borders; the Commons, in response, underlined their own urgent desire for good governance and the security of the realm; and, over the next year or so, such matters did indeed become a central concern of Henry V and his administration.

The Lancastrian dynasty was firmly established by 1413 and there was no serious rival to challenge the new king's authority. Nevertheless, during the early months of his reign, Henry V seems to have been acutely aware of any hint of sedition or threat of invasion, perhaps not entirely without justification. A contemporary Latin poem makes it clear the second Lancastrian was by no means universally popular, criticising both his grasping ministers and his unruly soldiery, while, so an eyewitness of the king's coronation reported to the Monk of Saint-Denis, there were many who still maintained the superiority of the young Earl of March's claim to the throne and, he predicted, a civil war might well ensue. Both popular versifiers in England and French chroniclers also specifically drew attention to the potential threat from a Scotland housing, as it did, both fugitives from Lancastrian rule and a pseudo-Richard (a man claiming to be Richard II). Fear of a plan formulated by Ricardian exiles and their Scottish hosts to foment rebellion in England and rescue the imprisoned James I of Scotland, moreover, probably helps to explain Henry V's arrest of a group of obscure conspirators only a few weeks into the reign. Their leader, an English yeoman John Whitelock, was subsequently brought to trial in King's Bench in July 1413 accused of plotting rebellion, conspiring to assassinate Henry V, favouring the king's enemies in Scotland and backing Thomas Ward (the pseudo-Richard) as true king of England. Interestingly, although this obscure conspiracy never seriously threatened his security, Henry was furious when Whitelock managed to escape; by the autumn of 1413 recognizances of good behaviour had been required of several leading English magnates; and the ceremonial reburial of Richard II's body in Westminster Abbey, in December 1413, probably had more than just symbolic significance.

Perhaps the greatest threat to Henry V's authority in 1413/14, if not his security, was posed by the proto-Protestant Lollards and their high profile leader Sir John Oldcastle. More probably, their importance was much exaggerated by contemporary and near-contemporary biographers and chroniclers, particularly clerics such as the anonymous author of the *Gesta Henrici Quinti*, Thomas Elmham and Thomas Walsingham who were genuinely horrified by Lollard beliefs, behaviour and the threat of heresy to the established church. No doubt, too, Henry V recognised the sheer propaganda value of presenting an image of himself as God's agent, and the church's secular protector, against forces of evil directed against both crown and people. As a result, it is often far from easy to separate fact from fiction, exaggeration from accurate reporting, in the narratives that have come down to us, central though they must remain to any reconstruction of events. Of Henry V's own strict and unflinching orthodoxy, however, there can be no doubt. Indeed, even before his accession he ranged himself firmly behind the established church and its defenders, not least in supporting Archbishop Thomas Arundel's purge of Lollards from Oxford University (the heresy's spiritual home ever since John Wycliffe first promulgated his unorthodox theological ideas there in the 1370s) in 1411. Prince Henry of Monmouth's traditional religious beliefs and their significance are perhaps most graphically demonstrated by his reaction to the Badby case in 1410, colourfully reported by Thomas Walsingham. John Badby, a Worcestershire artisan arrested for his Lollard sympathies, was brought to trial before Archbishop Arundel, condemned as a heretic and, when he refused to recant, handed over to the secular authorities for execution. Even contemporary records note the Prince of Wales's role in the affair while, according to Walsingham, once Badby had been condemned and imprisoned:

> ...Prince Henry, the king's eldest son, who was in London at the time, went to see him, and urged and advised him to come to his senses. But, lost in his own mists, he ignored this great prince's advice and chose rather to be burned than pay reverence to a living sacrament. So he was kept in prison before being consigned to consuming flames, which made him moan pitifully from the middle of the fire. The prince was moved by his terrible shouting, and ordered the timber to be taken off the fire, to remove the heat from him. He offered the man comfort, although he was nearly dead, promising that even now he could live, and receive a pardon and three pennies from the royal exchequer for every day of his life, if he would only come to his senses and recant. But the wretched man, rekindling his breath, spat on this generous offer, doubtless because he was possessed by an evil spirit. So Prince Henry ordered him to be put back on the flames and to receive no more mercy.[10]

Henry of Monmouth's presence at Smithfield to witness the burning of an obscure Lollard is surely evidence of both the prince's personal orthodoxy and his firm backing for the church's stance against heresy; moreover, since he was virtually running the government in 1410, it also provides an early pointer to his later stance, as king, towards religious dissent and its treasonable connotations for secular authority. Yet, paradoxically, the Lollard leader Sir John Oldcastle, a former companion-in-arms of the Prince of Wales, was at the same time enjoying his personal protection.

Contemporary and near-contemporary commentators made no attempt to disguise their hostility towards, and loathing for, Sir John

Oldcastle: the *Gesta Henrici Quinti*, for instance, vigorously denounced this 'man of sedition' and 'follower of Satan' who, poisoned by 'Wycliffite malevolence', proved such an 'enemy and subverter of the church'; Adam Usk remarked indignantly on the 'pestilential teachings' of the Lollards and 'the heretic' Sir John Oldcastle 'who despised the sacrament of the altar, the Blessed Virgin and confession'; an anony-mous London chronicler condemned Oldcastle and his affinity for conspiring the 'destruction of all holy church'; and Tito Livio's inform-ants convinced him that Sir John and his supporters 'made war against the priests, the church, the king and the entire kingdom'. While serving Henry of Monmouth during his Welsh campaigns, Oldcastle seems to have become not only a trusted lieutenant of the prince but also his close companion and, no doubt, this royal connection helps explain his marriage, in 1408, to a wealthy heiress: as a result he acquired both extensive estates and the title Lord Cobham. Even the *Gesta* admitted that, before Henry V's accession, Oldcastle was 'one of the most valued and intimate members' of his household, despite his 'slaughtering and pillaging the Welsh', securing his knighthood and 'flattering fortune' only by marriage and, 'swollen with the lust to dominate' as he was, always striving to 'fulfil his filthily corrupt design under a cloak of sanc-tity'. Perhaps, prior to 1413, Henry V turned a blind eye to Oldcastle's Lollard leanings; less plausibly, he may even have been unaware of them. Once king, however, he could no longer ignore a matter so potentially damaging to his preferred royal image and, when forced to choose between fidelity as a lord to a former companion-in-arms and duty as a Christian ruler to eradicate heresy, he did not shirk the decision. When Oldcastle, even after a series of personal interviews with his lord, refused to recant, the king (probably genuinely appalled to hear a prominent member of his own entourage voicing such strongly held Lollard opinions) sanctioned his arrest and imprisonment by the ecclesi-astical authorities in the summer of 1413. A few weeks later Oldcastle was arraigned before Archbishop Thomas Arundel and a panel of fellow ecclesiastics. Repeatedly pressed during the course of the trial, he vehe-mently denounced the pope as the head of Antichrist, the archbishops and bishops as his limbs, and the friars as his tail; as for his own judges, they were quite simply traitors to God! As a result, so the *Gesta* tells us, the tribunal, 'supported by the authority of the king', condemned:

…this traitor to God and man as a heretic (he being convicted by his own confession, nay, indeed, by his own vehement and obstinate assertion) and handed over to the secular arm for further punishment according to the established laws of the realm.[11]

Whether as a last-ditch lifeline to a former close associate or more probably, as Thomas Walsingham believed, because he did not want a sinner lost irrevocably for lack of time for repentance, the king even now granted Oldcastle a forty day stay of execution. It proved a futile gesture since, during the night of 19 October 1413, probably with the aid of outside supporters, he escaped from the Tower of London, went into hiding and, before long, began planning his revenge.

Less than three months after Sir John Oldcastle's break-out from the Tower came an abortive Lollard insurrection, two events which, for Henry V's government, contemporary commentators and, indeed, historians ever since have been regarded as irrevocably interconnected. Once he had 'escaped over the walls at night', declared Adam Usk, the newly convicted heretic:

…began sending out letters and messengers secretly encouraging his followers to join him at an open space called Ficket's Field, so that they could launch an attack against the king, destroy him, and all the prelates and the churches. But the king was informed of their plans and arrived there first that night with an armed force, so that when they [the rebels] came along, large numbers of them were rounded up, drawn and hanged.[12]

The *Gesta Henrici Quinti* reported even more dramatically how 'that man of bloody and unheard-of treachery' Sir John Oldcastle:

…resolved to make a surprise attack upon the king and his men and consign all indiscriminately to death by the sword. However, the treason of that follower of Satan having been discovered and resistance organised, God delivered the innocent from the hands of the ungodly.[13]

The fullest, and perhaps best informed, account of the affair, particularly its denouement, is to be found in the writings of the St Albans' monk Thomas Walsingham. Throughout his weeks of concealment, the chronicler tells us, Oldcastle was plotting revenge against the king until eventually:

> …while the king kept Christmas at Eltham, the Lollards, making a conspiracy, resolved to take or slay him unawares with his brothers. But certain of the conspirators warned the king of his danger, so that he quickly removed himself to Westminster, that place being safer and more populous. The Lollards met at nightfall in a field called St Giles near London, where it was reported that Sir John Oldcastle was waiting for his followers. There you might have seen crowds of men thronging the streets, drawn from all the counties of the realm by great promises of reward. Asked why they made such haste, they declared that they were rushing to meet Lord Cobham. But the king, not unaware of all this, at a well-chosen moment of the same night, ordered his followers to arm themselves… Entering the field shortly after midnight, [the king] established his position so as to be prepared for whatever might happen next day. Many who sought Lord Cobham's camp entered the royal camp by error [and] were taken prisoner. When the rebels heard that the king, with a strong force, had occupied a neighbouring field and captured many of their men, they were terrified, especially when no one from London came to join them [since] the king had ordered the closure of the city gates… Indeed, so it is said, had the king not done so as many as 50,000 servants and apprentices would have sallied forth against him. Thereupon the Lollards took to flight. The royal forces followed them, capturing some and killing others.[14]

Oldcastle himself escaped and remained on the run for almost three years until, so Adam Usk recorded, this heretic:

> …who had plotted the overthrow of the king and the kingdom was captured [and], having been brought before parliament and convocation, [he] was drawn on 14 December [1417] to the gallows and hanged there with an iron chain, being simultaneously, once and for all, consumed by a raging fire which was lit there, thus paying the penalty of both swords – and deservedly so.[15]

Clearly, the treatment of Sir John Oldcastle and Lollard conspiracy in contemporary and near-contemporary literary sources is far from impartial: all, to a greater or lesser extent, reflect royal propaganda condemning Lollardy, demonising Oldcastle and, above all, highlighting Henry V's prompt and entirely admirable reaction to a potentially lethal threat to both the English church and Lancastrian dynasty. In 1998 Paul Strohm, J.R.R. Tolkien Professor of English Language and Literature at Oxford University, even suggested the king may have deliberately invented the 'Oldcastle rising' of January 1414 as a handy means of consolidating royal authority, justifying the proscription of Lollards and headlining his own vital role as defender of Christian orthodoxy.[16] Such an extreme interpretation cannot be justified but, certainly, not only biographers and chroniclers but also the records of central government did very much take on board the 'official' line. The author of the *Gesta Henrici Quinti*, significantly, chose to begin his recital of Henry V's deeds with Oldcastle's plot to capture the king and seize the city of London; he emphasised how this devout Christian ruler, upholder and defender of the faith, was at the very outset placed 'in the furnace of tribulation' by his most intimate companion and his treacherous followers; and he revelled in the king's triumph over the Lollards as clear evidence of his status as the true and favoured instrument of God. Thomas Elmham, amidst a wealth of biblical imagery and polemic against the Lollards, deliberately juxtaposed Oldcastle, the Antichrist, and the Christ-like figure of Henry V. Tito Livio, in similar vein, proclaimed that Henry V's 'first battle was with heretics and others who were straying from the true doctrines of the church'; the king 'made an assault on the heretics and overcame them almost without a struggle'; and, as a result, 'the first great victory of this prince was gained for Christ and God's church against evil heretics'. Chroniclers such as Thomas Walsingham, Adam Usk and John Strecche, too, largely shared the compelling perspective of the king's biographers.

Distinguishing historical fact from propagandist hyperbole in all these accounts is virtually impossible but, with the help of surviving record evidence, modern historians have valiantly attempted to do so. Following his escape from custody in mid-October 1413, Oldcastle apparently despatched messages to Lollard congregations in the Midlands, West Country and South-east requesting that they gather

Dere shewith. howe after the cumming home of Erle Richard, from the holy londes
henry the 6th then beyng kyng of Englond, was secretely enfourmed of a preuey and
sodeyn insurreccion of traiterous heretikes whiche sodenly by myghte purposed to haue
taken & kept the kyng vnder their rule a subieccion, and after by his auctorite to haue
destroyed the churche of Englond, and to slee the state, and distribute their possessions
ayenst the honor of god, after their indiscrete advise and pleasure.

The betrayal of the Lollard conspiracy of 1413/4 to Henry V.

in St Giles' Field outside the walls of London during the night of 9–10 January 1414. By then, unless the story is indeed no more than a cunning royal fabrication, he planned that a group of conspirators, disguised as festive mummers, would have kidnapped (if not killed) the king and his brothers as they celebrated Twelfth Night (6 January) at Eltham palace, as a prelude to his Lollard supporters seizing power a few days later and setting in motion root-and-branch reform of the church. Through good intelligence, we are led to believe, Henry V got wind of Oldcastle's schemes, the attempt to capture him and his brothers was thwarted and, by the time insurgents began gathering in earnest, he was fully prepared to resist them. Just how many putative rebels turned up is far from clear but, certainly, nowhere near the 'crowds of men' from 'all countries of the realm' reported by Thomas Walsingham. At most there were probably a few hundred; little, if any, organised fighting took place; and, although about eighty men were arrested, fewer than fifty suffered burning as heretics. In the aftermath of this fiasco of a rebellion, however, there was a sharp increase in the prosecution of Lollards; rumours of Lollard plots occasionally surfaced over the next two or three years but none materialised; and, although Oldcastle remained at large until recaptured at Welshpool in November 1417, he was more an irritation than a threat. His condemnation as a notorious heretic and traitor by the Lords in parliament, and execution in London, rapidly followed. If Lollardy had ever constituted a serious menace to Henry V's government, the death of Sir John Oldcastle finally put paid to it. Indeed, its real political significance had probably always been as a handy propaganda weapon for the crown: now, the king's role as defender of Christian orthodoxy and protector of the established church was clear for all to see; more importantly, perhaps, so was his determination to deal ruthlessly with any perceived threat to the Lancastrian dynasty.

At the end of July 1415, when Henry V's preparations for invading France were virtually complete, news of the so-called Southampton conspiracy reached his ears at nearby Portchester castle and, again, his reaction was swift and decisive. For the anonymous author of the *Gesta Henrici Quinti*, who was in the king's entourage at the time, it was another divinely inspired trial of 'the constancy of His Elect'. God, he declared, now once more deliberately allowed Henry 'to be tested and smitten' by a 'hammer-blow causing great perturbation' when:

...our adversary the Devil entered into the hearts of certain men close at hand, namely the lords Richard Earl of Cambridge, his cousin-german, Henry Lord Scrope, an intimate member of his own household and one who was almost second to none in the kingdom among those in the king's confidence, and also Thomas Grey, a knight famous and noble if only he had not been dishonoured by this stench of treason. These men, in their brutal madness and mad brutality, tainted with a lust for power, but even more so by the stench of French promises or bribes, had conspired all too viciously and inhumanly, not only to prevent the intended expedition [to France] but also to inflict disaster by killing the king.

Fortunately, however, God 'soon delivered the just from the ungodly and revealed the Judas-like iniquity of these evil men through the Lord Mortimer, the Earl of March, whose innocence they had assaulted as part of this murderous design'. The *Gesta*, no doubt reflecting rumours circulating at the time or even royal propaganda, clearly believed the Southampton conspirators enjoyed financial backing from France designed to thwart the king's invasion plans. An anonymous *Brut* chronicler, too, reported that:

...Richard Earl of Cambridge, brother to the Duke of York, Lord Scrope, treasurer of England, and Sir Thomas Grey had received a huge sum of money, that is to say a million of gold, to betray the king and his brother to the Frenchmen.

Adam Usk was even more explicit, declaring that, shortly before embarking for France, Henry V was met:

...by the ambassadors of the King of France. They pretended to be seeking peace but, in fact, bribed a number of the king's councillors, the brother of the Duke of York, and Lords Scrope and Grey, with a large sum of gold, to kill him, or at least to put a stop to his expedition. Their plot was revealed by the Earl of March.

For an indignant Thomas Walsingham, likewise, sheer greed provided the main motivation for 'three of the most powerful' of the king's magnates, 'in whom he specially trusted', to conspire to betray and kill him:

The first and chief of them was Henry Lord Scrope, in whose faith and constancy the king had trusted his whole heart. [Yet] he entered into negotiations with the enemy, as a hidden foe to his lord the king, whom he soothed with false assurances… He had as fellow conspirators Richard Earl of Cambridge, brother of the Duke of York, and Thomas Grey, a northern knight. The king had created this Richard an earl and had enriched him with many goods and had honoured him outstandingly because of his lineage and parentage. But no good-will shown towards them, no benefits conferred upon them, could deter the traitors from preparing to kill so great a benefactor.

The Burgundian chronicler Enguerrand de Monstrelet, however, chose to put most stress on the conspirators' aim of replacing Henry V by Edmund Mortimer Earl of March. 'While the King of England was in Southampton with all his army ready to sail for the invasion of France', he learned, Henry V was informed that:

> …some of the chief lords of his household had conspired against him to place the Earl of March on the throne of England as the rightful heir to the late King Richard. It was a fact that the Earl of Cambridge with some others had plotted to seize the king and his brothers with that aim in view. They revealed their intentions to the Earl of March who immediately told the king, advising him to be on his guard or he would be betrayed, and gave the names of the conspirators.

In his own confession and plea for mercy to Henry V Richard Earl of Cambridge, too, admitted that the conspirators' plan had been for Mortimer to go:

> …into the land of Wales, without your licence, taking upon him the sovereignty of this land, [issuing a proclamation] in the Earl [of March's] name against you, my liege lord, called by an untrue name 'Harry of Lancaster, usurper of England', with the intention of persuading people to draw to him and away from you. [Moreover, it was intended to bring] that person which they named King Richard out of Scotland, with a power of Scots, their power together seeming to them sufficient to give you a battle.[17]

Virtually all contemporary and near-contemporary commentators report the failure of the Southampton plot, and its inevitable consequences, with every sign of satisfaction. By the will of God, declared Thomas Walsingham, the conspirators were discovered 'before they were able to accomplish their crime and, by the judgement of their peers, they were ordered to be beheaded'; once their plot had been revealed, echoed Adam Usk, 'they suffered the fate which they justly merited for such treason'; and, according to the *Genta Henrici Quinti*, 'after they had made public confession and sentence had been pronounced, the lords Richard Earl of Cambridge and Thomas Grey underwent punishment by beheading'. As for Henry Lord Scrope, 'the more culpable an enemy because the more intimate a friend', such was the 'infamy of his offence' that, prior to decapitation at 'the place of execution' in Southampton, he was 'drawn through the middle of the town'. Apart from his own brothers, remarked Walsingham, there was 'hardly anyone among the English people so dear' to Henry V, as the king 'openly proved by the display of affection he frequently showed to him'; Monstrelet learned that, so close were the two, Scrope 'slept each night in the king's room'; and his fellow Burgundian chronicler Jean le Fevre, too, noted how Henry V greatly loved this man 'who many times had slept with the king and in his chamber'. Within two months of the baron's execution, indeed, Henry Lord Scrope was remembered in the mayor of York's register as a man 'whom the king had loved more than all others' and to whom 'he had shown signs of the greatest favour'.

T.B. Pugh, the only recent historian to tackle the Southampton plot in real depth, rejected most literary sources with contempt. Indeed, he declared in 1988, none of the fifteenth-century chroniclers show any understanding of the grievances that led to the conspirators' bid to overthrow Henry V and their reporting of facts, too, often leaves a great deal to be desired. Even the author of the *Gesta Henrici Quinti*, despite being in the neighbourhood of Southampton in late July and early August 1415, was both unreliable and inaccurate when recollecting the conspiracy: for instance, his allegation that Cambridge and his associates were corrupted by French bribes lacks any sound foundation; he wrongly depicted Edmund Mortimer Earl of March as innocent of conspiracy; and he mistakenly recorded that Thomas Grey, as well as Cambridge and Scrope, was tried and executed for treason on Monday 5 August when, in fact, he had met his fate the previous Friday. Nor can

Thomas Walsingham, although also writing within a few years of the events, be relied upon. For Pugh, record evidence – particularly the very full confessions made by all three leading conspirators and the details of their treason trials preserved on the 1415 parliament roll – provide an altogether more reliable guide.

Largely on the basis of such evidence, he concluded that the Southampton conspiracy had virtually collapsed even before its betrayal to the king by Edmund Mortimer Earl of March. There was no plot to assassinate Henry V and his three brothers; rather, this was a story deliberately concocted to ensure Cambridge, Scrope and Grey could not escape the death penalty. Nor was there ever any real prospect of the conspirators launching a successful rebellion against the king: the timid, unambitious and inept Mortimer could never have provided a convincing alternative to the young and vigorous Henry V; Cambridge was a political nonentity, lacking the territorial power-base to foment provincial insurrection himself and entirely unrealistic in his hopes of a Welsh rising, Scottish intervention or the exiled Henry Percy Earl of Northumberland's capacity to raise northern England; and, anyway, the English nobility had already demonstrated its firm commitment to the Lancastrian dynasty. Indeed, the whole affair was largely a product of fantasy, delusion and its leaders' personal griev-ances: Mortimer resented the large fine recently exacted from him for failing to secure royal permission to marry; Cambridge's legitimate expectations of a landed endowment commensurate with his newly acquired title had been thwarted; Grey was simply covetous; and, as for Scrope (who had probably never belonged to Henry V's inner circle), not only his motives but even his role in the conspiracy remain a mys-tery. As for the indictments against the conspirators, they were carefully framed to ensure condemnations for treachery; Grey was tried, con-victed and beheaded with almost indecent haste on Friday 2 August; and the guilty verdicts brought in on Cambridge and Scrope (by a court of peers presided over by the king's own brother Thomas Duke of Clarence on Monday 5 August) were a foregone conclusion too, as was their execution on the very same day.

Clearly, there remains plenty of room for controversy about the Southampton plot. Pugh's rejection of the testimony of contemporary and near-contemporary commentators was too cavalier; the evidence of confessions and letters designed to save the conspirators' skins seems no less suspect; and the records of indictments, trials and executions obviously reflect the government's preferred version of events. Not in doubt is the swiftness and implacability of Henry V's reaction to the conspiracy, news of which was probably revealed to him at Portchester castle on 31 July 1415. Perhaps Edmund Mortimer did indeed betray plans to seize, or even kill, the king and his brothers; more plausibly, government agents warned Henry that an unholy alliance of aristocratic malcontents, Ricardian loyalists, Welsh rebels, Scottish adversaries, even Oldcastle and the Lollards, might launch a series of coordinated risings during his absence in France unless he reacted decisively now; and even after the Southampton conspirators had been seized, tried and executed, if we are to believe Thomas Walsingham, dissidents continued 'to raise their tails, vomit blasphemies about the king, speak out bombastically, and post threatening bills on the doors of churches and in other locations'. Yet Henry V clearly recognised, too, the propagandist potential of a high profile response to what may well have been, in reality, a hopelessly flawed and futile project to emulate the series of rebellions that had so disturbed the early years of his father's reign. They had failed; so did this; and the king could embark for France reassured that any potential resistance at home had been quelled. Moreover, although probably more than a mere armchair conspiracy, his throne had never been seriously threatened: indeed, the rapid collapse of this plot, like Oldcastle's Lollard rising the previous year, mainly serves to demonstrate just how little real opposition to Lancastrian rule there now was. Mortimer had been, at most, a nervous early party to the affair; Henry V speedily pardoned him (perhaps because he had, as reported, helped blow the whistle on its leaders); and he never blotted his copybook again. Cambridge, Scrope and Grey paid the full penalty for their disloyalty but, interestingly, Cambridge's young heir Richard of York was nevertheless brought up in the royal household. Most importantly, the Southampton plot had no sequel; the king's fleet set sail for France on 11 August 1415, less than a week after the executions of Cambridge and Scrope; and, over the next few years, Henry V could pursue his ambitions across the Channel confident that he left behind him a largely united kingdom.

Richard Beauchamp Earl of Warwick's appointment as captain of Calais by Henry V, February 1414.

10

POLITICS AND GOVERNMENT
IN ENGLAND

Politics and government in England during the reign of Henry V receive but scant attention in the pages of contemporary and near-contemporary biographies and chronicles: they, like the king himself, focussed mainly on Anglo-French diplomacy, the Agincourt campaign, the conquest of Normandy and the military legacy of the Treaty of Troyes. This is hardly surprising, reflecting as it does both the thrust of royal propaganda and the fact that, for over half his reign, Henry V was out of the country: for about three months in 1415, for three and a half years from July 1417 to February 1421 and, again, from July 1421 until the king's death at the end of August 1422. Yet the king never neglected domestic matters and there is a wealth of record evidence available for the study of Lancastrian administration, parliament, government finance, the legal system, and the relationship between crown and provinces. Even before his accession he had experience of the workings of the royal council (nearest medieval equivalent to a modern cabinet), most notably in 1410/11 when he virtually headed it on Henry IV's behalf and, although in 1413 he naturally favoured men like Henry Beaufort Bishop of Winchester (his first chancellor) who had served him as Prince of Wales, his administration also included many tried and trusted servants of his father. He clearly recognised talent and rewarded it; his council, whether the king was in England or not, proved itself a trustworthy and efficient organ of government; and, both at the centre and in the localities, he built up a competent and reliable team of administrators. The king himself was brisk, business-like, well informed and capable of maintaining a close scrutiny over all aspects of government. Even routine matters did not escape his attention and, while perfectly prepared to delegate authority, he never relinquished the reins of government completely. Most notably, when campaigning in France he directed a steady stream of instructions and letters (occasionally written in his own hand and frequently at his dictation) to his ministers and servants at home: in July 1419, for instance, he demanded (in response to a complaint of misgovernment) that his representatives in England 'call the justices' to their presence and 'by their advice' ensure the matter was equitably dealt with; in September 1419 he peremptorily insisted that an annuity be paid 'without delay and in haste'; and, in 1420, he required that all petitions to parliament be submitted to him for his personal attention. All in all Henry V breathed new life into royal government: he scrutinised his officials, punished corruption and, always, insisted on the crown's rights and dues; yet, at the same time and despite a notably restrained exercise of his wide powers of patronage, he both inspired the confidence, and won the loyalty, of England's ruling elite.

During the early years of Henry IV's reign crown/parliament relations had often been difficult as the king struggled to establish a new dynasty and the Commons pressed hard for conciliar reform, better financial management and improved defences. Henry V realised that, if he was to overcome a legacy of parliamentary suspicion and resentment stretching back to the last years of Edward III in the 1370s, he would need to adopt a fresh stratagem designed to foster cooperation with, and win the confidence of, the Commons. Already, when exercising power on his father's behalf in 1410 and 1411, he had begun to appreciate the value of managing parliament in the government's interests. Now, as king, he soon demonstrated a real flair for promoting cordial relations and mutual understanding between himself and his non-noble subjects, and ensuring that, when he embarked on his French campaigns, he could do so in a spirit of partnership with parliament. Even so, relations with his early parliaments in 1413 and 1414 were far from straightforward and his attempts to make the speaker of the Commons a virtual government agent, for instance, met real resistance: indeed William Stourton, speaker in Henry V's first parliament meeting at Westminster in May 1413, robustly reminded the king that, although his father had reacted positively on more than one occasion to the Commons' expressed desire for good governance, he had done little in practice to promote it. Chancellor Henry Beaufort clearly played a key role in calming parliamentary apprehensions and misgivings: in his opening speech he specifically promised that, if the king's reasonable requests for taxation were met, real efforts would be made to restore 'bone governance', promote sound financial management, enforce law and order, and defend the realm. And, in the king's second parliament meeting at Leicester in the spring of 1414, not only were specific measures enacted to root out the perceived threat of Lollardy and strengthen the machinery of law enforcement, real action to put them into practice soon followed. As a result cooperation, not conflict, became very much the mark of succeeding parliaments (at any rate until the Treaty of Troyes and its implications became an issue in 1420); regular, and generous, grants of taxation were forthcoming to help finance the king's French campaigns, almost without complaint; and, although little significant legislation resulted, Henry V certainly proved adept at managing parliament and responding sympathetically (if not necessarily productively) to its expressed concerns.

Clearly, Henry V's parliaments met in an atmosphere very different from that prevailing in his father's reign and this was partly down to the king himself. In successive opening speeches his chancellors, on his behalf, plugged the same propaganda line as the *Gesta Henrici Quinti* and, when in England, he may well have been present in person: here, they declared, was a king genuinely concerned for the well-being and good governance of his people; a man of action who was, nevertheless, prepared to heed advice before acting; and a ruler determined to defend the church, enforce the law and resolutely pursue his just claims across the Channel in France. Occasionally he made concessions to the Commons (but never at the expense of his own prerogative powers) and he may, even, have regarded the achievement of a smooth crown/parliament relationship as part of a joint enterprise to secure peace and stability at home. Yet, for Henry V, what mattered most of all was to win, and retain, the support of the political nation in parliament for his on-going French endeavours.

If Henry V's normally cordial relations with parliament stood in stark contrast to his father's tempestuous experiences of the institution, so did his management of the crown's finances. Lack of money, in fact, had proved an almost constant irritant in crown/parliament relations during Henry IV's early years: the Commons had criticised his excessive household expenses, developed the notion that redress of grievances should precede the supply of parliamentary cash and even attempted to direct how taxation be used. Significantly, when in control of the council in 1410/11, Prince Hal made a preliminary attempt to address parliament's grievances. Once king, so Adam Usk tells us, he obtained 'great sums from the general pardon'; when 'confirming annuities granted by his father he reserved the first year's yield for himself'; and, as for 'patents of grants reissued at the beginning of the reign', required fees were doubled. Records confirm, moreover, that Henry V did indeed seek to couple strict financial discipline with real efforts to increase the crown's revenues; he maintained a close personal interest in the enhancement, collection and spending of his income; and he even scrutinised royal accounts himself when he felt it was necessary. No new financial machinery or sources of income were developed in Henry V's reign; rather, the king sought to make the existing system work more effectively and maximise yields from traditional crown revenues: royal estates, customs duties, feudal prerogatives and the profits of justice. Even so, regular income, no matter how carefully nurtured, could never prove sufficient to finance the costs of war (especially the expensive and sustained campaigns Henry V mounted in France): no doubt, however, his success in restoring the crown's solvency on the home front helps explain why parliament proved so generous in granting the taxation, and his richer subjects so ready to make the loans, that were essential if his ambitions across the Channel were to be realised.

During the later years of Henry IV's reign there was mounting concern about the prevalence of lawlessness and the urgent need to restore public order in England. Indeed, this was probably the major problem facing Henry V on his accession, particularly since the establishment of peace and security at home was an obvious and essential preliminary to any renewal of the war with France. Such a view had certainly been expressed by Thomas Hoccleve a couple of years earlier in his *Regement of Princes*, specifically dedicated to Henry of Monmouth in 1411: the rule of law, he then declared, had virtually vanished from the land; in every shire, under the protection of great lords, bands of armed men were taking the law into their own hands; and, unless rapid measures were taken to remedy the situation, the kingdom would be lost. Moreover, when parliament met in May 1413, the Commons also chose to highlight Henry IV's repeatedly broken promises to restore law and order and petitioned the new king to suppress disorder without delay. Yet it was only in the aftermath of the abortive Lollard rising of January 1414 that Henry V inaugurated determined measures to tackle the problem. When parliament assembled once more at Leicester at the end of April 1414 the principal theme was law enforcement. Chancellor Beaufort chose 'he has set his heart to keep the laws' as his opening text and legislation was brought forward 'for the chastisement and punishment of the rioters, murderers and other malefactors who more than ever abound in many parts of the kingdom'. More significantly, perhaps, the central criminal court of King's Bench accompanied the king to Leicester and, immediately after the close of parliament, Henry V and his justices embarked on a vigorous programme of law enforcement in the west Midlands and elsewhere: indeed, the king presided in person over some sessions. Yet, arguably, all he had achieved by the time parliament met again in November 1414 was to confine chronic disorder in the realm within more acceptable limits than hitherto. By then, too, Henry V's attention was becoming ever more focussed on France: all other business, including judicial administration, had probably now become secondary to renewing the Hundred Years War. Indeed, it could well be that the judicial visitations of 1414 had been intended all along as a necessary preparation for this: settling the realm at home so that he could wage war abroad without fear of insurrection. Significantly, Beaufort's opening address in November 1414 had both a martial tone and particularly highlighted the notion of Henry V as a just ruler well worthy of God's support. 'Strive for justice and God will fight on your side', he declared, 'for without justice the republic is not ruled'. The general pardon promulgated in parliament in December 1414, moreover, certainly suggests that the king's principal aim was the restoration of social harmony rather than the punishment of crime. For the next few months until he left England for France, even more than before, reconciliation became his watchword, particularly when it came to magnates and gentry. In the early fifteenth century the crown was heavily dependent on local nobility in the provinces for the enforcement of law and order; yet, all too often, they themselves were the principal promoters of private feuds and local disorder. Hence why Henry V – by the imposition of recognizances as guarantees of future good behaviour, for instance, and the firm encouragement of arbitration as a means of settling disputes – made such determined efforts to curtail the phenomenon of elite violence. Pardons, too, had a vital role to play, particularly if their issue was made conditional on the performance of military service overseas. Even notorious criminals could obtain pardons providing they agreed, in return, to fight for Henry V in France. Indeed, the king may even have believed that channelling the energies of serious disturbers of the peace at home into fruitful (and potentially lucrative) campaigning abroad was the best way of restoring law and order in the shires.

Many years after Henry V's death the chronicler John Harding certainly looked back nostalgically on his reign as an era of peace and stability in England:

> Above all things, he kept the law and peace,
> Throughout all England, that no insurrection
> Nor any riots were not made to cease.
> No neighbours' war remained without correction
> But peaceably all under his protection
> Complaints of wrongs always in general
> Reformed were under his justice equal.

In fact, concluded Harding:

> The peace at home and law so well maintained
> Were root and head of all his great conquest.[18]

Clearly, so very positive a verdict must be treated with at least a degree of caution. Nevertheless, the success of Henry V's law enforcement policies is indeed demonstrated by the relative infrequency of serious disorder at home during his long absences abroad between 1415 and 1422; he made far more effective use of existing judicial machinery (he was no more an innovator here than in the financial sphere) than his father ever had; and, although public order was by no means perfectly maintained (there were plenty of complaints of the excesses of soldiers, for instance, and private feuds did not disappear completely), the second Lancastrian did prove that England was not ungovernable and his reign stands out as one of the few periods of relatively good order in the fifteenth century.

Although Henry V achieved much in England between 1413 and 1420, there are distinct signs of impending crisis at home during the king's last years, particularly on the financial front. As early as 1416 parliament had begun to express concern about the volume of taxation it was being called upon to levy and, in both December 1420 and May 1421, Henry V probably judged it prudent not even to ask the Commons for further subsidies. 1421, in fact, was the first year in his reign when no new parliamentary taxation was collected. Yet, by then, the royal finances had clearly become severely strained by the relentless cost of campaign and conquest in France: he had accumulated substantial debts; his government's credit worthiness had weakened alarmingly; and arrears of pay to both soldiers and civilians had mounted, and were still mounting, relentlessly. As a result, when the king returned to England for a few months in 1421 he had no choice but to launch a personal, and sustained, charm offensive in London and the provinces in order to raise desperately needed cash. If we are to believe Adam Usk, indeed, the king had now begun 'fleecing anyone with money, rich or poor, throughout the realm, in readiness for his return to France', so much so that his 'unbearable extortions' were provoking 'dark – though private – mutterings and curses'.

There are certainly plenty of indications that crown/parliament relations were becoming increasingly strained by the end of 1420, not least as a result of the Treaty of Troyes and its implications. Already, in 1419, the Commons had granted taxation for defensive purposes only and insisted that, in doing so, they were not committing themselves to future wars in France. The next parliament, called to Westminster in December 1420, proved much the most critical Henry V's government had yet faced. Humphrey Duke of Gloucester, deputising for his absent elder brother, was urged to persuade the king to return home from France as soon as possible (for the first time in three and a half years), probably reflecting growing feelings that England was in real danger of being relegated to permanent second place in Henry V's order of priorities. No less significantly, the Commons specifically demanded confirmation of Edward III's undertaking of 1340 that Englishmen should never be subject to the king by virtue of his *French* title, nor should English liberties be in any way compromised. Moreover when, in May 1421, parliament at last ratified the terms of the Treaty of Troyes, the Commons again insisted that Henry V declare he had no intention of introducing French laws and customs into England. Clearly, similar considerations also help explain parliament's increasing reluctance to grant subsidies: as far as the Commons were concerned, as a result of the Treaty of Troyes what had hitherto been a war between two nations had now become a war between Henry V (as regent of France) and the French king's rebellious subjects, a war in which the English people no longer had any part to play. In a nutshell, fighting in France should henceforth be financed by Frenchmen! Not until December 1421, in fact, was parliament prevailed upon to vote what turned out to be a final subsidy to Henry V and, again, it was specifically earmarked for the defence of England.

Henry V, for most of his reign at least, did demonstrate that English medieval government could be made to work far more effectively than it had in his father's time. Yet he had nothing new to offer and, in his last years, serious cracks were clearly beginning to emerge. Parliament could still prove difficult even for him to handle; his financial situation became ever more insecure; and, since he could never afford even a police force let alone a standing army, the implementation of a coercive system of justice inevitably eluded him (and, to the end, there were still parts of the country – for instance, the Welsh and Scottish borders – where the king's peace continued to be frequently broken). Once his son Henry VI came of age, and turned out to be the most inept of all England's later medieval kings, it soon became apparent that deep-seated defects in English government and administration were still very much there.

II

RENEWAL OF THE
HUNDRED YEARS WAR

Ever since 1066, when a Norman duke became king of England by right of conquest, English territories across the Channel had fuelled intermittent Anglo-French warfare. As a result of Henry II of England's marriage to Eleanor of Aquitaine in the mid-twelfth century, the Angevin empire was born and the potential for hostilities became greater still. Even after King John lost his northern French possessions (Normandy, Maine, Anjou and Touraine) to Philip Augustus early in the thirteenth century, the duchy of Aquitaine (or Gascony) remained in English hands, much to the chagrin of the French monarchy. Eventually, by the Treaty of Paris (1259), Louis IX of France agreed that Henry III of England should retain the province but on new terms: henceforth the sovereignty of Aquitaine was to be vested in the French crown, the English king acknowledging his own ducal status as a French feudal vassal. Inevitably, such a relationship soon resulted in renewed conflict, not least since, as the power of the French monarchy grew in the later thirteenth and early fourteenth centuries, the position of the English king/duke seemed ever more anomalous. The English crown, for its part, increasingly began to press for full sovereignty and, by the mid-1330s, this had become a very vexed issue indeed. The final straw came when, in May 1337, Philip VI of France declared Aquitaine confiscated on the grounds that Edward III had adamantly refused to acknowledge his obligations as a French prince, the English king ostentatiously defied 'Philip of Valois who calls himself King of France' and the Hundred Years War began. The situation was further exacerbated when, in 1340, Edward III also claimed the French throne (as grandson of Philip IV of France). After over twenty years of warfare, during which the English won a major naval victory (at Sluys in 1340) and twice defeated the French in the field (at the battles of Crecy in 1346 and Poitiers in 1356), the Treaty of Bretigny was sealed in 1360.

Bretigny was the high-water mark of English success in France in the fourteenth century: it gave Edward a greatly enlarged Aquitaine in full sovereignty, not to mention additional territories in France, in return for abandoning his claim to the French crown (which he may never have seriously coveted anyway). Peace only lasted until 1369, however, by which time France was under the vigorous rule of Charles V while Edward III was already entering an early dotage; consequently, in the renewed war, there was a notable French resurgence and, by the time Edward died in 1377, the English situation in France had been transformed and virtually all the gains of the Treaty of Bretigny set at nought. During the next three decades Richard II, Henry IV and, indeed, Prince Henry of Monmouth probably shared a common objective: realising, once and for all, the goal of an English Aquitaine in full sovereignty. Perhaps, when he negotiated a marriage to Charles VI's young daughter Isabella and a lengthy truce with France in 1396, Richard II believed the matter had been resolved. Henry IV's seizure of the English crown in 1399 rapidly put paid to that: indeed, for the next few years, the French did all they could to exploit the new Lancastrian king's difficulties at home to their own advantage. By 1411, however, the boot was firmly on the other foot. Ever since he had first gone beserk in 1392 and slaughtered several of his hunting compan-ions, Charles VI of France had suffered increasingly frequent bouts of mental instability and a bitter struggle for power between two power-ful French aristocratic factions – the Armagnacs (or Orleanists) and the Burgundians – resulted; in 1407 Louis Duke of Orleans, Charles VI's brother, was murdered on the orders of his princely rival John the Fearless Duke of Burgundy; and, in 1410, France dissolved into civil war. Inevitably, both Armagnacs and Burgundians soon appealed to England for support and in October 1411 the Prince of Wales, as head of his ailing father's council, despatched an English force to aid John the Fearless (possibly in return for a Burgundian promise not only to recognise Lancastrian sovereignty in Aquitaine but even assist in the recovery of long lost Normandy). When Henry IV rallied and ousted his eldest son from power in November 1411, however, the prince's pro-Burgundian stance was rapidly abandoned in favour of an alliance with the Armagnacs. Not that the king's objectives differed overmuch. Under the terms of the Treaty of Bourges in May 1412, indeed, the Armagnacs not only recognised that Aquitaine was English but specifically acknowledged Henry IV's *ancestral* right to the province. In return, a major pro-Armagnac expedition led by the king's second son Thomas Duke of Clarence sailed for France in August 1412, only to find, on arrival, that Armagnac/Burgundian hostilities had temporarily ceased! As a result the English force achieved precisely nothing and the Treaty of Bourges, probably never worth much in practice anyway, now became a complete dead letter. Nevertheless, the potential vulnerability of a faction-ridden France under the hapless Charles VI had been graphically exposed and Henry V was just the man to take full advantage of so tempting a prospect.

Although there is no contemporary or near-contemporary evidence to support the suggestion, in the opening scene of William Shakespeare's *Henry V*, that leading churchmen deliberately encouraged Henry to embark on his French adventures so as to prevent the confiscation of ecclesiastical property at home, Shakespeare's portrayal of a king invading France in pursuit of justice certainly can be traced back to the second Lancastrian's own times. Indeed, it is the central plank of Lancastrian pro-war propaganda. Henry V, it was stressed, had legitimate long-standing claims to territory in France (including Normandy and other lands seized by Philip Augustus from King John) and, more specifically, sovereign rights in Aquitaine and elsewhere clearly spelled out in the Treaty of Bretigny. The French, so the official line went, were unjustly and rebelliously resisting the English king's claims and denying his rights; if diplomacy failed to resolve the impasse, then force might legitimately be employed as a last resort; and if it came to the crunch, as an upright Christian prince enjoying God's full support, Henry V had a positive duty to fight a just war across the Channel. Indeed, on the eve of the Agincourt campaign, an anonymous poet declared that not only had the time now come to end Anglo-French negotiations but also that the king should openly pursue his rightful claim to the French crown. At almost every parliament of Henry V's reign, moreover, recovering royal rights in France furnished a major theme in chancellors' opening addresses: most notably, in March 1416, Henry Beaufort Bishop of Winchester declared that the king certainly wanted peace but a just peace recognising his legitimate claims across the Channel. Henry, he continued, had striven to achieve this objective by negotiation but unsuccessfully because the French were full of pride. Hence why the king had resorted to the sword; his great victories at Harfleur and Agincourt had proved God favoured the English; and yet, the chancellor concluded, 'we make war so that we may have peace, because the end of war is peace'. Diplomatic correspondence frequently makes precisely the same points. At the end of July 1415, for instance, in a letter despatched from Southampton to Charles VI of France, Henry V made clear his intention 'to have the rights which generations of our predecessors have left to us' rather than 'suffer the crown of England to be disinherited'. Indeed, he declared:

> We are not so blinded by fear that we should not be ready to fight for the justice of our cause: but the law of Deuteronomy has ordained that whoever prepares to attack a city must first offer it peace. We therefore exhort you, according to the perfect teaching of the Gospel 'Friend pay me what thou owest' and in order that the deluge of human blood be saved, that restitution be made of the inheritance and of the rights that have been cruelly taken away from us or at least of those which on previous occasions through our ambassadors and envoys we have already demanded of you and with which we are content out of respect for God and in the interests of peace.[19]

Earlier in the year, in a message to the mayor and aldermen of London dated 10 March, he had expressed similar sentiments, proclaiming his resolve, 'with no small army, to visit the parts beyond the sea, so that we may duly reconquer the lands pertaining to the heirship and crown of our realm, which have been for so long, in this time of our predecessors, by enormous wrong withheld'. On his death bed in August 1422, moreover, Henry V was still affirming that he had waged war not from any desire for worldly glory but simply in order to prosecute his just title in France and obtain 'peace and my own rights'.

The *Gesta Henrici Quinti* provides the clearest and most compelling rendering of the government line on Henry V's aims and intentions across the Channel, always representing the king as seeking peace with justice and only resorting to war when prolonged negotiations with the obstinate and rebellious French had failed. Indeed, declared the *Gesta*, before launching his invasion of France in 1415 'to recover his duchy of Normandy, which belongs to him entirely by a right dating from the time of William the Conqueror' but withheld 'for a long time past against God and all justice by the violence of the French', he ordered the transcription of:

> ...the pacts and covenants not so long ago entered into between King Henry IV of England, his father, and certain of the great princes of France [in the Treaty of Bourges in 1412] on the subject of his divine right and claim to the duchy of Aquitaine, from which they had rashly departed against their oaths, signatures and seals. And he sent some of these transcripts to the General Council [of Constance] and the Emperor Sigismund, and to other Catholic princes, that all Christendom might know what great acts of injustice the French in their duplicity had inflicted on him, and that he was being compelled, reluctantly and against his will, to raise his standard against the rebels.

The chaplain also specifically highlighted Henry Beaufort Bishop of Winchester's parliamentary declaration of March 1416 that 'the title of the crown of England to the kingdom of France had been divinely made plain' by Edward III's naval victory at Sluys in 1340, his son the Black Prince's triumph at Poitiers in 1356 and, most recently, by Henry V himself at Agincourt, where 'the unwarlike host of the French' had been put to flight and 'the sword of the French yielded to the sceptre of England'. And when, in November 1416, the *Gesta* recorded the king's 'unbreakable resolve to go overseas' once more in the following summer 'to subdue the stubborn and more than adamantine obduracy of the French', he made the heart-felt plea that God:

> ...grant that, just as our king, under His protection and by His judgement in respect of the public enemies of his crown, had already triumphed twice, so may he triumph yet a third time, to the end that the two Swords, the sword of the French and the sword of England, may return to the rightful government of a single ruler, cease from their own destruction, and turn as soon as possible against the unsubdued and bloody faces of the heathen.

Richard Beauchamp's appointment as an envoy to the Council of Constance by Henry V, October 1414. Henry V took a close personal interest in the deliberations of the council (which eventually, in November 1417, secured the election of Pope Martin V and the ending of the Great Schism) and his delegates acted very much in accordance with the king's instructions.

Similar sentiments, moreover, permeate the pages of many early fifteenth-century English literary sources. Thomas Walsingham, for instance, went out of his way to stress that, as England had won a series of victories against France since Edward III's time, the English cause clearly enjoyed, and continued to enjoy under Henry V, demonstrable divine approval. In the second year of his reign, declared Adam Usk, Henry V:

> ...sent a solemn embassy to France [to] demand from the French king those hereditary lands of his which were situated in his king-dom, and to ask for his daughter in marriage so that a proper peace might be made; but they were treated with derision, and returned to England without achieving any progress, whereupon the king, and the heroes of the realm, in their fury, began to direct their wrath against France.

An anonymous *Brut* chronicler emphasised that Henry V's claim to Normandy and other territories in France, wrongfully withheld from him, was by 'true title of conquest and right heritage'; John Harding believed that, since the time of that 'prince peerless' and 'flower of earthly worthiness' Edward III, the right of English kings to France 'by succession of blood and generation' had been clear; and, so Tito Livio learned:

> ...when affairs had been properly settled in Ireland, Scotland and Wales, Henry decided to win back the kingdom of France which belonged to him by birthright. First, however, he sought advice in all the schools and universities from men learned in divine and human law whether he might justly and without fear of wrongdoing seek to regain the crown of France by force of arms. The king then sent an embassy to France with instructions to present his claim to a council of the French and, if by any chance the French should refuse him jus-tice, to announce to them that King Henry would come with an army to claim his rights.[20]

Most French chroniclers seem to have been in little doubt that, from the beginning, Henry V was aiming at the French throne. Following the battle of Agincourt, declared the Monk of Saint-Denis, Henry V enthusiastically urged his troops 'to preserve a memory of that brilliant success as a clear witness of the justice of his cause and of the efforts which he was making to recover the lands of his ancestors which had been unjustly usurped'. According to this same commentator, however, English ambassadors to France in July 1414 had also demanded that the French 'restore to him the crown and kingdom of France which belonged to him'; moreover, he added:

> ...although these claims of the king [of England] were so ridiculous, for he was claiming a title which had never belonged to his predecessors, as is abundantly proved in old chronicles, yet they did not fail to discuss the matter seriously.

Jean Juvenal des Ursins, similarly, recorded that, on the eve of Agincourt, Henry V told his captains and men that:

> ...from time immemorial his predecessors had maintained their right to the kingdom of France, and that in good and just title it had fallen to him to conquer it, [but that] he wished to conquer gently all that belonged to him, not to cause any destruction at all. For this reason he said to them that he had true hope of God of winning the battle because his enemies were all full of sin and did not fear their maker at all.

As for Enguerrand de Monstrelet, he reported that, in response to a French embassy in 1415, Henry V made it clear that:

> ...unless the King of France would give, as a marriage portion with his daughter, the duchies of Aquitaine, of Normandy, of Anjou, of Tours, the counties of Ponthieu, Mans and Poitou, and every other part that had formerly belonged to the English monarchs, the king would not desist from his intended invasion of France, but would despoil the whole of that kingdom, which had been unjustly withheld from him, and that he should depend on his sword for the accomplishment of this and for depriving King Charles of his crown.[21]

French commentators, not surprisingly, were also often eager to emphasise the extent to which Henry V deliberately exploited the political situation in France during Charles VI's reign. The chronicler Pierre Fenin, for instance, highlighted the fact that, when he 'issued his orders in England and assembled a great force of English' in 1415, the king 'knew all too well the discord which existed between the lords in France and that they were constantly struggling to destroy each other'. An anonymous Parisian chronicler, similarly, recorded his conviction that 'the king of England would never have dared to set foot in France but for the dissensions that sprang from this unhappy name' of Armagnac. And, when looking back on earlier decades, an anonymous French tract of the mid-1450s certainly identified great divisions between 'lords of the blood' as responsible for 'terrible and long-lasting war', while Henry V's 'great conquests in this kingdom' also resulted, in part at least, from the fact that 'our king' Charles VII was 'young of years and still a child'.

No contemporary or near-contemporary French literary source, interestingly enough, contains any reference to the most famous tale associated with Henry V's renewal of the Hundred Years War: the story that French envoys deliberately provoked the king by an insulting present of tennis balls. As so often we have William Shakespeare to thank for particularly highlighting this, not least Henry V's robust response to the dauphin's effrontery:

> When we have matched our rackets to these balls
> We will in France, by God's grace, play a set
> Shall strike his father's crown into the hazard...
> Yea, strike the Dauphin blind to look on us
> And tell the pleasant Prince this mock of his
> Hath turn'd his balls to gun-stones...

Whether authentic or not the incident, perhaps occurring in Lent 1415, can certainly be traced back to early fifteenth-century English sources. During Anglo-French negotiations prior to Henry V's first invasion of France, declared Thomas Elmham in his *Liber Metricus*, the dauphin did indeed send a gift of tennis balls; the king, according to the chronicler Thomas Otterbourne, was at Kenilworth at the time of their arrival; and the story appears in early fifteenth-century ballads as well. An anonymous *Brut* chronicler, moreover, not only tells us that the balls were sent but that Henry V returned the compliment when, at the siege of Harfleur, he 'played at tennis with his hard gunstones'. The fullest early record of the incident is to be found in John Strecche's chronicle. In the second year of his reign, Strecche reported, the king:

> ...sent to France certain ambassadors in state, a bishop, two doctors and two knights in fitting array. They deliberated with the King of France and his council concerning a marriage to be celebrated between Henry, King of England, and the noble Lady Catherine, daughter of the King of France; but these envoys of the English king had only a brief discussion with the French on this matter, without arriving at any conclusion consistent with the honour or to the advantage of our king, and so they returned home. For these Frenchmen, puffed up with pride and lacking in foresight, hurling mocking words at the ambassadors of the King of England, foolishly said to them that, as Henry was only a young man, they would send him little balls to play with and soft cushions to rest on until he should have grown to a man's strength.[22]

The implication of this, clearly, is that Henry V was still too immature to constitute any sort of threat to France. Hardly surprisingly, if we are to believe Strecche, the king responded indignantly that within a few months he would 'play with such balls in the Frenchmen's own streets that they will stop joking and, for their mocking game, win nothing but grief'.

John Strecche, probably writing very soon after Henry V's death, was certainly well placed, at Kenilworth, to hear gossip emanating from the royal household when the king was in residence at the local castle: it is not entirely inconceivable, therefore, that the tennis balls story may have a degree of authenticity, perhaps originating in a chance remark over-heard by an English envoy to France and later retailed in courtly circles at home as evidence of French pride and insolence. Interestingly, too, this early source reports not that little balls were actually despatched to England but that Henry V's envoys were merely taunted by the threat of such a present. Yet even the notion of the dauphin sneering at the English king's youthfulness hardly squares with the fact that he himself was the younger of the two by several years. There is no mention of the incident in contemporary records or letters; neither the *Gesta Henrici Quinti* nor Thomas Walsingham make any specific reference to it; and, perhaps most significantly, no French chronicle contains the story either. Indeed, the tale might be no more than English propaganda providing yet another justification for Henry V to punish the French for their outrageous arrogance or, maybe, it is simply an example of the sort of courtly tittle-tattle John Strecche found so irresistible.

At the time of Henry V's accession, if we are to believe Jean Juvenal des Ursins, even the English princes were divided 'by the quarrel between Burgundy and Orleans, for the dukes of Clarence and Gloucester, the king's brothers, and with them the duke of York, favoured the Orleanists, while the king and the duke of Bedford, likewise his brother, were inclined to the Burgundians'. Divisions within the English royal family rapidly disappeared once Henry IV was dead but the on-going Armagnac/Burgundian feud in France clearly continued to provide an essential context for Henry V's diplomatic, and ultimately military, endeavours in France, and the king certainly had every intention of exploiting French political weakness to his own advantage. Precisely what Henry V's aims and intentions were when he invaded France in August 1415, and whether he had had full scale renewal of the Hundred Years War in mind from the very beginning of his reign, remains the subject of considerable historical controversy. The sincerity of the king's belief in the justice of his territorial claims in France, not only his right to Aquitaine in full sovereignty (under the terms of the Treaty of Bretigny) but also his titles to Normandy and other French provinces lost by King John over two centuries earlier, seems beyond question. Nor can there be much doubt about his single-minded determination to recover what he believed to be his own: indeed, France became virtually an obsession with him. Perhaps he also saw war in France as a handy means of healing wounds at home and uniting the country in pursuit of a glorious martial enterprise. Clearly, he very much had in mind a final, and lasting, settlement of the problems that had dogged Anglo-French relations for so long; he realised that, at a time when France was seriously divided internally under a king so mentally challenged on occasion that he believed himself to be made of glass, the potential for achieving this had never been greater; and his ultimate goal, all along, might well have been the French crown. If so, the prolonged negotiations preceding the king's invasion of 1415 could be no more than a diplomatic smokescreen to disguise Henry V's true intentions: hence why he set his territorial demands higher than any French government would concede and why, when it came to the crunch, he consistently rejected whatever terms were offered. Or perhaps, as many historians have argued, the crown was never more than a bargaining counter and Henry V, a realist as well as an opportunist, could have been persuaded to settle for less. Yet, since the king did so very often reiterate his right to the Valois throne, this is by no means certain.

Even as Prince of Wales Henry V had recognised the potential of turning France's political turmoil and intermittent civil war to England's advantage. In 1411 he had opted to support John the Fearless Duke of Burgundy in return for Burgundian backing of Lancastrian territorial claims across the Channel and his early diplomatic moves as king also tended to focus on the Burgundian faction. Not that he was under any pressure in 1413 to pursue foreign ambitions, let alone renew Edward III's bid for the Valois throne or launch an invasion of France: domestic matters, in fact, loomed largest during the king's first year and, significantly, no taxation for military purposes was even requested of Henry V's first parliament.

Although the king may well have intended from the start to focus on Anglo-French relations as soon as he could, it was not until the spring of 1414 that he made his first serious move when negotiations for a Burgundian alliance in return for concessions on Aquitaine got under-way. By the summer of 1414 when Burgundy tentatively agreed to aid Henry V to recover what was rightfully his under the terms of Bretigny, however, the king had already begun making determined overtures to the Armagnacs as well. In August 1414 Henry V sent an embassy to Charles VI and the Armagnac-dominated French council in Paris: it formally claimed the Valois throne, a huge dowry for the marriage of the French king's daughter Catherine of Valois to the English king and the whole of the Angevin empire as it had existed in the later twelfth century. During the course of negotiations the claim to the French crown was judiciously dropped for the time being but England's territorial demands barely changed; no agreement was reached; and, in September 1414, Armagnacs and Burgundians temporarily patched up their quarrel. Clearly, when negotiating simultaneously with Burgundians and Armagnacs, Henry was, at the very least, aiming to maximise the extent of French territorial concessions by promoting competition for his support. That his demands were eventually rejected by both factions was probably no more than he expected or calculated upon and, by the autumn of 1414 at the latest, he was seriously planning a full-scale invasion of France anyway. Chancellor Beaufort, when addressing parliament in November 1414, not only announced publicly Henry V's decision to prosecute war in France as the logical culmination of his efforts to ensure the rights of his English subjects and restore order in the realm but also proclaimed the righteousness of the king's cause and called for wise counsel, strong military support and, most importantly, a generous grant of taxation. In response, the speaker of the Commons urged Henry V to open new negotiations with the French for a peaceful settlement, if possible, before resorting to military force; however, parliament also responded very positively to the king's request for cash. Since military preparations for a major campaign across the Channel required many months to complete, Henry V did indeed reopen negotiations with France in March 1415, even reducing his demands: this was almost certainly a propaganda ploy designed to influence public opinion both at home and abroad, for the king probably calculated that whatever he asked for was liable to be refused so long as Armagnac/Burgundian rivalry remained in abeyance. He was right. Once more there was no meeting of diplomatic minds and if, as has been suggested, the French were as bellicose as the English at this time, perhaps the dauphin did deliberately provoke Henry V by threatening to send him an insulting present of tennis balls! When the king's military preparations were virtually complete, a French embassy turned up at his headquarters near Southampton in June 1415. This time it might well have been the French who were seeking the propaganda spotlight: the territorial concessions they offered were derisory, English sovereignty in Aquitaine and elsewhere does not even seem to have been on the agenda, and Henry V's right to the Valois throne was again robustly denied. No wonder the king now upped his own demands from what he had asked for in March: indeed, he issued an ultimatum that, if Normandy, Maine, Anjou, Touraine, Ponthieu, Poitou and Aquitaine were not promptly surrendered to him in full sovereignty and a fifty-year truce agreed, he would commence the conquest of France. Not surprisingly, this brought negotiations to a peremptory end; Henry V once more declared that, since the French were still determined to deny him justice, military force must be employed; and, on 6 July 1415, he formally declared war on France.

12

AGINCOURT CAMPAIGN
AND ITS AFTERMATH

Precisely what Henry V's military objectives were when he set sail from Southampton early in August 1415 are far from clear: indeed, even the expedition's destination may have remained a secret known only to the king and his closest advisers until after his fleet embarked. Maybe he had originally intended to launch a two-pronged campaign in both Normandy and Aquitaine but, lacking the resources, opted for a more limited strategy. Maybe he was eager from the start to seek out and engage the French in battle in the hope of repeating Edward III's great victories at Crecy and Poitiers. Maybe, as the *Gesta Henrici Quinti* suggests, he deliberately targeted Harfleur 'in order to recover his duchy of Normandy' before, perhaps, launching a major *chevauchée* (or plundering raid) towards Paris or Bordeaux. Or maybe, and most probably, Henry V's military aims in the summer of 1415 were essentially opportunistic, his ultimate goal always dependent on the outcome of early campaigning. Certainly, the king seems to have relished the prospect of conquest across the Channel and, of course, he had had plenty of experience of life on campaign in Wales during his formative years, as well as fighting at the battle of Shrewsbury in 1403 when only a teenager. No English king had campaigned personally in France, though, since 1359. As early as the summer of 1414 Henry V began amassing military stores and equipment, particularly artillery and siege engines; by the spring of 1415, even while Anglo-French negotiations were still in progress, recruiting forces to muster at Southampton was well underway; and, by the end of July, the king had gathered together an army of between 9,000 and 12,000 men and a fleet of perhaps 1,500 vessels to transport them. The fact that this force, the largest to leave England since Edward III's time, included many aristocrats, knights and esquires of the king's own household and men, mainly archers, recruited principally from crown estates (indented for up to a year's service) suggests Henry V may well have anticipated a long campaign and territorial conquests; yet, in August 1415, he did not have sufficient available cash for even six months, let alone a year, across the Channel.

'Seeing that the wind was blowing in his favour', reported the *Gesta Henrici Quinti* (whose anonymous author accompanied the royal army throughout the Agincourt campaign), Henry V 'spread his sails to the breeze with about 1,500 ships' on Sunday 11 August; moreover, he added, 'as we were leaving the coast of the Isle of Wight behind, swans were seen swimming among the fleet', a 'happy augury for the task we had under-taken'. It soon became evident that Harfleur, 'the key to all Normandy' as Enguerrand de Monstrelet put it, was the king's first target and a well chosen one at that: situated at the mouth of the Seine, it was the main French base for hostile operations in the Channel and, clearly, its capture would greatly improve the security of English shipping; moreover, once in Henry V's hands it could not only provide a vital base for stores and equipment but also open up a direct route to Normandy's capital Rouen and, even, Paris if all went well. The best and most detailed record of the ensuing five-week siege (19 August–23 September) is to be found in the *Gesta Henrici Quinti* and its clerical author was particularly anxious to explain and justify Henry V's behaviour throughout. At its commence-ment, so this anonymous royal chaplain and eyewitness assures us:

> ...our king, who sought not war but peace, in order to arm with the shield of innocence the just cause of the great enterprise upon which he had embarked, offered, in accordance with the twentieth chapter of the Deuteronomic law, peace to the besieged if, freely and without coercion, they would open their gates to him and, as was their duty, restore that town, which was a noble and hereditary portion of his crown of England and of his duchy of Normandy.[23]

When the king's offer was refused, the siege began.

Clearly, Henry V himself was very much in charge of operations: 'he did not allow his eyelids to close in sleep', declared the *Gesta*, but 'stayed awake night and day until, having prepared and positioned his guns close to the walls', he 'aimed them at the face of the town'; indeed, according to the *First English Life,* 'the king daily and nightly in his own person visited and searched the watches, orders and stations of every part of his host', praising the diligent and chastising the negligent. Moreover, when further negotiations also failed and 'the king saw that the enemy could not be overcome by comparatively mild sufferings', the *Gesta* tells us, he decided 'to proceed to sterner measures against this stiff-necked people'. Certainly, Harfleur seems to have been very heavily bombarded. Henry V, so Adam Usk learned, launched vigorous and sustained assaults, 'subduing the surrounding area with underground mines and shattering the town itself and its walls with his siege engines and cannons'. The English guns were of a truly 'monstrous greatness', echoed the Monk of Saint-Denis, firing 'enormous stones enveloped in thick clouds of foul smoke' and emitting a 'terrifying noise' as if 'vomited from the very jaws of hell'!

Despite Henry V's vigorous and unflagging command, and relentless bombardment, Harfleur held out for longer than anticipated and his own besieging army, as well as the town's inhabitants, clearly suffered considerably. Indeed, if we are to believe Adam Usk:

> Many died of dysentery during the siege [and] thousands of others returned home. Some went legitimately, having got permission to do so, while others were invalided home because they were sick, but there were some who, disgraceful to relate, simply deserted the army, to the king's fury.

Eventually, as conditions within the walls worsened and it became clear that no French force was coming to its relief, Harfleur surrendered on 22 September 1415. An anonymous London chronicler and possible eyewitness describes how, when a delegation brought the keys of the town to Henry V and were belatedly ushered into his presence, he completely ignored them:

> ...until they had long knelt. Then the king gave them a reward with his look, indicated to the Earl of Dorset that he should take the keys from them, and so he did.

As Henry V himself approached the gates of Harfleur next day, so the Burgundian Enguerrand de Monstrelet learned, he:

...dismounted from his horse, ordered his shoes to be removed and in that state went on foot to the parish church of Saint Martin, where he offered devout prayers to God and gave thanks for the success of his enterprise. He then had all the nobles and men-at-arms who were in the town made prisoner and shortly after turned most of them out of the town dressed only in their doublets... Next the greater part of the townsmen were made prisoner and forced to ransom themselves for large sums, then driven from the town with most of the women and children... It was a pitiful sight to see the misery of these people as they left their town and their belongings behind. The priests and the clergy were likewise dismissed. As for the wealth that was found in the town, this was immense: it was all taken over by the king, who shared it out as he chose.

Adam Usk, too, remarked on Henry V's severity in interpreting contemporary laws of war once 'the town, its inhabitants – stripped naked and with halters and nooses around their necks – and all their goods were surrendered to him'; indeed, according to Usk at least, the king 'expelled all the native inhabitants and replaced them with English people'. Yet the Monk of Saint-Denis, interestingly enough, was no less struck by the fact that Henry V on entering Harfleur:

...treated knights and esquires whom he had captured with more generosity than one might have expected... He ordered the lives of unarmed citizens to be spared... He left the youngest and most robust men for the defence of the town... As for women, he allowed them, out of compassion for their sex, to go off in full freedom and without impediment, with their clothes and all they could carry.

Even this not unsympathetic chronicler pointed out, however, that not only did the king despatch the wealthiest citizens to England 'until they paid ransom' but also that he peremptorily expelled 'the sick, the poor and the elderly'.[24]

On the very day Harfleur surrendered Henry V himself sent an upbeat report of the siege and its outcome to the mayor and aldermen of London:

...we came before our town of Harfleur on Saturday 17 August last and laid siege to it, [by] the good diligence of our faithful lieges, who are presently in our company, and by the force and enforcement of our cannons and ordnance. The men who were in the town made much effort to come to an agreement with us but, nonetheless, we made the decision to launch an assault on the town on Wednesday 18 September. Those in the town realised this and made even greater efforts than before to come to an agreement with us and, in order to avoid the shedding of human blood on both sides, we were inclined to hear their effort. [Agreement was reached] and the keys of the town were handed over to us and those within the town submitted to our mercy without condition...

Urging the Londoners to give 'humble thanks to Almighty God for this news' he added, significantly, his hope 'to do our duty to achieve our rights in this area as soon as possible' by the 'fine power and good diligence of our faithful people overseas'.[25]

Soon after Harfleur's surrender, reported the *Gesta Henrici Quinti*, Henry V, very much in line with the chivalric warrior-king image he so self-consciously sought to project, sent a 'single herald' to the French dauphin challenging him to 'a duel between them man to man' so as to avoid 'the shedding of human blood'; in order to secure peace, echoed Thomas Elmham in his *Liber Metricus*, the king:

...sought either to gain his rights without war or to give duel alone in the field, and if the dauphin should concede victory, Henry would return the proper right of the crown to him, which he would give to his father [Charles VI] during his own lifetime but for no longer, and on the latter's death it should be returned to Henry. But neither the king of the French nor the dauphin sent a response [during the eight day period specified].

Presumably, no one would have been more surprised than the English king had a positive response been received but when it was not, so the *Gesta* tells us, he resolved to commence 'a march through his duchy of Normandy towards his town of Calais'. The Monk of Saint-Denis, in similar vein, recorded that Henry V:

...decided to go home after putting a garrison in the town [of Harfleur]. A mortal epidemic brought about by intolerable shortages had already carried off many of his troops including those of high rank, and as winter approached he was persuaded to break off military operations and to seek winter quarters. On the advice of his most important men, he did not wish to trust to the dubious fate of military engagement with troops so unequal in number. So he decided to go to Calais...

According to Tito Livio, moreover, the king adopted a tone of real bravado when addressing his magnates in a council of war:

I have the spirit of a very strong man, more willing to enter all dangers rather than anyone should impugn the reputation of your king. We shall go with the judgement of God, unharmed and safe even if they try to hinder us, we shall triumph as victors with great praise.[26]

Yet, so Pseudo-Elmham learned in the 1440s, at first 'the majority of the councillors were of the opinion that a decision should be made not to march on'; only after Henry V had vigorously asserted the contrary opinion and, 'since nobody dared to contradict the king's decision', did they finally conclude that the army 'should pass from Harfleur to Calais, following the overland route'. It was an immensely risky strategy and Henry V's precise motives for adopting it are far from clear. Most of the council probably did believe, as the *Gesta Henrici Quinti* emphasised, that 'it would be highly dangerous for him in this way to send his small force, daily growing smaller, against the multitude of the French which, constantly growing larger, would surely enclose them on every side like sheep in folds'. Just how depleted was the king's army? The estimates in French chronicles certainly cannot be relied upon: Enguerrand de Monstrelet, for instance, suggests 2,000 men-at-arms and 13,000 archers, while Jean Juvenal des Ursins' figures (4,000 men-at-arms and 16,000–18,000 archers) are even more fanciful. Nearer to the truth, surely, is Thomas Walsingham's 8,000 men and the *Gesta*'s 'no more than 900 lances and 5,000 archers able to draw sword or fit to fight' even more so. Henry V's wisest option, under the circumstances, would have been to return to England by the direct sea route. Yet this would not have suited his carefully constructed image at all. Perhaps John Harding's remark that the king 'homeward went through France like a man', or Adam Usk's conclusion that 'committing himself to God and the fortunes of the sword', he 'set out bravely like a lion with barely ten thousand soldiers', got to the heart of the matter.

Once he had determined on a trek across country, Henry V's options were clearly limited: it was probably too late in the campaigning season to contemplate marching towards Paris or Bordeaux and, already, substantial French forces were beginning to gather at Rouen. Anyway, so depleted, sick and weary was his army, a full-scale *chevauchée à la* Edward III was almost certainly out of the question. A successful march to Calais might, at least, cock a snook at the French and help counter the charge that, apart from the seizure of Harfleur, the expedition had not only been expensive but largely futile. It was certainly a high risk strategy and its eventual outcome probably far better than even Henry V had anticipated. Whatever his hopes a few weeks earlier, he was not now seeking a battle or even the conquest of territory: getting his small force to Calais relatively unscathed was very much the name of the game. Leaving Harfleur between 6 and 8 October 1415, the king certainly did not wish to provoke areas through which he marched: he made no attempt to mount any further sieges or assaults, avoided castles and fortified towns and, according to the *Gesta Henrici Quinti*, gave orders that 'under pain of death, no man should burn or lay waste, or take anything save what was necessary for the march, or capture any rebels save only those that he might happen to find offering resistance'. Indeed, so the royal chaplain reported, when he learned that 'a certain robber, an Englishman', had 'carried off from a church (perhaps thinking it was made of gold) a pyx of copper-gilt in which the Host was reserved, that pyx having been found in his sleeve', by the king's command and after sentence had been passed, the man 'met his death by hanging'. Yet the *Gesta* also tells us that, when the inhabitants of certain hamlets refused to pay ransom, he ordered them to be 'set on fire and utterly destroyed'; an anonymous Parisian chronicler learned that, during the trek, the English 'devastated and robbed all the countryside' (although, he added, French troops 'did as much harm to the poor people as the English'); and Jean Juvenal des Ursins declared, predictably, that, as it marched, Henry V's army committed 'countless evil deeds, burning, killing people, capturing and abducting children'.

Henry V's force, according to Thomas Walsingham, was a 'very small band who were thin from hunger, from the bloody flux and from fever' and, before long, French troops were trailing the king; indeed, if we are to believe Thomas Elmham's *Liber Metricus*:

> Everywhere the bridges and causeways were broken by the enemy [and, while] their company continued to grow, [there] were scarcely eight days' supplies for the king. The French devastated farms, vineyards and food supplies, [for] they were keen to harry the people by hunger so that they might ruin them completely by making them weak and without even fighting.

The English were probably lucky not to be confronted earlier than 25 October 1415: even as it was, and perhaps as a consequence of poor scouting, Henry V had to make a long diversion to get across the Somme on 19 October; French heralds challenged him, the following day, to fix a date and place for battle; and a major engagement in the field became virtually inevitable when, on 24 October, the king found his route blocked by a large army. By then, according to the *Gesta Henrici Quinti*, Henry V's puny force was physically and mentally exhausted and, if we are to believe French chroniclers, the king even made a desperate last ditch attempt to negotiate his way out of trouble. The English, declared Jean Juvenal des Ursins, made:

> ...several offers that they might be allowed to pass in peace. They even offered, or so it is said, to quit Harfleur and return it to the possession of the French king, and to restore the prisoners without demanding ransom, or to come to a final peace and to deliver hostages to guarantee all that they now promised.

The Monk of Saint-Denis, similarly, reported the sending of representatives to the French lords on 24 October:

> ...to offer them reparation for all the damage which they had caused and the restitution of all that they had taken on condition that they would agree to let them return freely to their own country. The annals of earlier reigns ought to have served as lessons for the lords of France that the rejection of such reasonable conditions had often

been cause for repentance… But having too much confidence in their forces, and guided by the poor advice of some of their company, they rebuffed all proposals for peace and made reply to the king of England that they would give battle on the next day.[27]

Significantly, perhaps, the *Gesta Henrici Quinti* makes no reference to any such negotiations and, clearly, even if they did take place, nothing came of them.

Although there is no contemporary evidence for the Shakespearean story that Henry V spent the night before Agincourt making the rounds of his troops in disguise, both English and French commentators do supply no less vivid anecdotes. Thomas Elmham, for instance, tells us that, as 'black night was almost descending and did not allow for fighting', the king:

> …bivouacked in silence and ordered his men to keep silent. He silently approached the village where he might pitch camp. That rainy night the people there, without bread, overflowed with the offering of prayers and vigils to the Lord. The enemy, pondering that the English were spending the night in silence, thought therefore that the king was intending to flee. They rode quickly over the field by several routes [and threw] dice to determine which [of the English] they should each have.

Enguerrand de Monstrelet, by contrast, chose to highlight the eerie quietness in French ranks compared with the music-loving English troops. The French army, he believed, had:

> …few musical instruments for their amusement and scarcely any of their horses neighed all night – which many took to be an omen of evil to come. The English played music on their trumpets and other instruments throughout the night, and the whole neighbourhood re-echoed with the sound of it. Although they were weary, and suffered from cold and hunger and other discomforts, they did not neglect to make their peace with God and tearfully to confess their sins; and many of them received the body of Our Lord, for, as many prisoners afterwards revealed, they thought they faced certain death on the next day.

Clearly, it needed all Henry V's skill as morale-booster and soldier to inspire his men and French and English commentators alike bear witness to his success. Before hostilities commenced, so the Monk of Saint-Denis tells us, he urged them to be 'mindful of the valour' their ancestors had shown at Crecy and Poitiers and, 'rather than being scared of doing business with so many princes and barons, be of firm hope that their large number will turn, as in the past, to their shame and eternal confusion'. The king exhorted his troops to be 'good men in battle and do their duty', reported Jean Juvenal des Ursins, 'inspired them to defend themselves well' and 'boosted their courage tremendously'. 'Bearing his own arms', recorded Thomas Elmham, Henry V 'put his own crown on his head' and 'signed himself with the cross, thus giving courage to his men'; Tito Livio emphasised the king's rallying cry to his men to be 'brave in heart' and 'fight with all their might'; and, according to the *Brut*, he declared:

> 'Now is a good time, for all England is praying for us. Therefore be of good cheer and let us go into battle'. Then he said in a high voice: 'In the name of Almighty God and St George, advance banners. St George, give us this day your help'.[28]

There is no shortage of contemporary and near-contemporary descriptions of the battle of Agincourt, both English and French; moreover, although no account provides comprehensive coverage and authors frequently disagree on detail (supplying very different estimates of the size of the two armies, for instance, and the number of men killed in the field), it is possible to reconstruct what happened on 25 October 1415 with considerable confidence, not least the personal role and behaviour of Henry V himself. Several reports, indeed, were written by eyewitnesses or drew on the recollections of men who were present at the battle. The anonymous author of the *Gesta Henrici Quinti*, who provides the earliest English narrative of Agincourt, specifically tells us that 'for as long as the conflict lasted I, who am now writing this, was then sitting on a horse at the rear of the battle', while the chronicler John Harding (although he did not put pen to paper until the 1440s) may well have been among the nine thousand English soldiers who, he reported, 'fought full sore' and 'proudly battled with a hundred thousand' Frenchmen 'in array' that day. The Burgundian chronicler Jean Le Fevre, who probably accompanied Henry V's army in a heraldic capacity, recollected many years later that 'I stayed with the English' after the battle and 'heard many notable knights speak of it', and Jean Waurin tells us that, at the age of fifteen, he was also present at Agincourt, probably serving as a page 'in the assembly on the French side': both Le Fevre and Waurin, however, drew heavily on Enguerrand de Monstrelet's earlier chronicle, as well as heavily plagiarising each other! The Monk of Saint-Denis, although not an eyewitness, penned the earliest and most original French account of the battle and its significance; Thomas Elmham's *Liber Metricus* was of similar date; and Thomas Walsingham, too, was writing within Henry V's own lifetime. Rather later came Tito Livio's *Vita Henrici Quinti* and the *Brut* – but Livio must surely have obtained information about the battle from his patron Humphrey Duke of Gloucester (who was undoubtedly present), while vernacular English chroniclers drew not only on eyewitness reports but also contemporary newsletters and ballads. On the personal role and behaviour of Henry V at Agincourt, graphic evocations certainly abound. Tito Livio, for instance, tells us that on the morning of the battle:

> The king put on a helmet and placed over it an elegant gold crown encrusted with various precious gems and with the insignia of the English. He then seated himself on a white horse. Following him, the most noble horses were led forth with gold saddles, with fine harnesses and most valuable trappings as was the royal custom, with similar insignia of the English and French kingdoms all over.

During the action, moreover, 'the renowned king never spared himself but 'fought like an unvanquished lion' and 'received many blows on his helmet and elsewhere'. Interestingly enough, Thomas Elmham had already recorded some twenty years earlier that 'the crown of the king was broken off his helmet by an axe', as well as anticipating Livio by reporting that:

> ...the brother of the king, the noble Duke Humphrey, was wounded in the groin. Gore flowed down from the wound. Having fallen to the ground, the king stood over him to assist him. He was in this battle the defender of his brother.

And, no less vividly, Thomas Walsingham declared that during the battle:

> The king himself, not so much as a king but as a knight, yet perform-
> ing the duties of both, flung himself against the enemy. He both
> inflicted and received cruel wounds, offering an example in his own
> person to his men by his bravery in scattering the opposing battle
> lines with a battle axe.[29]

Early in the morning of 25 October 1415 Henry V found himself facing a fresh and numerically much superior French army encamped on ground of its own choosing. Even so, the terrain was hardly promis-ing. Not only was the battle fought in 'a field which was newly sown with wheat', declared Thomas Walsingham, but it was also 'extremely difficult to stand or to advance' because of the 'softness of the ground' and the 'muddiness of the place'. 'As the night had seen much rain', echoed the Norman chronicler Pierre Cochon, 'the ground was so soft that the men-at-arms sank into it by at least a foot'; the Monk of Saint-Denis portrayed French forces 'marching through the middle of the mud where they sank up to their knees'; and Jean Juvenal des Ursins, even more vividly, tells us how his fellow countrymen:

> ...came to a field where the ground was very soft for it had been rain-
> ing. The French were heavily armed and sank into the ground right
> to the thick of their legs, which caused them much labour for they
> could scarcely move their legs and pull them out of the ground.[30]

Fifteenth-century commentators' estimates of the size of armies at bat-tles are notoriously unreliable and Agincourt is no exception. The *Brut*'s figure of 120,000 French is clearly a gross exaggeration; the *Gesta Henrici Quinti* and Thomas Elmham suggest 60,000; and Jean Le Fevre's estimate of 50,000 is lower still. On the English force there is more agreement; 7,000 men according to Thomas Elmham and the *Brut*, no more than 6,000 on the *Gesta*'s reckoning. What is abundantly evident, as Pierre Fenin put it, is that 'the French were incomparably greater in number than the English', but by just how much remains far from clear. For several hours, it seems, the two armies simply faced each other across a muddy quagmire, shut in by woods on both sides. The

English, perforce, adopted a defensive position: a single dismounted line of men-at-arms, interspersed by wedges of archers, and further protected against the threat of a French cavalry charge by sharpened stakes driven into the ground. Although drawn up on a wider front, so numerous were the French that the enclosing woods forced them into three divisions, one behind the other, mainly on foot but with squads of armoured cavalry on each flank. From the beginning Henry V was very much in command of the English army and throughout he adopted a high personal profile: indeed, as John Harding put it (here echoing Thomas Elmham), he fought so courageously 'with his own hands' that day that a 'piece of his crown was broken', only later found in the field and returned to him. The French, by contrast, had no single commander and, if we are to believe Pierre Fenin, so confident were they of success and so eager for glory that they 'put the majority of their nobles and the flower of their men' in the vanguard, leaving whole units further back virtually leaderless. As a result, so the Monk of Saint-Denis learned, the French van found itself 'so tightly packed that those who were in the third rank could scarcely use their swords'; the English, by contrast, were 'lightly armed and their ranks were not too crowded' and, consequently, enjoyed 'freedom of movement' to 'deal mortal blows with ease'. Enguerrand de Monstrelet reported, similarly, that 'when the two armies were close to each other the French were so tightly packed that they could not raise their arms to strike the enemy, except for some of those in the front, who had cut their lances in half in order to make them more manageable in close combat'.

Eventually, after almost three hours, Henry V broke the deadlock and advanced, halting within shooting distance in order to shower the enemy with arrows. This provoked a disastrous French cavalry charge, vividly recounted by both English and French commentators. Thomas Elmham, for instance, tells how:

> ...the troops of the French rushed forward against the archers. In the face of a storm of arrows they began to turn back. Their nobility in the front, divided into three groups, advanced towards our banners in the three positions. Our arrows carried and penetrated, and the enemy was worn out under the weight of their armour. Some of our king's trustworthy men pressed down the enemy who penetrated the

line with axes and the latter fell down. The living were pushed towards death. The living went under the dead. The battle lines piled in. The English rose up against the companies of the French as they came to grips. The French fell before the power of the English. Flight from there was not open to them. They killed them, they captured them and kept them for ransoming...

When some of the French fell at the front, early in the battle, declared the Gesta Henrici Quinti even more graphically:

...so great was the undisciplined violence and pressure of the mass of men behind that the living fell on top of the dead, and others falling on top of the living were killed as well, with the result that, in each of the three places where the strong contingents guarding our standards were, such a great heap grew of the slain and of those lying crushed in between that our men climbed up those heaps, which had risen above a man's height, and butchered their enemies down below with swords, axes and other weapons.

Thomas Walsingham particularly focussed on the fact that it was French *cavalry* who came unstuck:

[The French] advanced in terrifying fashion into the field, sending the mounted men ahead who were to overwhelm our archers by the armoured breasts of their horses and trample them under foot. But, by God's will, things turned out other than they had hoped. The archers simultaneously shot arrows against the advancing knights so that the leading horses were scattered in that great storm of hail... The horses were pierced by iron... Many of the French fell...

Among French narrators of the action, the Monk of Saint-Denis was certainly critical of the thousand well-mounted French men-at-arms who, 'to their eternal shame', simply 'turned and fled' at the first volley of English arrows; Jean Juvenal des Ursins recorded gloomily that, when 'the noble French fell one on top of the other, many were suffocated and others killed or taken'; and, according to an anonymous Norman chronicler, so thick was the shower of English arrows falling on armoured French horsemen directed to resist them that:

...they were compelled to retreat amongst their own people, by which they broke their vanguard, which was close by ready for action. At the same moment both the horsemen and the footsoldiers ran to fall upon and pillage the horses and baggage of the English which they had left in the rear during the battle. Such was the commencement of the battle in the valley [near Agincourt], where the ground was so soft that the French foundered in it, for which cause and from their line being broken by their own horse, they could not again join battle, but were more and more defeated... It was then a pitiful sight to behold the dead and the wounded who covered the field, and the number of men-at-arms who turned and fled.[31]

At this stage, too, the English took many French prisoners.

Clearly, this was a critical turning-point in the battle. According to the *Gesta Henrici Quinti*:

...a shout went up that the enemy's mounted rearguard (in incomparable number and still fresh) were re-establishing their position and line of battle in order to launch an attack on us, few and weary as we were. And immediately, regardless of distinction of person, the prisoners, save for the dukes of Orleans and Bourbon, certain other illustrious men [and] a few others, were killed by the swords either of their captors or of others following after, lest they should involve us in utter disaster in the fighting that would ensue.

Interestingly, the *Gesta* makes no mention of any *royal* command to kill French prisoners. Nor does Thomas Elmham: since 'many new battle lines threatened to enter the fray', he reported, and since 'there was indeed a great throng of people', the English 'killed the French they had taken prisoner for the sake of protecting their rear'. Tito Livio, too, makes no mention of the king:

Considering that the English were exhausted by so long and hard a fight, and because they saw that they held so many prisoners (so many that they came to the same number as themselves), they feared that they might have to fight another battle against both the prisoners and the enemy. So they put many to death, including many rich and noble men.

Yet the order must surely have come from Henry V himself and, indeed, an early fifteenth-century *Brut* chronicler specifically tells us that, when 'news came to the king that there was a new battle of Frenchmen drawn up ready' to renew the action, he immediately 'had it proclaimed that every man should kill the prisoners that he had taken and straightway drew up his battle line again ready to fight with the French'; moreover, he added, 'when they saw that our men were killing their prisoners, they withdrew, and broke up their battle line and their whole army'. French chroniclers certainly had no doubt that responsibility for the massacre lay firmly with Henry V. When a large group of French warriors 'made a movement to the rear in order to withdraw from the blind fury of the victors', reported the Monk of Saint-Denis, the English king:

> ...believed that they were intending to return to the charge and so ordered that all the prisoners should be killed. This order was executed quickly and the carnage lasted until he had realised and seen with his own eyes that all the men were thinking of flight rather than of continuing the conflict.

Enguerrand de Monstrelet, in similar vein, tells us that, fearing a fresh French attack, Henry V 'had it announced with a trumpet call that every Englishman should kill his prisoners so that they could not possibly rejoin their own side'; in response, 'all the French prisoners were immediately massacred'. And, according to Jean Waurin:

> ...when they were least expecting it, the English experienced a moment of very great danger, for a large detachment from the French rear-guard [returned] and, in good order, advanced with determination upon those holding the field. When the king of England saw them coming, he immediately ordered that every man who had a prisoner should kill him, something which they did not willingly do, for they intended to ransom them for great sums. But when the king heard this, he ordered a man and two hundred archers to go into the host to ensure that the prisoners, whoever they were, should be killed. This esquire, without refusing or delaying a moment, went to accomplish his sovereign master's will...

This was 'a most terrible thing', Waurin concluded, 'for all those French noblemen were decapitated and inhumanly mutilated there in cold blood'.[32]

Just how many French prisoners there were is far from clear (the Monk of Saint-Denis suggests 1,400; Monstrelet, Le Fevre and Waurin 1,600); the number actually slaughtered is unknown; and the justification for such a massacre, as well as the implications for Henry V's chivalric warrior-king reputation, has certainly been vigorously debated ever since. The subsequent French resurgence, when it came, seems to have been at best a half-hearted affair; indeed, it swiftly turned into a full-scale flight and, against all the odds, Henry V had won. If we are to believe Thomas Elmham, moreover, English casualties in a battle where 'the smaller army overcame the many thousand' were tiny:

> ...the Duke of York was overcome by the whirlwind of war. The king washed his body for burial with royal care. The young Earl of Suffolk died there also. Scarcely thirty other English fell by the sword.

On the French side, by contrast, 'a bishop, three dukes, six counts and no less than 800 barons, 1,000 knights and also 7,500 of the men of noble rank fell'. The *Gesta Henrici Quinti* suggests three dukes, five counts, 'more than ninety barons and bannerets, whose names are set down in a volume of records, and upwards of 1,500 knights according to their own estimate, and between 4,000 and 5,000 other gentlemen, almost the whole nobility among the soldiery of France', died that day. On the English side, however, there were found slain in the field:

> ...no more than nine or ten persons, apart from the illustrious and most prudent prince the Lord Edward Duke of York, the Lord Michael Earl of Suffolk (a brave young man), and two newly dubbed knights who had fallen in the line of battle.[33]

Clearly, such figures need to be treated with extreme caution, if not discounted altogether. Yet even French chroniclers highlight the lowness of English casualties compared to the huge total of French fatalities on 25 October 1415.

Contemporary and near-contemporary English commentators certainly sounded a note of triumphalism when reporting Agincourt and highlighted the outstanding military leadership and personal bravery of Henry V. Yet they also tended to stress no less emphatically that, against the odds as it was, the king's victory was a clear sign of God's favour for his just cause. 'Far be it from our people to ascribe the triumph to their own glory or strength', declared the *Gesta Henrici Quinti*; rather, 'let it be ascribed to God alone from Whom is every victory.' The king himself gave 'ceaseless thanks to Him who had bestowed an unexpected victory', echoed Thomas Walsingham. And, so Tito Livio learned, not only did Henry V praise God 'for the great victory accorded to him' but also:

> ...because that day was the commemoration by the church of the blessed Crispin and Crispinian, and it seemed to him it was through their intercession to God that he had obtained so great a victory over the enemy, he ordered that for as long as he lived commemoration of them was to be made in the masses which he heard every single day.

Early fifteenth-century French chroniclers, not surprisingly, were appalled at so great a defeat by so inferior an army: indeed, for the patriotic Pierre Cochon not only was Agincourt 'the ugliest and most wretched event that had happened in France over the last thousand years', the fact that Henry V's 'pride was greatly boosted by having such good fortune' only served to compound the disaster. Several commentators highlighted the foolish vanity and over-confidence of the French nobility who, in their desire for glory, attacked the English without caution and came a cropper as a result. Pierre Fenin noted despairingly that 'many evils later arose' as a result of the failure of 'the flower of gentility' at Agincourt: yet, despite so humiliating a defeat, 'dissension between Duke John of Burgundy and the lords of the royal blood' nevertheless continued unabated. Jean Juvenal des Ursins, even more bitterly, recollected that:

> ...several were shocked by the fact that the Duke of Burgundy, who had been quite close to the area where the battle was fought, had not been present or sent assistance. It was commonly reported that he was not bothered in the slightest... In Paris there were even some who

seemed pleased and expressed signs of joy, saying that the Armagnacs had been defeated and the Duke of Burgundy would this time increase his position... Men of worth said that God wanted to bring down the pride of the many... That event was the most shameful which had ever happened to the kingdom of France.

Perhaps the most balanced French verdict was also among the earliest. The Monk of Saint-Denis, indeed, paid specific tribute to Henry V himself who, after the battle was won, deliberately:

> ...assembled his victorious troops and, after making a sign that they should all be silent, thanked them for having so bravely risked their lives in his service and encouraged them to preserve a memory of that brilliant success. [He] also urged them not to attribute their victory to their own strengths but to accord all the merit to the special grace of God who had delivered into their small company such a great multitude of the French and had brought low the latter's insolence and pride. He added that they must thank God that almost none of their own men had fallen on the field. He declared himself horrified that so much blood had been spilled and that he felt great compassion for all the deaths and especially those of his comrades in arms.

This chronicler certainly went out of his way to provide a comprehensive list of reasons for French failure: the sins of the nation provoking divine retribution; political divisions in France; contempt for the English; the pride of the French nobility; lack of sleep the night before the battle; torrential rain resulting in a water-logged field (disastrous conditions for heavily armoured men); and even the rashness of the young who, during the battle, simply ignored the advice of their elders. No wonder the result was utter humiliation when:

> ...the nobility of France was taken prisoner and put to ransom as a vile troop of slaves or else perished under the blows of a faceless soldiery. O eternal dishonour! O disaster for ever to be deplored!

And when news of this sad outcome became known to the French king and his subjects:

...there was general consternation. Each felt a bitter sadness in thinking that the kingdom had been deprived of so many of its illustrious defenders and that the revenues, already much diminished in order to pay the troops, would be completely ruined by the ransoming of the prisoners. But what was most galling was to think that the reverse would make France feeble and the laughing stock of other countries.[34]

'When the King of England found himself master of the field and all the French who were not dead or captured had fled in various directions', declared Enguerrand de Monstrelet:

...he made a circuit of the battlefield accompanied by some of his nobles. While his men were engaged in stripping the dead of their armour, he sent for the French herald Mountjoy, and several other English and French heralds, and said: 'It is not we but God Almighty who has ordered this great slaughter, to punish the French for their sins.' [Then] the king asked them the name of the fortress he could see not far off, and they replied that it was called Agincourt. 'Every battle', said the king, 'must bear the name of the fortress nearest to which it was fought, and this battle shall for now and all time be known as the battle of Agincourt.'

The day after Agincourt the English resumed their march to Calais, albeit 'at least three-quarters of them worn out with fighting, hunger and disease': thus, concluded Monstrelet, Henry V 'returned to Calais after his victory without meeting any obstruction on his journey'. On arrival there with his French prisoners on 29 October 1415, so the *Brut* tells us, the king 'thanked God for his glorious victory, and St George who had helped him to fight and who had been seen above in the air on the day that they fought', while, according to Tito Livio:

...the most vigorous king was received by his people at Calais with great and appropriate joy. There his knights and the others were restored with food, drink, sleep and rest, for a short time. The king consulted his men whether, as ought to follow a great victory, he should go on to besiege neighbouring towns and castles or whether, because much of his army was troubled by the bloody flux and hampered by a lack of supplies, as well as having many wounded, he should lead the army back home where they could recover for a few months. The unanimous opinion was that two great victories showed that God had the king's rights close to his heart, and that divine aid would not be lacking in the future to give further honour to the king and his rights. As a result, all of them considered that they should go back home.

During a notably rough Channel crossing, moreover, Henry V proved his stomach 'as good and as whole' on water as on land since he endured 'the rage and boisterousness of the sea without discomfort'. Probably landing at Dover on 15 November, he proceeded to Barham Down where, according to the *Brut*, representatives of the Cinque ports:

> ...met him with 10,000 men fully armed and arrayed. Then said the Duke of Orleans: 'What, shall we now go again to battle?'. The king answered, saying: 'Nay, these are the children of my country come to welcome me home'. At that place the Cinque ports presented the king with a ship that contained gold. Then he rode on to Canterbury where a procession met him outside the town, bringing him to Christ Church. The king made an offering at St Thomas's shrine and from there rode on to Eltham from where he made his way to London.[35]

Already, on 4 November 1415, Henry Beaufort Bishop of Winchester had heaped praise on Henry V for his successful siege of Harfleur ('the strongest town in that part of the world and the greatest enemy to the king's lieges') and his 'glorious and marvellous victory' at Agincourt in an opening speech to parliament; several vernacular ballads celebrating the king's brilliant campaign and triumphant return were probably composed at this time, most notably the so-called Agincourt Carol; and even the chronicler Adam Usk inserted a patriotic Latin poem into his text:

> People of England, cease your work and pray,
> For the glorious victory of Crispin's day;
> Despite their scorn for Englishmen's renown,
> The odious might of France came crashing down.

Invidious race of French, your scorn but taught
Our brave king's heart to turn that scorn to naught.
To him it gave new heart, you it benumbed;
Praise be to Christ, from whom these gifts have come!
Thus artifice is vanquished, witchcraft gone,
Dull, downcast minds drink bitter, deep and long.

London-based chroniclers, not surprisingly, focussed particularly on Henry V's entry into the capital on 23 November; Adam Usk seems to have been an eyewitness of the spectacular pageantry that greeted him; and, most importantly, there is a remarkably detailed account of the king's splendid reception in the *Gesta Henrici Quinti*. According to Adam Usk, Henry V was received:

...one mile outside the city by the clergy in procession, and four miles from the city, at a place called Blackheath, by ten thousand of the people, nobles and citizens mounted on horses and brightly dressed in red, wearing hoods of black and white, their hearts leaping with joy. At the entrance to London bridge there stood an enormous armed figure [and] his wife next to him...These two stood like guards outside the gate, bearing the royal arms; in the middle of the bridge, in front of the drawbridge, stood two bulwarks, with a lion armed with a lance on the right-hand one, and an antelope bearing the royal arms around his neck on the other; and, beyond the bridge, stood a fully armed figure of St George... Ornate aqueducts running with wine provided relief for those who wished to drink. At the cross in the middle of Cheap, [there] was a three-storeyed building mounted by a remarkable series of ladders, to which towers and bulwarks and the coats of arms of the kingdom and its princes were attached... Six citizens, magnificently dressed, came out of its iron gates carrying two basins made of gold and filled with gold, which were offered to the king. As he approached the lower conduit, chanting virgins came dancing to meet him, accompanied by choirs and drums and golden viols, just as in King David's time, after the slaying of Goliath. What more can I say? The city wore its brightest aspect, and happiness filled the people – and rightly so.

Like Adam Usk, the clerical author of the *Gesta Henrici Quinti* probably witnessed the spectacular civic festivities of Saturday 23 November

1415 in person, as well as drawing on the pageant's official programme. Indeed, he reported:

> ...so great was the throng of people in Cheapside, from one end to the other, that the horsemen were only just able, although not without difficulty, to ride through. And the upper rooms and windows on both sides were packed with some of the noblest ladies and women-folk of the kingdom, and men of honour and renown, who had assembled for this pleasing spectacle, and who were so very becomingly and elegantly decked out in cloth of gold, fine linen, and scarlet, and other rich apparel of various kinds, that no one could recall there having previously been in London a greater assemblage or a more noble array.

What particularly struck the royal chaplain, however, was Henry V's *personal* demeanour and behaviour amidst all the revelry:

> ...the king himself, wearing a gown of purple, proceeded, not in exalted pride and with an imposing escort or impressively large retinue, but with an impassive countenance and at a dignified pace, and with only a few of the most trusted members of his household in obedience... Indeed, from his quiet demeanour, gentle pace, and sober progress, it might have been gathered that the king, silently pondering the matter in his heart, was rendering thanks to God alone, not to man.

When the king approached St Paul's Cathedral, according to Thomas Walsingham, he was:

> ...solemnly received in procession by twelve bishops, who advanced towards him and led him to the high altar. Once his devotion was complete, he returned to the churchyard where, meanwhile, horses had been prepared for him and his men. Having mounted a charger, he set out for Westminster, riding thence in mounted procession through the middle of London. When he reached there, it was amazing that there ran up to meet him the greatest multitude of people that was ever seen in London.[36]

Clearly, Henry V's reputation as a soldier was greatly enhanced by the Agincourt campaign in general and his victory in the field on 25 October 1415 in particular. The taking of Harfleur gave English merchants a degree of safety at sea they had not enjoyed for years and, for a man whose only previous experience of a pitched battle had been at Shrewsbury in 1403 (when he was a mere sixteen years old), Agincourt certainly was an extraordinary achievement. After all, an exhausted, hungry and heavily out-numbered English force did indeed rout a fresh and well-provisioned French army: as a result, Henry V's prestige (both at home and abroad) was enormously enhanced, while the French judiciously avoided further set-piece confrontations once fighting resumed (at any rate until Thomas Duke of Clarence's foolish decision to provoke them to battle at Baugé in March 1421). Yet Henry V's victory at Agincourt owed more to French folly than the king's generalship and, even then, catastrophe was only narrowly averted. Strategically, the battle achieved virtually nothing since Henry simply lacked the capacity to follow it up: resumption of his march to Calais, and return to England, was the only realistic option open to him. Not until July 1417, moreover, was the king at last able to mount a second invasion of France.

13

CONQUEST OF NORMANDY

Throughout 1416 Henry V remained in England but Anglo-French relations, and the pursuit of his dynastic and territorial claims across the Channel, continued to provide his prime focus of attention, not least during a four month visit by the Holy Roman Emperor Sigismund who, Adam Usk noted succinctly, came to London 'via the kingdom of France in the hope of establishing peace between the realms'. Since December 1415, in fact, 'the most Christian and super-illustrious Sigismund' (as the *Gesta Henrici Quinti* dubs him) had been in Paris striving to reconcile Anglo-French differences but with little success: the French, in the aftermath of Agincourt, were in anything but a conciliatory mood. At the end of April 1416 he sailed for England, clearly in the hope of persuading Henry V to modify *his* demands, and when he arrived at Dover on 1 May, so the *First English Life* tells us (on the 'credible report' of the Earl of Ormonde), the king's brother Humphrey Duke of Gloucester deliberately waded into the sea, with sword drawn, in order to prevent the emperor's landing until he had given assurance that he would make no attempt to exercise imperial powers in the English realm: a colourful story, certainly, but perhaps (if true) an early indication of Gloucester's later and well-documented jingoistic nationalism. Accompanied by about a thousand men on horseback, apparently, Sigismund then travelled to London via Canterbury, Rochester, Dartford and Blackheath where, according to the *Brut*:

> ...the mayor, aldermen and sheriffs, with the worthy crafts of London,
> by the king's commandment, met with him, in the best array that they

could, on horseback, and there they welcomed him and brought him to London with much honour and reverence…And there was a worthy meeting between the emperor and the king; and there they kissed together, and embraced each other; and then the king took the emperor by the hand; and so they came riding through the city of London to St Paul's… Then they took their horses and rode to Westminster; and there the king lodged the emperor in his own palace, and there rested him a great while, and all at the king's cost.

Tito Livio, similarly, tells us that:

When King Sigismund came into the outskirts of London [on 7 May 1416], the most victorious King Henry came forth to meet him with all regal pomp, attended by his brothers, their highnesses the dukes of Clarence, Bedford and Gloucester, and other members of the royal family. The two kings greeted one another with the utmost gentility… Then they progressed to the city where a vast crowd of people was gathered, eager to see the foreign king. Indeed, those most invincible kings and the other royal princes who attended them were scarcely able to make their way even through the broadest squares, so great was the throng of onlookers. Finally they arrived at the palace of Westminster where all the king's treasures were displayed with royal magnificence and splendour in honour of the visit of the King of the Romans.

Clearly, Henry V was determined to impress his eminent German visitor, and at whatever cost: indeed, Livio continues, such was their 'mutual affection and regard' that, 'at his own request', Sigismund was even admitted to the Order of the Garter at Windsor on 24 May 1416. The king's main aim, however, was to convince the emperor of the justice of his cause in France and in this, seemingly, he completely succeeded. Before long, if we are to believe the *Gesta Henrici Quinti*, Sigismund:

…gloried in the exploits of our king no less than he abominated the machinations and trickery of the French. And there was no secret, no matter how close, which the one concealed from the other; and it is the general belief, praise be to God, that never before was there a greater trust or affection between two Christian princes.[37]

On 15 August 1416, in fact, the two put their seals to a formal treaty of alliance at Canterbury: Sigismund abandoned his efforts at mediation between England and France; both men agreed to support each other's employment, in the future, of all lawful means in pursuit of their respective claims to rights and lands at present withheld by the French; and for both, too, there was the clear implication of mutual assistance in quest of such legitimate objectives.

On the very day the Treaty of Canterbury was concluded, ironically enough, the king's brother John Duke of Bedford won a major victory over the French at sea. 'Under cover of pretended negotiations for peace', reported the *Gesta Henrici Quinti*, the French, 'having in the meantime summoned in great numbers carracks from Genoa and other galleys and vessels from allied states, assembled a powerful fleet and, when it had entered the mouth of the Seine, laid siege to the town of Harfleur'; Henry V, on 22 July 1416, appointed 'the illustrious prince his brother, the Duke of Bedford, as the leader of his naval force and the one responsible for relieving the siege'; and when, 'in the early dawn' of 15 August, the two fleets had:

> ...drawn close to one another in the mouth of the River Seine, and then, having grappled, had come to grips; and when, following an exchange of missiles, iron gads, stones, and other weapons of offence, the fury of the combatants had reached boiling-point; at last, after a long-drawn-out and bitter fight of five or six hours, during which, of them some fifteen hundred souls had been slain and about four hundred made prisoner, and of our men nearly a hundred had been killed under the heavy rain of missiles, and when three great carracks had been captured and one hulk sunk, by God's command victory was yielded to the English and the remainder of the many ships of the enemy fled to Honfleur on the other side of the River Seine.[38]

The so-called battle of the Seine was probably the most spectacular naval confrontation of the entire Hundred Years War: involving substantial fleets on both sides (at any rate by fifteenth-century standards), it certainly lasted several hours and did, indeed, result in the loss of both men and vessels. Once it was over half the surviving English fleet entered the harbour of Harfleur; the rest – and the wounded John Duke of Bedford – sailed home triumphantly; and, as a result of this

Fighting at sea, possibly the battle of the Seine, August 1416. As a result of this naval victory by Henry V's brother John Duke of Bedford, the French blockade of Harfleur was ended and the way opened up for the king's subsequent invasion and conquest of Normandy.

great victory, not only was the French blockade of Harfleur ended but the way was also opened up for Henry V's subsequent invasion and conquest of Normandy.

Soon after bringing news of his brother Bedford's naval triumph to Sigismund at Canterbury, Henry V accompanied his foreign guest to Dover where, on 25 August, the emperor embarked for Calais. Before leaving, so Adam Usk learned, 'with his own hands' Sigismund:

> ...distributed around the streets numerous proclamations worded as follows; 'Farewell, O happy England, rejoice in your glorious triumph.' For, worshipping Jesus as you do, with angelic nature and glorious praise, you are rightly designated as blessed. This praise which I offer you, you have most assuredly merited'.

That the emperor's 'retainers on horseback' had 'wanted to bless our nation so warmly and spontaneously' by scattering such broadsheets 'unobtrusively along the streets and thoroughfares' of Canterbury, the *Gesta Henrici Quinti* added, was because 'their affection and esteem for us had grown as much as had ours for them'. A few days later, on 4 September 1416, Henry V himself sailed from Sandwich for Calais; moreover, according to the *Gesta*, 'when the emperor, having in the morning been informed of the king's coming, had waited for a long time at the shore to see his eagerly desired face, and the king, being very close, had disembarked, each of them rushed with great joy into the other's embrace'. The purpose of their visit was a conference with John the Fearless Duke of Burgundy. By this time, clearly, all hopes of reconciliation with Charles VI and the Armagnacs had been abandoned, despite the fact that, as Sigismund sadly informed the Valois king on 6 September, 'in order to obtain peace between the realms of France and England, we have often spent sleepless nights, and have turned breakfast into dinner, to see if by ourselves, or by conferring with others, we might find any means of securing peace between you and him'. Just what happened when Henry V and John the Fearless met, for several days, early in October 1416 is far from clear. Henry's hopes of the meeting, at least, are indicated by a surviving memorandum: that Burgundy, once finally convinced of the English king's right to the French crown and justification for mounting a new campaign against Charles VI, would agree to aid him secretly at first and later, when he had acquired a solid territorial footing in France, openly by performing homage to him. According to Enguerrand de Monstrelet, Henry V offered Burgundy a share in his future French conquests but the offer was refused. If we are to believe the *Gesta Henrici Quinti*, however, John the Fearless was guilty of blatant deception:

> What kind of conclusion these enigmatic talks and exchanges produced went no further than the king's breast or the reticence with which he kept his counsel. I who am writing know that the general view was that Burgundy had all this time detained our king with ambiguities and prevarications and had so left him, and that in the end, like all Frenchmen, he would be found a double-dealer, one person in public and another in private.

Almost certainly, no formal agreement resulted from these negotiations, although the Burgundian duke did endorse a six-month truce extension and might well have hinted at future support for Henry V. Soon afterwards, so the *Gesta* tells us, the king went down to the seashore 'escorted by the emperor and, after many mutual leave-takings and oft-repeated embraces from which, in tears, they could hardly be parted because of the ardour of their affections', he boarded ship and 'we spread our sails for Dover'.

Clearly, by the autumn of 1416, Henry V had finally resolved to launch a new invasion of France. When parliament convened at Westminster on 19 October, reported the *Gesta*, Chancellor Henry Beaufort, in his opening address, declared that:

> ...because a just peace could not be obtained by any manner of negotiation, there seemed to be no alternative but to have prompt recourse again to divine judgement in favour of accomplishing it by the sword, and to achieve this it would be necessary to ask for their expedient advice and service as well as for their wealth.

Parliament ended on 20 November, moreover, with the:

> ...final adoption of the king's unbreakable resolve to go overseas in the following summer to subdue the stubborn and more than adamantine obduracy of the French, which neither the tender milk of

goats nor the consuming wine of vengeance, nor yet the most thor-
oughgoing negotiations, could soften.[39]

For the next few months Henry V threw himself energetically into
financial and military preparations for the now looming campaign.
Parliament responded generously to Beaufort's exhortations by granting a double subsidy leviable within a year; the convocation of the
English church, similarly, voted substantial sums of money; and the
king's government pulled out all the stops in raising loans, not least
from wealthy individuals such as the chancellor himself. In January
1417 recruiting the army and assembling the fleet necessary to transport it to France began in earnest. Since much attention was devoted,
too, to ensuring the readiness of siege engines and artillery, as well as
arrangements for supplying the expeditionary force from England, it
soon became clear that this was to be a full-scale campaign of conquest.
Equally important, enthusiasm for the war had to be stimulated and
sustained and complaints about the frequency and burden of taxation,
even before the invasion began, countered: in May 1417, for instance,
the king prompted Henry Chichele Archbishop of Canterbury to issue
a mandate urging both clergy and laity to greater participation in
processions, litanies and prayers for victory since, despite earlier exhortations, such devotions were still being practised too tepidly. In June
1417, as military preparations at home neared completion, Henry V also
addressed head-on the problem of safely transporting his invading
force across the Channel. Since the battle of the Seine Harfleur had
remained firmly in English hands but it now came to the king's attention that a flotilla of mainly Genoese ships, lurking in the vicinity,
might still pose a threat. Hence why he despatched a preliminary task
force to deal with it. On 29 June, an anonymous London chronicler
recorded, John Holand Earl of Huntingdon:

> ...with certain other lords and their retinues fought with nine car-
> racks of Genoa, the greatest that were ever seen near these coasts, and
> defeated them; of which, thanked be God, he took three great ships
> with their masters, and the admiral of them all the Bastard of
> Bourbon, with all the treasure with which their wages should have
> been paid for a quarter of a year. And the other carracks all fled away.[40]

A month later Henry V himself, with an army of about 10,000 men, sailed from Southampton and, on 1 August 1417, he landed at Touques in Normandy just across the Seine estuary from Harfleur.

Enguerrand de Monstrelet was certainly in no doubt that, when 'King Henry, accompanied by his brothers the dukes of Clarence and Gloucester, a number of other nobles, and a numerous army' arrived in Normandy, it was 'with the intent to conquer the whole of that duchy'. Almost immediately the king despatched a formal challenge to Charles VI demanding restoration of his just rights in France but more significantly, as Monstrelet also noted, 'the royal castle of Touques was speedily invested on all sides' and surrendered within four days. This set the pattern for the whole campaign. Since his prime objective from the outset was conquest, Henry V's strategy marked a complete break with the past: siege warfare, rather than *chevauchées* or seeking out and confronting the French in battle, was very much the name of the game, designed to secure control of the principal fortresses and towns of Normandy, establish permanent garrisons in them and, once this was accomplished, subject the surrounding countryside to English rule as well. The impact of the king's single-minded and ruthless generalship, moreover, had certainly become deeply embedded in French folklore by the time Thomas Basin put pen to paper half a century later:

> It is not easy to convey what terror was inspired among the inhabitants [of Normandy] by the name of Englishmen alone – fear so sudden that nobody, or almost nobody, thought that there was any safety other than in flight. If in most of the towns and fortresses those captains who had garrisons had not shut the gates, and if the inhabitants had not been restrained by force as well as by fear, it is beyond question that many would have been left totally deserted as certainly happened in some places. Indeed the people, unnerved by a long period of peace and order, simple as they were, generally thought that the English were not men like everyone else but wild beasts, gigantic and ferocious, who were going to throw themselves on them and then devour them.[41]

Yet, at the time, Henry V himself clearly realised that the systematic conquest and colonisation of territory alone would not be enough to ensure a permanent occupation of north-western France. Indeed, if we are to believe Tito Livio, the king knew full well that if he 'subdued the land by arms without appeasing the minds of the gentlemen and commons, at the last he should bring all the land to desolation, which he intended not', preferring 'to lose all his right in the kingdom rather than be lord of a void and desolate country'.

Henry V's first major objective was the seizure of Caen, capital city of lower Normandy, and he wasted no time in laying siege to it. The king 'came before the town of Caen, which was very strong and populous, and made many attacks on it', declared Enguerrand de Monstrelet, until 'at length, by continued assaults, he took it by storm'. The siege lasted about a fortnight, in fact, and the English certainly did not pull their punches; Henry V's guns, so the Monk of Saint-Denis learned, 'threw enormous stones with a noise like thunder amid fearsome clouds of black smoke so that one might have thought they were being vomited forth by hell'; and its final capture on 4 September 1417, no French force appearing to relieve it, was certainly brutal. Worse still, it was widely reported on the continent, was the callous butchery of many of Caen's inhabitants that immediately followed the town's surrender. The Venetian commentator Antonio Morosini, for instance, tells us he received letters 'from divers parts' informing him that the English king 'ordered his subjects – barons and knights, and all his men-at-arms – to kill and cut to pieces everyone they found from the age of twelve upwards, without sparing anybody; no one', he added, 'had ever heard of such infamy being committed'. When writing personally to the mayor and aldermen of London the day after the city's capitulation, however, Henry V himself merely reported that 'God sent into our hands our town of Caen, by assault and with right little death of our people'. The *First English Life*, following Tito Livio, tells us predictably that once in control of the city the king issued a proclamation that whosoever would:

> ...return to their proper houses to live under the obedience of the King of England, and swore to be faithful liegemen to him and his heirs, should enjoy their houses and lands, and their former right and title... Which proclamation made, many Frenchmen, as well noblemen, citizens, burgesses, as commons, almost all the country, returned again in short time and swore fealty to the king... And thus with the king's goodwill they lived well and peaceably, and prospered as well and better than before.

'As I have heard of the report of the Earl of Ormonde', he also recorded:

> ...all the great riches of the town were left unspoiled, by the king's straight commandment, gathered together, and put into a great and strong house; whereof, when the door was securely locked, the king gave the key and all the substance to the Duke of Clarence, because by him the town was first taken, and to himself reserved nothing except a goodly French book.[42]

More recent admirers of Henry V, too, have been at pains to justify English behaviour in Caen: even if his troops did engage in wholesale massacre and looting, it is argued, this was no more than contemporary laws of war sanctioned under the circumstances; the butchering of the citizenry was not on the king's orders and, when it came to his attention, he commanded an end to such behaviour; and, as far as clergy, women and children were concerned, he was actually more merciful than a strict interpretation of the rules of war required. Nevertheless, it seems that at least two thousand people were massacred and, even after the king ordered the killing to stop, his men continued pillaging and looting the city. Perhaps it was all carefully calculated, even orchestrated up to a point: Henry V may have deliberately sanctioned a mixture of harshness and mercy in the hope of encouraging other Norman towns and fortresses to surrender without the need for similar sieges and assaults in the future.

'By taking the town of Caen', reported the Monk of Saint-Denis dramatically, 'the King of England inspired such terror in the Normans that they lost all courage': indeed, in the months that followed, English troops brought 'fire and blood and made everything to fall to them, by force of arms, by menace and by terror'. Anyone who rejected his summons to surrender and fell into his hands bearing arms, moreover, was 'put to death as guilty of *lèse-majesté*'; the young and the aged suffered 'cruel tortures before being chased into exile'; and, apart from those 'who resigned themselves to marrying Englishmen', even mothers were 'reduced to leaving the country with their children'. In the aftermath of Caen's capitulation, echoed Jean Juvenal des Ursins despairingly, 'there was no resistance, save for a few companions who held out in the woods' and 'whenever the English caught them, some they hauled off to fortresses, others they threw in the river'. The *First English Life*, by contrast, emphasised that 'in a short time all the country was brought with goodwill, love and favour under the king's dominion', while even the Monk of Saint-Denis was prepared to admit that many strong castles in Normandy surrendered to Henry V 'by dint of promises rather than naked force' since 'by his word as a prince he guaranteed, to everybody who yielded, exemption from taxes, freedom to concentrate on farming or commerce, and the re-establishment of privileges as they had been in the time of St Louis'(King Louis IX of France 1226–1270). Clearly, many smaller Norman towns did indeed put up little or no resistance to Henry V, for whatever reasons, in the autumn of 1417 and as a result fell easily into his hands. Falaise proved more of a challenge but, after a siege of several weeks, it finally capitulated in mid-February 1418. After a winter's campaigning, during which he judiciously rewarded his English supporters and those Normans who joined him by distributing confiscated 'rebel' estates among them (as well as making provision for the administration of areas succumbing to him), the king chose to spend Easter 1418 at Caen. Whilst there, moreover, he also made a particular point of celebrating the feast of St George and dubbing new knights in the local castle.

Enguerrand de Monstrelet, anxious to explain 'the facility of King Henry's conquests' in Normandy and the reasons why 'scarcely any place made a defence', chose to blame:

> ...the divisions that existed among the nobles, some taking part with the king [Charles VI], and others with the Duke of Burgundy, and therefore fearful of trusting each other. The [Armagnac] constable had, besides, drawn off the greater part of his forces in this district to Paris, to be prepared to meet the Duke of Burgundy, whom he daily expected in these parts with a large army.

Whatever his hopes at the time of their meeting in Calais during early October 1416, however, Henry V himself had so far received no direct support whatever from Burgundy. John the Fearless, clearly, was very much following his own agenda: the capture of Paris and seizure of Charles VI. Thus, while the English king continued campaigning in lower Normandy during the spring of 1418, the Burgundian duke launched his own attack on the Armagnacs in the Seine valley until finally, on 29 May, his forces took Paris, massacred his Armagnac enemies and secured control of the hapless Valois king. Henry V, meanwhile, despatched his brother Humphrey Duke of Gloucester to besiege Cherbourg: 'the strongest place in all Normandy and the best supplied with stores', so Monstrelet tells us, it eventually surrendered in September 1418 after holding out for five months. More immediately, the king himself laid siege to Louviers in June 1418 where, according to the Kenilworth chronicler John Strecche, he only narrowly escaped death when 'a gunner from within the town' fired a stone shattering the central pole of the Earl of Salisbury's tent (where he happened to be at the time). After this, Strecche continued, Henry V 'delivered many heavy assaults against the town', rapidly secured its surrender and, promptly, 'hung eight gunners on a gallows' as well as condemning nine more to perpetual imprisonment; then, without delay, the king:

> ...hastened, in royal manner with his army fittingly arrayed, to besiege the town of Pont de l'Arche. This is a strong city and nobly fortified. The town is situated on one of the banks of the Seine, and the castle of the town stands in a stately manner on the other, a strong bridge over the water joining the two, a bridge built and erected in marvellous fashion over the deep abyss, and a good defence in time of war. For no ships could come up the river, nor was any passage open to the town, without permission from those on the bridge and in the castle. When King Henry arrived at the place, he considered the position and erected his tents. And the king laid fierce siege to the town from the side on which was the castle, and daily for many days delivered assaults upon it. And after fifteen days the king took the town with its castle, after hard fighting, with the loss of many noble men.[43]

The castle of Pont de l'Arche fell, in fact, on 20 July 1418 after a three-week siege; soon afterwards Henry V managed to get his army across the river; and, at the end of July, he settled down to besiege the nearby Norman capital of Rouen.

For the anonymous author of the *First English Life* Rouen was 'the master city of all Normandy', while Henry V himself informed the mayor and aldermen of London on 10 August 1418, in a letter written in English 'under our signet in our host afore our city of Rouen', that 'we have laid siege to the city of Rouen, which is the most notable

place in France, save Paris'. Clearly, securing Rouen had deep psychological as well as military significance for the English king, not least
since the owner of its castle was traditionally Normandy's duke and the
city itself a natural focal point for ducal administration. The siege is
notably well documented in both English and French sources, moreover, and widely reported elsewhere in Europe, too, as a major event of
the time. Most notably, both Tito Livio and Pseudo-Elmham provide
narratives of it; so does Enguerrand de Monstrelet; and the chronicle of
John Strecche contains a substantial account as well. Strecche's description, however, derives almost entirely from the work of a contemporary
balladeer John Page, while an anonymous *Brut* chronicler simply incor-
porated Page's poem *verbatim* into his narrative. John Page, a soldier in
Henry V's army, experienced the rigours of the siege first-hand:

> ...I will tell you who are here
> If to my tale you will give ear
> How the fifth Henry who was our liege
> With his royal host he set a siege
> Unto Rouen, that rich city...
> For at the siege with the king I lay.

Page certainly provides a vivid, moving and detailed account of what
took place at Rouen over a period of almost six months; he had no
qualms about the justice of the king's cause; and, as for Henry V himself, he was a 'king most excellent' who was both 'manful while the war
does last' and 'merciful when the war is past'. Yet, no less clearly, Page
had every sympathy for the physical suffering and material destruction
experienced by the besieged inhabitants and their city.

Since Rouen had formidable defences and seemed well prepared to
withstand a siege, Henry V faced an awesome task when he began his
blockade of the city on 30 July 1418. He met the challenge with typical
thoroughness, mounting a strong watch at each gate, constructing towers bristling with artillery and surrounding the town with a ditch
hedged with stakes and filled with traps. The king also took care to
ensure his investing force was able to sustain a long blockade: the
prime purpose of his letter to London on 10 August, indeed, was to
request the mayor and aldermen to send 'in all haste' as many small vessels as they could 'with provisions and, especially, with drink' to

The siege of Rouen, July 1418 to January 1419. The capitulation of the 'master city of all Normandy' on 19 January 1419, after a long and implacable blockade by Henry V, made the duchy's conquest by the king virtually inevitable.

Harfleur and 'thence as far as they may up the Seine towards Rouen' for 'the refreshing of us and our host'. No such relief came to the city itself and as a result, so John Page tells us, by October the townsfolk were on the verge of famine:

> By that time their victuals waxed quite scarce.
> Meat and drink and other victual
> In that city began to fail...
> Their bread was nearly gone,
> And flesh save horsemeat had they none.
> They ate up dogs, they ate up cats;
> They ate up mice, horses and rats...
> Then to die they did begin,
> All that rich city within.
> They died so fast on every day
> That men could not all of them in the earth lay.
> Even if a child should otherwise be dead,
> The mother would not give it bread...

Soon afterwards many of the poor, old and infirm in Rouen were forced out of the town to save food. If the city authorities thought Henry V would feel morally obliged to feed them they were wrong. Although, if we are to believe Page, the king was greatly angered at such inhumane behaviour, since he regarded the refugees as the garrison's responsibility, he would not let them through English lines. Instead, he ordered his troops to herd them into the ditch he had dug outside the city walls and there they remained: only over the Christmas season did he temporarily relent and provide a certain amount of food and drink. Meanwhile, the situation within the walls also became ever more desperate and, when no aid was forthcoming either from John the Fearless Duke of Burgundy or the Dauphin Charles, a delegation of citizens was allowed out to meet with the king: they begged him to have mercy on them as their poor were starving and many were dead but Henry V, with unsmiling countenance, offered only the stark choice of starvation or surrender. By this time, moreover, the people in the ditch were in a very bad way indeed, not least since it had rained continuously for several weeks. As John Page put it:

There men might see a great pity,
A child of two or of three
Go about and beg his bread
For father and mother both were dead.
And under them the water stood
And yet they lay crying after food.
Some had starved in that place to death,
And some had stopped both eyes and breath,
And some were crooked in the knees
And were now as lean as any trees.
You saw a woman hold in her arm
Her own dead child, with nothing warm,
And babies sucking on the pap
Within a dead woman's lap.
There men might find it at last arrive
That twelve were dead to one alive.[44]

Although several French chroniclers suggest that, towards the end of the siege, the inhabitants of Rouen threatened to set fire to their city and leave Henry V nothing but smoking ruins, eventually, on 13 January 1419, terms of surrender were finally agreed: if no rescue came within eight days, the keys would be handed over and the town 'pay to our king £50,000'. No relief was forthcoming, so the city duly capitulated on 19 January and, with cries of 'Welcome, Rouen, our king's own right', the English passed through its gates.

Next day Henry V himself entered Rouen, an event colourfully reconstructed by Tito Livio:

[The] victorious king entered the town and fortress accompanied by a great crowd of dukes, nobles and other attendants. But first of all, lest some of his men should rush off to pillage the town, the king appointed officers to watch over every quarter of the city, that damage and rapine might be prevented. Henry V himself, moved to pity by the wretchedness of the townspeople, gave orders to his servants and retinue to fetch food for the crowd. A great quantity of victuals, brought at the most merciful wish of the king, came only just in time to revive the dying townspeople – and the most tenderhearted of princes had given instructions for the provision of food before anything else.

As for the men who had sought to defend Rouen over so many weeks, according to Enguerrand de Monstrelet they were ordered 'to march out by the gate leading towards the Seine' and then searched by royal officials who 'took all their money and valuables': indeed, he declared, 'some noblemen were even stripped of their handsome coats, made of marten silk or embroidered with gold, and made to exchange them for worthless old garments'. Specifically, Rouen's vicar-general Robert de Linet, who had publicly excommunicated Henry V and his army from the city walls, was handed over to the king and, so the *First English Life* tells us, paid for his rashness by being kept in chains for the rest of his life. Yet a fortnight after Rouen's fall, if we are to believe John Strecche, as the king prepared 'to make the ceremonial offering of his candle' at Candlemas (2 February 1419):

> ...the citizens of the city, plotting to take the life of King Henry, determined to arm themselves suddenly and to attack the king, seize him and kill him. Thanks be to God, their plot did not remain hidden from the king. For the king anticipated their evil design, and fell upon them with an armed band whilst they were arming in a secret place to kill him. And thus, even while they were plotting these evil deeds, the king captured them all and imprisoned them. And he sent fifty of the richest and most powerful of them to England and imprisoned them in various castles.[45]

Most of Rouen's population, however, seems to have welcomed the Lancastrian king with relief if not rejoicing; Tito Livio learned that he soon appointed 'such worthy men as his prefects that the city was quickly restored to the flourishing condition it had enjoyed in the past'; and back in England, Adam Usk reported, news of Henry V's victory resulted in triumphant processions and even dancing in the streets of London.

Once the fall of Rouen became known, resistance to Henry V in Normandy rapidly crumbled. Indeed, according to Enguerrand de Monstrelet, over the next few months Normandy was 'overrun by the English and laid waste with fire and sword', the king's troops seized much booty and the poor were 'left defenceless with no other resources than to offer up their prayers and lamentations to God'. Everywhere, declared the Monk of Saint-Denis, Normans now laid down their arms and submitted to 'the odious yoke of the English'. Early in February 1419, reported an anonymous chronicler living in Paris at the time, 'the English took Mantes and several nearby strongholds'; moreover, he added sadly, 'no one did anything about it because all the French lords were angry with each other, because the dauphin was at odds with his father on account of the Duke of Burgundy, who was with the king, and all the other princes of the blood royal had been taken prisoner by the English king at the battle of Agincourt'. Dieppe capitulated at about the same time as Mantes; other towns soon followed its example; and by June 1419 virtually the whole of Normandy was in English hands. Indeed, by then, Henry V had begun to advance into neighbouring regions as well. When negotiations to secure a reconciliation with John the Fearless failed, moreover, and the Burgundian duke responded by making a pact with the French dauphin to drive the English out of France once and for all, the king promptly stormed and sacked Pontoise on 30 July. As a result, commented Monstrelet, the English 'gained great riches' while, from Henry V's point of view, the seizure of Pontoise also had real military significance since, once he had installed a loyal garrison, it could prevent supplies reaching Paris, even threaten the French capital itself. An anonymous Parisian chronicler certainly gave vent to real emotion when reporting the event. Within a few days of Pontoise's fall, he declared, fleeing refugees arrived at the gates of Paris 'in a state of terror, some of them wounded, others faint with fear, and all looking more dead than alive': no wonder if, as they asserted, the English had 'killed everyone who crossed their path'. Indeed, the chronicler concluded despairingly, 'the only news one heard' at this time was about 'the ravages of the English', as they took towns and castles, spread ruin throughout the entire realm and sent everything, loot and prisoners, back to England in triumph.

During the conquest of Normandy the quality of Henry V's generalship became only too apparent, as he methodically reduced castles, fortresses and hostile towns, and then organised the rule of vanquished territory from these self-same strongholds. Throughout the campaign, moreover, the king maintained overall command of strategy, frequently demonstrated his considerable knowledge of the art of warfare (not least the lethal potential of artillery bombardment) and even directed many sieges and assaults in person. Once lands were under Henry V's control he required local inhabitants to recognise the legitimacy of his rule by swearing an oath of allegiance to their new lord. Those who refused were deprived of their estates, forced to leave the province and left with no option but to seek refuge in Valois-controlled territory. Yet, although the king pursued a deliberate policy of encouraging Englishmen to settle in Normandy, he also made a real effort to win over the natives by granting confiscated estates to his French supporters, appointing Normans to a range of administrative posts in the duchy and providing ordinary folk with a degree of legal protection against English garrisons. No less importantly, as the Ordinances of War he issued in 1419 demonstrate, Henry V put in place a remarkably sophisticated system of muster and review of troops firmly ordering his fighting men to be obedient to their superiors (not least by 'keeping such watches and guard-duties as required of them'). Even so, the campaign probably lasted longer than he had expected and absorbed all his energies for months on end; John the Fearless singularly failed to provide the overt support he had hoped for (although he clearly benefited from Armagnac/Burgundian feuding); and, despite all the king's efforts to stamp it out, bands of brigands continued to wage intermittent guerilla warfare even after the conquest of Normandy proper was complete. Henry V can hardly have anticipated, in August 1419, that in less than a year he would be regent of France and the recognised heir to the Valois throne.

14

TREATY OF TROYES
AND LAST YEARS

The conquest of Normandy was clearly Henry V's top priority throughout 1418 and the early months of 1419 but that did not prevent intermittent negotiations with both Armagnac and Burgundian factions for a diplomatic settlement of the king's claims in France. By and large, too, Henry continued his old game of playing one side off against the other while, at the same time, pushing steadily ahead with his military operations. When, at the end of May 1418, John the Fearless Duke of Burgundy seized Paris and secured control of the French king Charles VI he became, in effect, the ruler of France and, as such, responsible for stemming English military advance. The young Dauphin Charles, however, had managed to escape from Paris, join the Armagnacs and become the nominal leader of internal French resistance to the Burgundian duke. Over the next few months Armagnac/Burgundian feuding obviously worked very much to Henry V's advantage: neither faction had the strength to confront him without the support of the other and all attempts at reconciliation between them failed. In November 1418, with much of Normandy already in his hands, the English king put out diplomatic feelers to the Armagnacs at Alençon but, although substantial French concessions were offered, negotiations soon foundered, as so often in the past, on the vexed issue of sovereignty. By the spring of 1419 it had become evident that neither Armagnacs nor Burgundians could master their rivals, let alone mount effective resistance to the English invaders. Henry V, in consequence, continued to sweep all before him, particularly after the surrender of Rouen on 19 January. Once more the

Armagnacs indicated their willingness to negotiate but, at the end of May, it was a Burgundian initiative that finally elicited a positive response from the English king.

Although Charles VI himself was too incapacitated to attend, Queen Isabella and their daughter Catherine of Valois accompanied John the Fearless to meet Henry V face-to-face at Meulan on 29 May, hopefully to negotiate peace terms and seal the agreement by a royal betrothal. At their first encounter two days later, so several chroniclers reported, the English king could hardly have been more impressed by the young French princess: 'King Henry', declared Enguerrand de Monstrelet, was at once 'very desirous to marry her and not without cause for she was very handsome, of high birth, and of the most engaging manners'; Jean Waurin had no doubt he fell in love at first sight; and, according to the anonymous author of the *First English Life* too, 'the flame of love fired the heart of this martial king' as soon as he clapped eyes on her. Unfortunately, ensuing peace negotiations soon hit familiar obstacles and eventually, early in July 1419, collapsed altogether. A letter sent by Queen Isabella to the English king a few weeks later perhaps explains why. 'Although the offers you made were agreeable enough to us', she wrote, 'there was nevertheless great difficulty in the way of accepting them and concluding with you, for at the time all were advising that we should incline to our son'. Moreover, she added, had we accepted the terms on offer, 'all the lords, knights, cities and good towns would have abandoned us and joined our son' and, as a result, 'even greater war would have arisen'. In fact, even while negotiations with Henry V were still continuing, John the Fearless and Queen Isabella had already opened up a new dialogue with the Dauphin Charles. Unexpectedly, this produced a fragile Armagnac/Burgundian reconciliation on 11 July 1419 and, in response, Henry V resumed his military offensive with a vengeance on 30 July by seizing and sacking Pontoise. Soon afterwards Charles VI, his queen and daughter Catherine, fearing Paris itself might now come under attack, fled from the city and set up court at Troyes instead. Only a month after that, however, the murder of John the Fearless completely transformed the situation yet again.

In order to strengthen the earlier pact between them, John of Burgundy and the Dauphin Charles met at Montereau, south east of Paris, on 10 September 1419 where, following an altercation, a member of the dauphin's entourage slew the Burgundian duke in cold blood.

Marriage of Henry V and Catherine of Valois in the parish church of St John, Troyes, 2 June 1420, a direct result of the Treaty of Troyes ratified less than a fortnight earlier on 21 May.

Although Jean Juvenal des Ursins later chose to emphasise the dauphin's innocence in the matter, even suggesting young Charles was aghast when he learned of the murder, far more convincing is the pithy account penned by his own mother less than a fortnight after the event:

> ...after several embassies had been despatched to our son, Sunday 10 September last past was fixed as the day upon which they [John the Fearless and the dauphin] should meet upon the bridge of Montereau... After our cousin had given him a courteous and humble greeting, and had offered him himself, money and his friends, several armed men came out from a hiding place constructed in one of the rooms, and together struck our cousin, who was kneeling before our son, with axes, and there brutally murdered him against God, justice, reason, faith and law, and took prisoner the knights who had accompanied him to this fateful meeting.[46]

And a century later, in 1521, when showing the skull of John the Fearless to the then French king Francis I, a Carthusian monk apparently pointed to a gash and remarked: 'My lord, that is the hole through which the English entered France'.

The assassination of John Duke of Burgundy certainly resulted in a comprehensive metamorphosis of the political and diplomatic situation in France. When the new duke Philip learned of his father's death, Jean Juvenal des Ursins tells us, he was:

> ...very grieved and angry, and not without cause, and assembled his council to know what he ought to do. Moreover, he sent to the King of England to treat of peace even more fully than his father had offered, and in this hope a truce was made between the Duke of Burgundy, in the name of the king whom he abused [Charles VI], and the King of England. And their people considered themselves as all of the same party, English and Burgundians, in order to make mortal war on the dauphin and those who supported him, and avenge themselves for this death.

Queen Isabella of France, in a letter to Henry V written at Troyes on 22 September 1419, declared her firm intention to assist Duke Philip 'to avenge the unreasonable and cruel death' of his father. Already, she reported, 'we have found that the loyal barons, cities and good towns hereabouts are willing to support us'. Nevertheless, she added, since 'we are still desirous of preserving peace, amity and concord with you', we 'earnestly beseech you' to 'aid us in avenging this sad death' and 'not allow the delays which have occurred to cool your desire for the conclusion of peace in any way'. As for Henry V himself, if we are to believe Jean Waurin the king certainly regretted the removal of that 'good and loyal knight and prince of honour' John the Fearless; however, he also recognised at once that 'by his death, and the help of God and St George, we are at the achievement of our desire'. Whatever his ultimate ambitions before, moreover, the English king now openly set his sights on the French throne: just over a fortnight after the Burgundian duke's death, indeed, royal envoys once more reminded Charles VI's council of Henry V's claim not only to Normandy but the crown of France and also made abundantly clear his intention to secure *all* his just rights in the kingdom. Indeed, Henry V could probably have seized the French throne by force at this time had he wished. He made no attempt to do so. Instead, complex negotiations began with the Burgundian-dominated government in Paris, negotiations destined to last several weeks. Meanwhile, according to the *First English Life* (following Tito Livio), the king:

> ...gave himself not to rest and sloth but, with marvellous solicitude and diligence, he laboured continually. For almost no day passed but he visited some of the towns and strongholds... He ordained in all parts sufficient garrisons for their defence. He repaired their castles, towns and walls. He cleansed and secured their ditches.[47]

Moreover, the biographer added, English troops 'remained conquerors in the field' and, after slaying and maiming many of their adversaries, put the rest of them to flight.

By December 1419 Philip of Burgundy, despite serious misgivings, had finally come to the conclusion that he had no option but to meet Henry V's demands; otherwise, he was likely to lose control of Paris to the English and the royal court to the Dauphin Charles, as well as find himself isolated between two enemies who might well form an alliance against him. On 2 December, at Arras, he formally committed himself to supporting a peace settlement between Henry V and Charles VI: under its terms the English king would marry Catherine of Valois and become regent of France; on Charles VI's death he, not the dauphin, would succeed to the French throne; and, after Henry V's own death, the crown would duly pass to his and Catherine's heirs. In response, at Rouen on Christmas Day, Henry V publicly proclaimed the new Anglo-Burgundian alliance, reiterated his desire for peace and solemnly undertook to wed the French king's daughter; no less significantly, he promised to support and help advance Burgundian claims and rights within the kingdom of France. The centre of attention now switched to Troyes where the royal court, initially stupified by the news emanating from Arras and Rouen, eventually bowed to the inevitable and, by April 1420, all parties (except, of course, the Dauphin Charles and his Armagnac supporters) were ready to put their seals to a historic treaty.

Early in May 1420 Henry V set off for Troyes. En route, according to Georges Chastellain, he met Philip Duke of Burgundy for the first time; the two hit it off well; and, on 20 May, they arrived at the city where Charles VI, Queen Isabella and Catherine of Valois were already in residence. Soon afterwards the English king paid a courtesy visit to the Valois court where, so Chastellain tells us, he 'bowed very low' as he approached Catherine, 'kissed her with great joy' and, after a brief discussion, returned to his lodgings. Next day, in the cathedral of St Peter at Troyes, came the formal ratification of the first full Anglo-French peace treaty since Bretigny in 1360. Henry V, seemingly, demonstrated a characteristic concern for public relations on this momentous occasion: in order to prevent his soldiers disgracing themselves by drinking too much, Pseudo-Elmham learned, the king issued instructions that no Englishman take any wine unless it was watered down, while, according to Jean Waurin, at the ceremony itself the English nobility, bedecked in rich garments, rings and jewels, appeared far more resplendent than their French counterparts. Charles VI was unable to attend the ceremony but the English king, Queen Isabella and Philip of Burgundy played a full part, Henry and Catherine were formally betrothed and peace publicly proclaimed. Less than a fortnight later came the marriage of Henry V and his French bride and, significantly, it appears to have been an archetypically soldier's wedding, the king well attended by an essentially military entourage. On 2 June 1420, reported Jean Juvenal des Ursins:

...the King of England married Lady Catherine, and he willed that the ceremony should be carried out entirely according to the custom of France [in] the parish church of St John at Troyes... And instead of thirteen pence the king placed on the book thirteen nobles [1040 pence]. And at the offertory, with the candle, everyone gave three nobles; and he also gave to the church of St John two hundred nobles; and afterwards there was a feast with wine in the accustomed manner and the blessing of the nuptial couch.[48]

According to Enguerrand de Monstrelet, moreover, so great was the pomp and magnificence on display that day that it was as if Henry V had become 'king of all the world'!

The Treaty of Troyes very much reflected the transformed political and diplomatic climate in France brought about by the murder of John the Fearless and, in order to secure it, Henry V certainly demonstrated the powerful streak of opportunism in his nature. Under its terms the Lancastrian king abandoned his hereditary Plantagenet claim to the French throne and recognised, for the first time, the right of his erstwhile rival: Charles VI was to 'hold and possess' the 'crown and dignity of France' for the rest of his natural life; Henry V was to marry his 'most dear and most beloved daughter' Catherine; and, after the Valois king's death, 'the crown and realm of France' was to pass to them and their heirs in perpetuity as Charles VI's legitimate successors. In the meantime, since his father-in-law was 'so afflicted with various infirmities' that he 'may not in his own person arrange for the needs of France', Henry V was to act as his regent and, not only was the Dauphin Charles permanently excluded from succession to his father's throne, the English king committed himself (as regent) to:

...labour to put into obedience to our father-in-law all cities, towns, castles, places, counties and persons within the realm who are disobedient and rebellious, holding or belonging to the party commonly called Dauphin or Armagnac.[49]

Such terms clearly bear witness to Henry V's negotiating skills, particularly the need to make them firmly watertight (unlike the Treaty of Bretigny) and as widely acceptable as possible to the French people. The eventual outcome, in fact, was to be a dual monarchy of France and

England; the union of the Lancastrian and Valois crowns was to be purely personal; the kingdoms of England and France were to remain separate and continue to be ruled in accordance with their own ancient laws and customs; and all lands recovered from the Armagnacs were to revert to the French crown, and Normandy too, once Charles VI was dead. Philip of Burgundy, moreover, gained valuable territorial concessions under the terms of the treaty, as well as the promise of English assistance in avenging his father's death. As for Henry V himself he was, so Enguerrand de Monstrelet assures us, very well satisfied since he had now gained virtually everything he had ever hoped to achieve in France.

Inevitably, the significance of the Treaty of Troyes and, even more, its long-term viability (or otherwise) have been much debated. Clearly, once Charles VI was dead (and he was not expected to cling to life for long!), the treaty did indeed envisage the establishment of a dual monarchy: two separate kingdoms but both ruled by a single Lancastrian king. That, however, was for the future. More immediately, Henry V faced the challenge of making his French regency a reality and, despite his earlier conquests, this was never going to be easy. Even in Normandy there remained considerable opposition, and potential for resistance, to English rule. By turning the king into an overt participant in an on-going French civil war, moreover, the treaty also spawned problems for Henry V in England. Even after Troyes was sealed, the Dauphin Charles adamantly refused to accept it; so did his Armagnac supporters; and Henry V, in effect, found himself an ally of the Burgundian faction in its unceasing struggle for power. France had now split into two nations: a dauphinist south (which rejected Troyes) and an Anglo-Burgundian north (where the treaty was widely, if by no means universally, accepted); moreover, while many in the north now accepted Henry V as Charles VI's successor, much of the south firmly backed the dauphin as a future Valois king Charles VII.

No sooner had Henry V's marriage to Catherine of Valois been celebrated, Jean Juvenal des Ursins tells us, but 'a public proclamation was made that everyone should be ready armed and equipped by the following day' and, on 3 June 1420, the king left Troyes and resumed his campaign of conquest in France. Indeed, according to a contemporary Parisian chronicler, on the day after the nuptials:

...English and French knights intended to hold a tournament to celebrate the marriage of such a prince, as is usually done, but the King of England, for whose pleasure the tournament was meant, said of his own accord, in everyone's hearing: 'I beg my lord the king whose daughter I have married, and all his servants, and I command all my own servants that tomorrow morning we all of us be ready to go and besiege Sens, where my lord the king's enemies are. There we may all tilt and joust and prove our daring and courage, for there is no finer act of courage in the world than to punish evildoers so that poor people can live'.

The dauphinist stronghold of Sens offered little resistance, surrendering on 10 June. Nor did Montereau hold out for long: indeed, the town was stormed by an Anglo-Burgundian force on 24 June. Montereau's governor and most of its garrison took refuge in the adjoining castle but not before eleven men had been captured. Once more, if we are to believe Enguerrand de Monstrelet, Henry V showed no mercy:

> The King of England sent the prisoners from the town under strong guard to parley from the ditches with the men in the nearby castle and persuade the governor to surrender the place. When they were within hearing they fell on their knees and begged him piteously to yield, for by so doing he would save their lives and in any case he could not hold out much longer against such a large force. The governor replied that they would have to look after themselves as he was not going to surrender. Abandoning all hope of life, the prisoners then asked to speak with their wives, friends and relatives in the castle and everyone said goodbye with tears and lamentations. When they were brought back to the army the English king had a gallows erected and hanged them in full view of the castle.

At the same time, Monstrelet continued, the king:

> ...hanged a running footman who always followed him when he rode out, holding the bridle of his horse. He was a great favourite of the king but, having killed a knight in a quarrel, was punished.[50]

The fact that the knight had, apparently, been killed accidentally made no difference to the king: stern justice, even for a royal favourite, had to be done – and seen to be done.

Montereau finally surrendered on 1 July 1420. Henry V now proceeded down the Seine to Melun, a notably well-fortified town where, as Jean Juvenal des Ursins rightly reported, its captain Arnaud Guillaume the Sire de Barbazan, 'with many other knights and squires, had a great desire to hold out'; even the English king himself, he tells us, frankly acknowledged that 'these are valiant people and not easily overcome'. The siege of Melun, in fact, lasted over four months and the town's defenders certainly did mount a stubborn resistance, as Juvenal des Ursins learned (probably from one of his own relatives who was present); at one point, for instance, the Sire de Barbazan:

> ...ordered forty or fifty crossbowmen armed with good crossbows, the best in the town, to be on the walls facing the Burgundians, and a certain number of the remaining soldiers together with a body of the townsfolk to pour down large stones and boiling fat, whilst another body of the better armed and most valiant of the defenders were to leave by a false postern, which opened out of the city towards the trench. He further forbade them to shoot or enter the trenches until a trumpet was sounded within the city. At last there came a day when the two dukes, [Philip] of Burgundy and the Red Duke [of Bavaria], cried 'To the assault', and the trumpet sounded, and they leapt joyfully and confidently on to the edge of the trenches, threw down their ladders, and many of them proceeded to descend into them... When the Burgundians and Germans saw how those within the city were acting, they realised the folly of their enterprise, and sounded the retreat.

Clearly, then, Henry V's forces did suffer setbacks during the siege but, nevertheless, they kept up a relentless bombardment of Melun's defences and undertook extensive mining operations beneath its walls. Georges Chastellain, indeed, specifically describes an incident when 'the English king had a barrier erected in a mine, where he and the Duke of Burgundy, with a courage equal to their renown, fought for a long space hand-to-hand with strokes of sword and lance'. Perhaps the great cannon which, John Strecche tells us, Londoners provided for

Henry V played a crucial psychological as well as military role in bringing about Melun's eventual capitulation:

> As soon as this gun, called the *London*, arrived, the king ordered it to be loaded with powder and a great stone to be placed in its mouth, and [the powder] to be lit. At once the huge stone was hurled against the city, striking and demolishing a row of houses nearly a quarter of a mile long; the explosion itself split the gun and almost broke it to pieces.

In the end, however, famine and sickness rather than bombardment brought the town to its knees. By October 1420, Jean Juvenal des Ursins learned:

> ...those within the city were reduced to great distress and suffered from scarcity of food...They had been a whole month without bread, and had only horse-flesh to eat, a food of little or no nourishment, [so] those within were therefore forced to accept such terms as their enemies proposed. It was therefore decreed and arranged that they should escape with their lives, and without being forced to pay any ransom or fine. Only those who had consented to the death of John, the late Duke of Burgundy, were excepted from the terms.

Melun finally surrendered on 18 November and, clearly, during the long blockade there had been heavy losses on both sides: an anonymous London chronicler concluded, indeed, that this had been 'one of the worst that ever the king laid siege to', while, according to Thomas Walsingham, it resulted in 'a victory as destructive as glorious'. Juvenal des Ursins was certainly critical of Henry V's behaviour following Melun's fall, noting in particular the fate of a formerly loyal servant who had fought for the king at Agincourt but, unwisely, helped Armagnac friends to escape from the town: he was peremptorily beheaded without trial. As for the treatment of prisoners taken at Melun, it was outrageous:

> ...the hostages and anyone else whom [the English] had captured were brought to Paris by boat. Some were confined in the Bastille of St Antoine, others in the Palais, the Châtelet, the Temple and in

various other prisons... Several of them were put in deep ditches, especially at the Châtelet, and left there to die in hunger. And when they asked for food and screamed from hunger, people threw straw down to them and called them dogs.

'Which', he added, was 'a great disgrace to the King of England'.[51]

On Sunday 1 December 1420, according to an anonymous Parisian eyewitness, Henry V, his new wife Catherine, his brothers Clarence and Bedford, Charles VI, Queen Isabella and Philip of Burgundy:

> ...entered Paris in great state, for the street of Saint Denis by which they entered was draped from the second gate as far as Notre Dame and was a wonderful sight, and most of the people of Paris able to do so were clad in red robes... No princes were ever welcomed more joyfully than they for, in every street, they met processions of priests in copes and surplices carrying reliquaries and singing *Te Deum Laudamus* and *Benedictus qui venit*... And this was all done joyously and gladly, and the common people acted in a similar manner, for nothing done to win the favour of these lords was displeasing to them.

Yet this same commentator tells us that, during the Christmas festivities, while the English court in Paris displayed every sign of regality, the French royal family seemed pitifully down-at-heel by comparison. Enguerrand de Monstrelet, too, reported that:

> At the season of Christmas the two kings and their queens held open court in the city of Paris, the King of France in his Hotel de Saint-Pol, the King of England in the Louvre. But there was a vast difference between the state they kept, for the King of France was poorly served and attended by comparison with the great and mighty state he used to maintain, and on that day he received few visits apart from a small number of old servants and persons of low degree. How painful it must have been to the hearts of all true Frenchmen who were there to see this noble kingdom under the government of their old enemies through the misfortunes of war, and that for the present they were forced to live under foreign dominion.

As for Henry V and Queen Catherine, he added:

...it is scarcely possible to tell in detail of the state they kept that day, of the feasts and ceremony and luxury of their court or in that of the princes. Subjects of the noble kingdom of France came from all parts in the greatest humility to do the king honour, [and from] that time King Henry began to undertake the government and administration of the affairs of the kingdom of France.

By the time Georges Chastellain put pen to paper, he could hardly contain his indignation:

The city of Paris, ancient seat of France's royal majesty, now seemed to have changed name and situation because this king [Henry V] and his numerous English people had made of it a new London, no less by their rude and proud manner of conversation and behaviour as by their language. And they went through the city, which they held as masters, with their heads held high like stags, staring all round them, glorying at the shame and ill-fortune of the French, whose blood they had shed in such quantities at Agincourt and elsewhere, and so much of whose heritage they had taken from them by tyranny.[52]

While Henry V was holding court in Paris, however, news reached him of disturbing developments at home. When parliament met at Westminster in December 1420 it soon gave vent to mounting concern that England was now taking second place to France in the king's esteem and real anxiety about the domestic implications of the Treaty of Troyes. The Commons promptly petitioned Henry V, in fact, to confirm Edward III's promise that 'his realm of England and the people in it' should 'never in any time to come be put into subjection nor obedience to him, his heirs and successors as kings of *France*' and, on his absent brother's behalf, Humphrey Duke of Gloucester gave just such an assurance. Significantly, too, parliament not only failed to grant a subsidy but also requested Gloucester to persuade the king to return to England as soon as possible in order to crown his new queen. Clearly, then, there seems to have been little enthusiasm for Troyes nor the prospects it opened up: Henry V's English subjects saw no need to contribute further to a war he was now waging as Charles VI's regent and heir and, after an absence of more than three and a half years, many felt it was about time he returned home and attended to the needs of his own realm.

Early in 1421 Henry V, in response to parliament's concerns and also because of his now urgent need to replenish his war chest and recruit fresh troops, returned to England via Rouen and Calais. He and Catherine landed at Dover on 1 February and, so Enguerrand de Monstrelet assures us, he was welcomed home 'as if he had been an angel sent from God'. Their arrival in London later in the month was reminiscent of the king's reception in the capital following his great victory at Agincourt and, no doubt, deliberately so. According to an anonymous *Brut* chronicler, some 30,000 or more people, including the city's mayor and aldermen, greeted the couple at Blackheath and escorted them to London for Catherine's coronation on 23 February; a giant, various angels and nineteen virgins apparently awaited them on London Bridge; and next day, en route to Westminster, the queen was accorded 'all the royalty of sights that might be performed for her comfort and pleasure, every street being richly hung with cloth of gold, silks and velvets'. The queen's actual crowning in Westminster Abbey, so Enguerrand de Monstrelet learned, was 'performed with such splendid magnificence that the like had never been seen at any coronation since the time of that noble knight Arthur, King of the English'. So impressive was the ensuing banquet, moreover, that a *Brut* chronicler recorded its entire menu! Strangely enough, Henry V himself seems to have taken no part in the day's proceedings: perhaps he deliberately wished his French queen to occupy centre stage; perhaps his earlier affection for her was already waning; or, maybe, he simply felt his time was too valuable to waste participating in such ephemeral junketings.

Certainly, almost as soon as the celebrations were over, the royal couple set off on a whirlwind tour of the kingdom, nicely catalogued by John Strecche. The king, he tells us, first of all:

> ...visited Bristol, then other towns in the southern and western parts of England. And then he turned aside to his beloved castle of Kenilworth... And so he progressed to Coventry, then to Leicester, where he waited for a time for the arrival of the queen. She, after leaving Westminster, journeyed via Hertford, Bedford and Northampton to Leicester, where she joined Henry on the eve of Palm Sunday and, in that city, king and queen kept the feast of Easter. When it was over the king at once set off with his followers to the north. First he went to the

city of Nottingham, then to the town of Pontefract, and so to the city of York, to Beverley, and to Lincoln.

While still in Yorkshire, Henry V learned of his brother Thomas Duke of Clarence's defeat and death during an encounter with a Franco-Scottish force at Baugé in Anjou on 22 March 1421. In response, he now made his way back to London, taking in Lincoln, Lynn, Walsingham and Norwich en route. The queen, meanwhile, had also returned to the capital from Leicester, via Stamford, Huntingdon, Cambridge and Colchester. Thomas Walsingham believed that this had been, above all, a tour of holy places by a pious king but, in fact, Henry V's prime purpose throughout seems to have been to raise money and men for his French campaigns. John Strecche, indeed, specifically noted that 'the king and queen received precious gifts of gold and silver from the citizens and prelates of the towns' they visited; moreover, he added, 'the king demanded and received from the more powerful men of the realm, such as merchants and bishops, abbots and priors, great loans of money'. As for Enguerrand de Monstrelet, he learned that when:

> ...King Henry made a progress to the principal towns of his realm, he explained to them with much eloquence what grand deeds he had performed through his prowess in France and what yet remained to be done for the complete conquest of the kingdom... To complete this conquest, he said, two things were necessary, money and men: these requests were so liberally granted that, of the first, he very soon collected larger sums than had ever been seen so that they could scarcely be counted and, of the second, he enrolled all the most able youths in the country, and the most expert in drawing the bow, and, placing them under the command of his princes, knights and esquires, composed an army of full 30,000 combatants.[53]

Clearly, Monstrelet exaggerated the degree of Henry V's success in raising men and money during this tour but, equally evidently, he did indeed attract substantial sums in loans (thanks not least to the generosity of Henry Beaufort Bishop of Winchester) and recruit fresh troops (perhaps as many as 4,000), as well as taking the opportunity to settle magnate disputes, show off his new queen and visit several popular shrines. If we are to believe John Strecche, moreover, early in May 1421 both parliament and a convocation of clergy granted subsidies to the king. The church certainly did cough up cash but there is no record of any parliamentary subsidy at this time (although parliament did, at last, accept and approve the Treaty of Troyes as 'praiseworthy, necessary and useful'). Interestingly, too, Adam Usk remarked on the considerable hostility occasioned by Henry V's 'unbearable impositions', as well as predicting that in the end 'the great men and money of this kingdom' might well be 'miserably wasted in this enterprise'.

Early in June 1421 Henry V once more set sail for France, landing at Calais on 11 June. Clearly, his personal presence across the Channel was now urgently required and the task ahead of him formidable. At the end of January 1421 the Dauphin Charles had issued a defiant manifesto rejecting the Treaty of Troyes:

> For the honour of the fleur de lys there follow some considerations founded in right to rebut the damnable treaty which Henry of England has asked for and wishes to have... [The] right of the crown of France belongs clearly [to] the very noble prince Charles... [The] crown ought to be upheld and guarded by all faithful and loyal subjects of the crown... The damnable treaty that Henry of England has asked for under pretext of marriage with the daughter of the king of France and of total peace between the kingdoms of France and England is full of malignity, [and] tends to innumerable and perpetual divisions... The treaty must be resisted and prevented by every good Christian having ecclesiastical or temporal power...

On his return to England at the beginning of February 1421, Henry V had left his brother Thomas Duke of Clarence as his lieutenant in France; however, so Adam Usk learned:

> ...a stomach illness upset these arrangements, whereupon a certain person called the dauphin, putatively alleged to be the son of the king of France, gathered a party together to support his claims. [On 22 March at Baugé] he suddenly attacked and destroyed the duke and his army, [inflicting] great slaughter upon them, which caused much grief in England.

News of Clarence's defeat and death at Baugé certainly did cause considerable consternation in England and he himself did not escape criticism for his lack of foresight and caution. The duke had lost his life, declared a *Brut* chronicler, 'because he would not be governed', while, according to John Harding, when 'found by his enemies' he:

> ...arrayed his troops in fear and hurried to Baugé... There they alighted and fought with them at once. The duke was slain there that day... The English reinforcements came when all was over and rescued the dead men where they lay.[54]

Fortunately for Henry V, the French failed to take advantage of their victory, not least as a result of the efforts of Thomas Montagu Earl of Salisbury who, so Adam Usk tells us, was 'charged with his followers to avenge this slaughter' and is now 'fiercely avenging it with fire and sword' in order 'to keep the country safe'. Even so, Baugé had clearly shown that the English were not invincible in the field, at any rate when the king himself was absent, as well as putting a temporary halt to any further advance southwards.

Once back in France himself Henry V promptly embarked on the task of clearing the Armagnacs from such fortresses and towns as they still held in the vicinity of Paris. In September 1421, for instance, he besieged the dauphinist stronghold of Rougement: indeed, according to Georges Chastellain, he assaulted its garrison 'lethally from every side' and, although the castle's fortifications were 'the best possible', he nevertheless 'harried them to death'. Following the fortress's fall, moreover, his revenge was both swift and severe: the town was burnt to the ground, so it was reported, and its surviving defenders callously drowned in the nearby river. During August and September 1421, too, he vainly sought to bring the dauphin to battle by campaigning as far south as the Loire before, early in October, settling down to besiege the formidable Armagnac stronghold of Meaux. Perhaps the town's inhabitants provoked Henry V by complaining to Charles VI in Paris that he was already waging total war on them and setting all the local countryside on fire. The English king's response, if we are to believe Jean Juvenal des Ursins, was to declare that such was the 'custom of war', adding starkly that 'war without fire was like sausages without mustard'. Certainly, the ensuing blockade of Meaux was both grim and prolonged. The town's inhabitants, recorded the Monk of Saint-Denis:

> ...resisted the king and his army with energy and courage, and held
> the town against him for seven months. At this siege, many of the
> English died from natural causes or were killed and wounded in the
> assaults and combats that took place.

'From the commencement of the siege until the last moment when
they no longer had any hopes of relief from the dauphin', declared
Enguerrand de Monstrelet:

> ...the besieged poured torrents of abuse upon the English. Among
> other insults which they offered, they had an ass led on to the walls of
> the town and, by beating it, made it bray, and then cried out to the
> English that it was their king calling out for assistance, and told them
> to go to him. This conduct raised the king's indignation against them.

The braying donkey figured, too, in Jean Waurin's report of the siege, as
did a cornet player whose mocking of the English besieging force so
angered Henry V that he was promptly beheaded following Meaux's
capitulation. Pseudo-Elmham, moreover, recounts a possibly contemporary rumour that the English king's army never suffered so much
during any of his sieges than at Meaux. Clearly, it was not alone! Even
over Christmas and Epiphany 1421/2, a Parisian commentator noted,
Henry V:

> ...had his men pillaging all over Brie and, because of them and the
> other lot, no one could get any ploughing or sowing done anywhere.
> People complained to these lords often enough but they only sneered
> and laughed at them and their troops were then worse than ever.

Eventually, so the Monk of Saint-Denis learned, the Dauphin Charles
did send reinforcements who 'tried in vain to enter the town' but the
English 'barred the way and fell upon them'. Thereafter, he continued:

> The Frenchmen within the town, seeing that they were reduced to
> extremities, withdrew to the market place, which was separated from

The birth of Henry VI at Windsor, 6 December 1421.

the main town, and left the town to the English... After the capture of the town, the English entered the mills which were, as one might say, adjacent to the market and the bridge. There the Earl of Worcester was slain by a stone hurled from the market place and killed instantly... The market place at Meaux at last surrendered and fell into the hands of the English as the town had done.

Meaux finally capitulated on 10 May 1422 and, so the Saint-Denis chronicler tells us, although 'the lives of some Frenchmen were saved, others were punished by death and the rest taken to England or other parts of the kingdom and imprisoned'; moreover, 'all the goods both of the town and of the market place were looted' by Henry V and 'redistributed according to his pleasure'.[55] Specifically, if we are to believe Jean Juvenal des Ursins, large numbers of French captives were despatched to Paris where, like the men incarcerated in the city's prisons following the fall of Melun in November 1420, they received appalling treatment (chained together in twos by the legs, reported a Parisian chronicler, even 'piled up like pigs').

Soon after the siege of Meaux commenced, Juvenal des Ursins also reported, 'a marvellous pestilence of stomach flux' broke out among Henry V's troops and by the time the town surrendered his force had been severely weakened. Worse still, the king had probably contracted the illness which, within a few weeks, would kill him. Rumours reached Paris, in fact, that 'several great men', among them Henry V himself, had succumbed to smallpox; Thomas Walsingham believed that, 'as a result of long and excessive labours', the king developed 'an acute fever with violent dysentery'; and Jean Waurin learned that 'an inflammation called the disease of St Anthony', an infection caused by contaminated grain, 'seized him in the fundament'. More fancifully, a Scottish chronicler writing about twenty years after the king's death ascribed his demise to 'a cancerous illness which in the vernacular is called St Fiacre's disease'. Thomas Basin, similarly, believed Henry V was struck down by 'St Fiacre's Evil', a condition which 'swells the belly and legs hideously', because 'he had allowed his troops to sack and devastate the oratory of St Fiacre' near Meaux. Indeed, as the legend evolved, the king's illness and death came to be portrayed as a direct consequence of his decision to remove the relics of St Fiacre (a seventh-century missionary hermit) from their shrine near Meaux and transport them to England. Contemporaries and near-contemporaries probably had no real understanding of the nature of Henry V's last illness but acute fever and dysentery, brought on by the rigours of a prolonged siege in difficult conditions, fit the bill well enough.

Even had his strength and energy remained intact, Henry V's ambitious military plans might well have had to be curtailed in the months to come. As it was, Meaux turned out to be his final conquest. Painfully ill but at this stage probably still hoping for a complete recovery, the king took up residence in the royal castle at Bois de Vincennes a few miles to the east of Paris. It was not to be. When he did courageously set out to relieve Cosne-sur-Loire in July 1422, so Pseudo-Elmham tells us:

> ...because of the seriousness of his illness, he was too weak to ride and so he ordered himself to be carried in a litter drawn by horses such as invalids employ. But when he reached the town of Corbeil some days later he had become so ill that he was unable to proceed further against the enemy without the expenditure of his last strength... And when after a few days the seriousness of his illness grew much worse than before, he returned to the castle of Vincennes.

Once there he was forced to take to his bed and eventually, according to Thomas Walsingham, so chronic did his condition become that 'the doctors dared not give him internal medicine and despaired of his life'.

Although highly rhetorical, Pseudo-Elmham's description of Henry V's last days and death is certainly the most detailed, and probably the best informed, of several that have come down to us. 'Realising that the gravity of his illness would not cease until death itself', the biographer recorded sombrely, 'the devoted and prudent king prepared for his end by daily confessions and largesse of alms'. He spent his last days at Vincennes in the company of his brother John Duke of Bedford and veteran aristocratic (and military) companions such as Thomas Beaufort Duke of Exeter and Richard Beauchamp Earl of Warwick. Interestingly enough, he did not send for Queen Catherine (despite the fact she was in France at the time); moreover, although the future prospects of his infant son and heir Henry (born at Windsor on 6 December 1421) clearly did concern him at the end, his wife seems to have had no place in his last thoughts. As for the death bed speech put into Henry V's

Richard Beauchamp Earl of Warwick becomes Henry VI's tutor following the death of Henry V.

mouth by Pseudo-Elmham, even if not a literal rendering of the king's final oration, it might well reflect what his biographer learned from men who were present. 'In a firm voice', he tells us, the king declared:

It is certain that, according to the pleasure of the Saviour, I cannot avoid imminent death... If therefore I have ruled otherwise than I ought, or if I have done injustice to anyone, as I believe I have not, I humbly ask for pardon. For the good services rendered to me in these wars, I give thanks to you and all my fellow knights [and], if I had not been prevented by death, I had intended to give to each a fitting reward.

Clearly, Henry V was also anxious once more to explain and justify his French wars:

I exhort you to continue these wars until peace is gained. It was not ambitious lust for dominion, nor for empty glory, nor for worldly honour, nor any other cause, that drew me to these wars, but only that by suing for my just title, I might at once gain peace and my own rights. And before the wars were begun, I was fully instructed by men of the holiest life and wisest counsel that I ought and could with this intention begin the wars, prosecute them, and justly finish them, without danger to my soul.

As well as displaying a characteristic concern for his future eternal well-being, the king sought, too, to make provision for the govern-ment of England and France during his son's minority and for the security of the Lancastrian dynasty:

To my brother the Duke of Bedford I commit the custody and rule of France and the Duchy of Normandy until my son shall reach years of discretion. My brother the Duke of Gloucester shall be the protector and defender of England. I will and decree that my uncles the Duke of Exeter and Henry Beaufort Bishop of Winchester, along with the Earl of Warwick, shall be the tutors of my son.

Moreover, Pseudo-Elmham added, Henry V then 'showed his will, first made in England [on 10 June 1421 at Dover], to those present,

Here sheweth howe kyng henry the vj kyng in his tendre age / was crowned kyng of Englond at westm[ynster] w[ith] greet solempnyte ./.

The coronation of Henry VI in Westminster Abbey, 6 November 1429.

together with attested codicils [added on 26 August 1422], in which he bequeathed large sums to pay the debts of himself and his father and also the arrears of pay of his household'. That done, he ceased to 'concern himself and his senses with the affairs of this world' until:

> ...at last, amidst many and great works of pious contemplation, he received the sacrament of the Body and Blood of the Lord and of extreme unction with a contrite heart and the humility of a penitent spirit. And when he laboured in his last moments he cried out, 'Thou liest! Thou liest! My portion is with the Lord Jesus Christ!', as if he spoke boldly to an evil spirit. Then breathing his last breath and devoutly clasping the crucifix he cried, in a strong voice, 'Into thy hands thou hast redeemed the term', and passed away perfectly and devoutly.

More succinctly, Thomas Walsingham tells much the same story:

> Seeing that his death was approaching, the king called together his dukes and others who were able to be present... He made wise arrangements, wrote his will and provided for his debts to be paid from his treasuries and numerous jewels. After taking holy communion and the other sacraments that were the duty of a Christian, in true penitence, proper faith, certain hope, perfect charity and right remembrance, he gave up his soul to his creator.[56]

Henry V died during the night of 31 August 1422 at Vincennes. According to Pseudo-Elmham, so emaciated by illness was his body that there was hardly any flesh to putrefy; consequently, the corpse was allowed to remain intact (complete even with intestines) before being:

> ...steeped in aromatic herbs and balsam, enveloped in waxed linen and lead, and placed, wrapped in a silk cloth, in a wooden coffin. This was carried in a funeral carriage draped with black, and on top lay a large effigy of the king in royal vestments wearing a crown and holding a sceptre. Thus, escorted by princes and magnates, it set out for England.

On the afternoon of 14 September 1422, so a Parisian commentator noted, Henry V's coffin was:

The coronation of Henry VI, the only English monarch ever to be crowned king of France in Paris, 16 December 1431.

...taken to St Denis, without entering Paris, and on the next day [his] obsequies were performed at St-Denis-en-France. A hundred torches were kept burning all the way there, in the churches. From St Denis his body was taken to Pontoise and thence to Rouen.

At both St Denis and Rouen the late king's coffin lay in state for a time before, on 5 October, the cortège left Rouen, travelled slowly to Calais, and finally crossed to Dover on 31 October. Catherine of Valois, so strangely absent from her husband's side at his death, did accompany Henry V's body back to England. London records, interestingly, report the careful preparations for the funeral in the capital on 5 November:

[The] mayor, sheriffs, recorder, aldermen and officers, and the more sufficient persons of the whole city, shall proceed on foot as far as St George's Bar, clothed in black vestments, together with 300 torches, borne by 300 persons clothed in white gowns and hoods, and there reverently salute the corpse, following it the first day as far as St Paul's church, where the funeral obsequies take place, and the second day to Westminster, [where] throughout the streets shall stand on either side men with lighted torches, and the chaplains of the churches shall stand at the doors of the churches dressed in their richest vestments and bearing in their hands censers of gold and silver, whilst they solemnly chant the *venite* and incense the corpse as it passes.[57]

After a solemn requiem mass, Henry V's body was finally laid to rest in Westminster Abbey on 7 November 1422.

III

HENRY V
IN RETROSPECT

15

PERSONALITY

[By 1413] all men had for some time looked to him and succeeding generations have seldom doubted that, according to the standards of his day, he was all that a king should be... He was endowed with the highest attributes of manhood... He was more deeply loved by his subjects of all classes than any king has been in England.[1]

S uch was the great twentieth-century warlord Sir Winston Churchill's verdict on Henry V in his splendid *History of the English Speaking Peoples*. Yet the second Lancastrian was probably a more complex man and a less stereotypically virtuous later medieval king than Churchill – or, indeed, many contemporary and near-contemporary commentators – would have us believe. Clearly, he had real charisma and personal magnetism; he enjoyed the confidence, even inspired the devotion, of those close to him; and he successfully sold himself, or an image of himself, to the English people as well: for instance, by encouraging the English language, by promoting notions of English national sentiment, and by presenting an essentially imperialist war in France as the fulfilment of England's divinely directed destiny. Equally clearly, he possessed enormous energy and a great capacity for hard work, not least when it came to the detailed business of government; his personal courage and bravery are beyond question (as early as 1403, at the age of sixteen, he received a severe wound at the battle of Shrewsbury); and, during his long years of relentless campaigning in France, he demonstrated formidable staying power even when faced by real adversity and, towards the end, a fatal disease. An able and businesslike administrator and a good man-manager, he both recognised talent and rewarded loyalty. Most of the time, the king was honest and upright in his dealings; he was decisive in planning, and effective in delivering, policy (whether at home or abroad); his care for friends and retainers, and concern for the welfare of his troops, is evident from his correspondence; and, when it suited him, he could be merciful and forgiving. As for his personal behaviour, Henry V seems to have been notably abstemious in food and drink; his much vaunted premarital chastity certainly won the approval of several clerical commentators; and, although he probably had little time for relaxation (and may even have lost the taste for it after he became king), records reveal that, when at ease in the company of his inner circle, he not only played cards, backgammon and chess but also wagered (and lost!) significant sums of money.

Despite all the praise heaped upon him in the pages of contemporary and near-contemporary biographies and chronicles, however, there is also evidence of altogether less admirable traits in Henry V's character and behaviour. Very much the autocrat (as his letters demonstrate only too graphically), he could be domineering, inflexible, ruthless, vindictive and, on occasion, inhumane even by the not very exacting standards of the early fifteenth century: the ruthless hanging (or perhaps even crucifixion) of eight gunners following the fall of Louviers in 1418, for instance, and the vindictive beheading of a mere trumpeter after Meaux's capitulation in 1422, look suspiciously like cruel acts of personal vengeance. Although capable of charm and friendliness (as even French chroniclers report), he could also be cold and aloof, particularly on ceremonial occasions, as well as distinctly touchy if he felt his royal dignity in any way impugned: Enguerrand de Monstrelet, indeed, preserves a telling anecdote of Henry V publicly reprimanding a Burgundian lord for daring to look him full in the face! Clearly, too, he was capable of guile and deceit, intolerant of dissent and perfectly prepared to punish, even remove, those whose loyalty he suspected; men feared his anger and, if they were smart, avoided questioning the wisdom of his judgements or the rightness of his decisions; and, particularly in his last years, he behaved ever more arbitrarily, succumbing to rapaciousness and, perhaps, even fanaticism in his singleminded and relentless pursuit of his French ambitions.

Virtually all Henry V's contemporaries, English and French alike, agree that, as a military commander, he was exceptionally gifted:

meticulous in planning, inspiring in the field and, above all, a master of
the art of siege-craft. Although Agincourt was of French not English
making, and the king's victory owed a great deal to enemy mistakes
and sheer good fortune on the day, the battle's outcome certainly
enhanced his reputation as a general both at home and abroad. Henry
V's qualities as a campaign manager and coordinator of day-to-day
military operations on the ground really began to show themselves,
however, in the long, slow, grim war of sieges that followed his second
invasion of France in 1417, where we find the king systematically capturing fortified strongholds and, once they were in his hands, gradually
consolidating his control over the surrounding countryside. Such an
endeavour needed fighting forces that were both loyal and disciplined
and here, too, Henry V very much proved his mettle as a commander.
While capable of delegating military authority and enjoying the services
of many able captains, moreover, he was always very much a hands-on
general, master-minding strategy, overseeing diplomatic negotiations
and maintaining firm control over the deployment of manpower,
the enforcement of discipline and the redistribution of conquered
territories. Even so, as a military commander he did take inordinate
risks, not least by marching from Harfleur to Calais in the autumn of
1415 when he came dangerously close to being out-generalled.
Throughout, too, he was much aided by the political situation in France
and, eventually, his military ambitions ran out of control and his last
campaign, at least, proved futile.

Even if Henry V, in reality, sacrificed many men and a great deal of
money in pursuit of objectives that were ultimately unrealisable, he
never ceased to project an image of himself as the veritable personifica-
tion of later medieval ideals of chivalric warrior kingship; moreover, so
many contemporary and near-contemporary literary sources would
have us believe, the king and his aristocratic supporters always strove to
behave in accordance with a practical chivalric code of behaviour and
well-established laws of war. Chivalric kings and their nobility were
expected to be virtuous, courageous and, above all, skilful warriors;
they were obliged to employ their arms in the service of God, whether
defending Christ's church against heretics and infidels, upholding justice, pursuing legitimate claims of right or, even, defending the weak
and oppressed; and, in their relations with each other and their knightly
supporters (and even their opponents), they were duty bound to

behave honourably and generously, not least when it came to the distribution of largesse. Nevertheless, this was very much an aristocratic culture of violence, an elitist culture, and the lower ranks of society were not part of it nor did chivalric rules of conduct apply to them or their treatment. For instance, when besieging a town (as happened over and over again during Henry V's French campaigns, of course), besiegers were required to proclaim the justice of their cause and provide the besieged with every opportunity for honourable surrender: yet, if a town refused to submit to a claim of right, its inhabitants must suffer the consequences (however dire they might be). Similarly, if nobles and knights were taken prisoner as a result of military defeat, they must be treated respectfully and, once appropriate ransoms had been paid, released from captivity: yet ordinary rank-and-file soldiers need be afforded no such consideration, nor civilians who became the innocent victims of combat; villages and towns might legitimately be pillaged; and the seizure of booty was an entirely justifiable perquisite of war. This was no simple black-and-white code, however; shades of grey abound all over the place: hence why there is so much room for disagreement, even at the time, about precisely what was and what was not chivalrous behaviour, and just what the laws of war did or did not allow.

Contemporary and near-contemporary literary sources certainly abound in stories of the chivalric acts and chivalrous behaviour of Henry V, while the king himself frequently employed the language of honourable conduct. When writing to Charles VI shortly before sailing for France in the summer of 1415, for instance, he appealed to the French king for restitution 'of the inheritance and rights cruelly taken away from us' so as to prevent 'the deluge of human blood' invasion might bring; similarly, in a letter to the mayor and aldermen of London in September 1415, he specifically referred to his earlier negotiations with the men of Harfleur for the town's voluntary surrender 'in order to avoid the shedding of human blood'. The battle of Agincourt provided an all too obvious focus for tales of chivalrous behaviour, particularly by the English king: during the fighting, declared the *Gesta Henrici Quinti*, Henry V himself performed great feats of strength in the field; he fought 'not so much as a king but as a knight', echoed Thomas Walsingham, fulfilling the duties of both, indeed, by inflicting and receiving many wounds and providing an excellent role model for his men 'by his bravery in scattering the opposing lines with a battle axe';

and Tito Livio, too, learned that the king 'fought against the enemy with great ardour, receiving many blows on his helmet and armour'. Once the battle was won, so the Monk of Saint-Denis reported, Henry V 'declared himself horrified that so much blood had been spilt', expressed 'great compassion for all the deaths' and mourned, most of all, fatalities among his own comrades-in-arms. According to the same chronicler, moreover, the king also showed 'the utmost tact, respect and kindness' towards captured French nobles and knights awaiting ransom. The many sieges undertaken by Henry V also provided ample opportunities for chivalrous behaviour and chivalric acts. On entering Harfleur in September 1415, the Monk of Saint-Denis tells us, the king 'treated the knights and esquires whom he had captured with more generosity than one might have expected' and 'ordered the lives of unarmed citizens to be spared' (although, the chronicler added, he also took 'the wealthiest of them' to England as prisoners). When he entered Rouen in January 1419, according to Tito Livio, Henry V promptly took measures to prevent his soldiers pillaging the town and, 'moved to pity by the wretchedness of the townspeople, gave orders to his servants and retinue to fetch food for the crowd'. As for Georges Chastellain, he was certainly impressed by the king's personal bravery at the siege of Melun in 1420 where 'he and the Duke of Burgundy, with a courage equal to their renown, fought for a long space hand-to-hand' against 'two of the most valiant and tried soldiers of the time'.

Yet, although Henry V could on occasion be more merciful than contemporary laws of war required, his personal code of chivalry seems to have fallen short of what Maurice Keen (the most eminent recent historian of medieval chivalry and the laws of war) has called the 'hereditary and honourable duty' of a king 'to be ready to draw the sword to defend the weak and oppressed'.[2] For him, as the *Gesta Henrici Quinti* emphasised more than once, God's inflexible orders to the people of Israel in Deuteronomy seem to have been paramount, not least the notion that it was entirely the fault of the inhabitants of a besieged town if their failure instantly to surrender to a claim of right resulted in dire consequences: indeed, the king himself specifically cited the 'law of Deuteronomy' as justification for his behaviour in his own correspondence and, certainly, a number of royal decisions and deeds must surely call into question Henry V's reputation as a chivalric warrior king. Following the fall of Harfleur in 1415, according to the

Monk of Saint-Denis, the victor expelled 'the sick, the poor and the elderly', while, if we are to believe Adam Usk, he drove out 'all the native inhabitants and replaced them with English people'. Even if, under contemporary rules of war, military necessity may have justified Henry V's massacre of French prisoners at Agincourt, such an act of callous ruthlessness certainly squares uneasily with the king's chivalric image. The wholesale slaughter of many of Caen's inhabitants following the town's surrender in 1417 elicited criticism even in England; the king's calculated indifference to the fate of men, women and children expelled from Rouen in the autumn of 1418 is reprehensible by any standards; and his savage reprisals against the defenders of Pontoise in 1419, Melun in 1420, Rougement in 1421 and Meaux in 1422 point, at the very least, to Henry V's growing vindictiveness and casual inhumanity.

Not only English biographers and chroniclers but French commentators, too, were impressed by Henry V's passion for justice: the Monk of Saint-Denis, for instance, declared him 'a scrupulous dispenser of justice'; Pierre Fenin remarked on his 'great will to keep justice'; and even Georges Chastellain conceded that he was 'the prince of justice'. What particularly impressed the French, seemingly, was the king's resolve that justice be impartial, regardless of social status, perhaps because they themselves over recent years had become so unaccustomed to judicious government. Certainly, Henry V's determination to promote, and practise, impartial justice was plugged for all it was worth and not without justification; his record as an arbitrator in magnate disputes is impressive; and his efforts to curb lawlessness in the English provinces and protect even his ordinary subjects from acts of injustice is well documented. Nor did he exempt his own friends and entourage; his former companion-in-arms Sir John Oldcastle, for instance, was eventually tracked down and executed for heresy and treason; Henry Lord Scrope's involvement in the Southampton conspiracy of 1415, however tenuous, brought a rapid and humiliating nemesis; and a similar fate befell royal servants, however close to the king, who failed to obey his ordinances while serving in France. Yet although, by and large, Henry V's justice may have been impartial, it was also stern and unbending, as well as frequently high-handed; moreover, on more than one occasion, his behaviour clearly fell sadly short of his own high standards.

Most remarkable, perhaps, is the king's treatment of his long-time mentor and counsellor Henry Beaufort Bishop of Winchester. When, in December 1417, Pope Martin V offered Beaufort a cardinal's hat, neither he nor the king can have been too surprised: Beaufort was, after all, an obvious choice and had richly deserved his elevation. What was probably unexpected was his appointment, at the same time, as a papal legate and, soon afterwards, his exemption (as bishop of Winchester) from the jurisdiction of the archbishopric of Canterbury. As far as Henry V was concerned, this amounted to unwarranted and unwelcome papal interference in internal English ecclesiastical affairs and a challenge to his own authority in the English realm; he angrily forbade Beaufort to accept appointment as either cardinal or legate; and he made it clear that, if the bishop disobeyed royal orders, Beaufort risked humiliation and ruin at the king's hands. Even after Beaufort capitulated to royal pressure, pledged his unflinching loyalty to the crown and firmly committed himself to behave impeccably in the future, he remained under suspicion. Not until 1421, and only after he had loaned his nephew the enormous sum of £22,000, was he at last formally reconciled with the king. Clearly, there was a fundamental principle at stake in this affair; nevertheless, it is hard to escape the conclusion that Henry V's determination to deny a red hat to Beaufort (who had served him loyally and effectively for years) was not only harsh but downright vindictive. Equally cavalier, as well as blatantly financially motivated, was the king's treatment of wealthy dowagers such as Alice Countess of Oxford, Anne Countess of Stafford and Beatrice Lady Talbot. Nor, on occasion, did Henry V behave much better towards members of his own family.

During Henry IV's lifetime, and particularly towards the end of that king's reign, relations between father and son often seem to have been uneasy at best, downright hostile at worst. Perhaps this helps explain, but can hardly justify, Henry V's discreditable failure to pay his father's debts. Since her marriage to the first Lancastrian in 1402 Joan of Navarre, by contrast, had apparently been on the best of terms with her stepson and, after her husband's death in 1413, continued to be treated with every mark of respect by the new king. Yet, in the autumn of 1419, the queen dowager was suddenly arrested on the charge that she had 'compassed and imagined the death of our lord the king in the most high and horrible manner'. In October 1419, declared Thomas Walsingham:

...the king's stepmother was accused by certain persons of some
wickedness that she had contrived to the injury of the king. All her
attendants were removed, and she was committed to the custody of
Sir John Pelham who, hiring five new attendants, put her into the castle of Pevensey, there to be kept under his control.[3]

London chroniclers reported, specifically, that she had attempted 'by
sorcery and necromancy to destroy the king'. The charges were almost
certainly false and Joan was never brought to trial. Instead, she was
peremptorily deprived of her dower lands and imprisoned for nearly
three years in Leeds castle in Kent. Such a ruthless and wilful act of
injustice can only be explained by sheer greed: even though his stepmother's captivity was comfortable enough, Henry V was able to
pocket nearly £6,000 a year at her expense (more than 10% of the
crown's income at the time). Eventually, as he contemplated imminent
death in July 1422, the king ordered both Joan of Navarre's release and
the restoration of her possessions, 'lest it should be a charge upon our
conscience', a clear admission that he had indeed treated his stepmother harshly and unjustly. As several chroniclers suggest, Henry V
may have been genuinely charmed when he first met Catherine of
Valois at the end of May 1419 and may even have fallen in love with
her. Once married, however, his ardour soon cooled, perhaps because
the new queen's personality and intelligence fell well short of her
beauty. Yet he probably never took a mistress nor did he sire any
bastards. Maybe, indeed, the king only felt really comfortable in male,
particularly military, company. Even when he and Catherine were in
England in 1421 they were apart much of the time; the king did not
attend the queen's coronation; and, on his return to France, he left his
now pregnant wife behind. Early in 1422, after Henry VI's birth,
Catherine herself did travel back to France: yet, even though she was
staying with her parents at Senlis as he lay dying in the nearby castle of
Bois de Vincennes, the king never sent for her.

Clearly, Henry V's religious convictions reached well beyond the
conventions even of early fifteenth-century England; his fear of the
proto-Protestant Lollards was genuine and heart-felt; he founded
notably austere religious houses; he played a significant role in bringing
the Papal Schism to an end; and his hopes of leading a new crusade to
the Holy Land were the product of a very deep, if very traditionally

focussed, piety. As early as 1408 an Oxford academic Richard Ullerston, when dedicating a treatise on the moral and spiritual requirements of a knight to the Prince of Wales, specifically referred to young Henry's 'desire for spiritual study' and commended him for his familiarity with the scriptures. 'From the very beginning of his assumption of government', declared the clerical author of the *Gesta Henrici Quinti*:

> ...so fervently had he been devoted to the hearing of divine praises and to his own private prayers that, once he had begun them, there was not anyone, even from amongst his nobles and magnates, who was able, by conversation however brief, at any time to interrupt them. There cannot, therefore, be denied by the Prince of princes to a prince who, in the judgement of all men, is of such goodness and obedience, whatever he may justly ask of him.[4]

The Benedictine monk of Westminster, in his *Versus Rythmici*, was no less impressed by the regularity and diligence of Henry V's attendance at mass, his weekly confession, his frequent fasting and his liberality in almsgiving. And, according to the St Albans' monk Thomas Walsingham, the king was 'generous in constructing buildings and founding monasteries, munificent in his gifts and, above all, pursued and attacked enemies of the church': indeed, so supportive was he of the religious establishment and its teachings that the Lollards dubbed him 'the priests' king'.

Contemporary and near-contemporary clerical commentators certainly plugged Henry V's religious orthodoxy and his conviction that he enjoyed divine favour for all they were worth. Royal propaganda also laid great emphasis on the notion of the English church as a veritable pillar of the realm ruled over by a king determined both to protect its rights and liberties and stamp out the threat of heresy: Henry V, in fact, saw himself as very much the secular master of the church, exercising entirely legitimate authority over spiritual as well as temporal matters, and fully entitled to resist any papal interference in his freedom of action. Certainly, the king became actively involved in all manner of ecclesiastical affairs, encouraging religious reform, promoting new liturgies and, most importantly, choosing bishops who frequently combined firm belief in royal leadership of the church, spiritual integrity and the capacity to exercise diocesan authority. No less noteworthy was his close supervision of services in his private chapel, his care in selecting confessors, his admiration for holy hermits, his approval of the austere Carthusian order, his concern to reform Benedictine monasticism and his enthusiasm for religious shrines. Nor can his personal piety seriously be doubted. Yet Henry V's religious beliefs, although clearly based on very considerable knowledge and understanding of the Christian faith, were also narrowly orthodox and deeply conventional: indeed, so intense was his religiosity and so extreme his devotion that he cannot easily escape the charge of out-and-out bigotry. His piety, moreover, was not free from superstition: he greatly feared witchcraft and black magic; sorcerers were prosecuted in the courts on his orders; and his intolerance of religious dissent, especially Lollardy, resulted in the merciless persecution of nonconformists. Certainly, too, he had a puritanical, even messianic, streak in him, nicely illustrated by a story told by the anonymous author of the *First English Life* and attributed by him to the Earl of Ormonde. In May 1419, the biographer reports, the Spanish Dominican friar Vincent Ferrer, perhaps the greatest Christian evangelist of his day, came to Caen and preached before the king and his court. Wearing his hood drawn over his face lest fear prevent him saying 'all he had fixed his mind upon', he proceeded to rebuke the king in no uncertain terms for ruthlessly killing so many innocent men and women. Henry V, apparently, listened impassively but, once the sermon was over, summoned Ferrer to his presence and vehemently declared: 'I am the scourge of God sent to punish the people of God for their sins'. After engaging in no doubt robust debate for some three hours, Ferrer eventually emerged and publicly proclaimed:

> This morning, before I came hither, I believed that the king your master had been the greatest tyrant among all Christian princes; but now I perceive the contrary, for I assure you he is the most perfect and acceptable to God of all those here present, and his quarrel is so just that undoubtedly God is and shall be his aid in these years.[5]

Even if this tale is more legend than fact, it certainly highlights only too graphically the force of Henry V's personality and the king's absolute conviction of his divinely ordained status as the true servant of God.

Clearly linked to Henry V's religious devotion was his enthusiasm for sacred music and interest in theology. Both his parents had been music lovers; as a young lad he had learned to play the harp and perhaps other musical instruments; and, as king, not only did his chapel become a focus for musical innovation, English royal musicians came to enjoy a European reputation. In October 1420 he bought harps for both himself and his new queen; in September 1421 he purchased another and ordered that it be sent to him in France; and, wherever he went, he seems to have been accompanied by musicians and minstrels. Moreover, the king appears to have been as much a patron of scholars, poets and actors as musicians, as well as contributing to the rebuilding of the nave of Westminster Abbey. From boyhood, too, Henry V seems to have had a real taste for reading, and serious reading at that, not only in English but also French and Latin. As king, his library appears to have been amply stocked and his books, so well-informed contemporaries believed, much read: as the monk of Westminster put it, 'often reading books, he surrenders himself to an honourable reputation'. Henry V also borrowed books from others, even gaining a certain notoriety for his dilatoriness in returning them: at the time of his death, apparently, he had failed to return two chronicles of the crusades lent by his aunt Joan Countess of Westmorland and still had in his possession a complete set of the works of Pope Gregory the Great formerly belonging to Thomas Arundel Archbishop of Canterbury. As for Henry V's own books, they are known to have included volumes on theology, history, law, chivalry and hunting and, specifically, he certainly owned copies of Cicero's *Rhetoric*. St Augustine's *City of God* and Chaucer's *Troilus*. By later medieval standards, in fact, the king's reputation as a well-read, cultivated, even learned, layman was not without justification and he certainly played a pivotal role in promoting the English language.

Early in Henry VI's reign a eulogistic epitaph was entered in the records of the new king's council proclaiming his father 'the most Christian warrior of the church, the sun of prudence, the exemplar of justice, the most invincible king, the flower and glory of all knighthood'. Yet, throughout his reign, everything else had been subordinated to the overriding, and probably ultimately unrealistic, objective of restoring traditional English rights in France by a man convinced that he was indeed carrying out the wishes of the Almighty. Henry V had both the strengths and failings of a medieval warlord, a man who clearly enjoyed campaigning and felt most at ease in the company of his comrades-in-arms, and a king who was driven – in his personal and political as well as his military life – by a narrowly focussed enthusiasm and determination that came perilously close to out-and-out fanaticism. According to Georges Chastellain, moreover, during the siege of Melun in 1420 Henry V and Philip of Burgundy found common ground in a shared dream of mounting a crusade against the infidel and pledged themselves to set out for the Holy Land as soon as the French war was finally won. On his death bed, too, the English king reportedly asserted that, had he lived, he would have united Christendom against the Turks, led a new expedition to free the Holy Places, and 'built again the walls of Jerusalem'. Fanciful the hope may have been but a sentiment entirely consistent with what we know of Henry V's character, beliefs and personality.

16

ACHIEVEMENTS AND FAILURES

When Henry V came to the throne in 1413, declared Sir Winston Churchill in his *History of the English Speaking Peoples*:

> ...England was wearied by feuds and brawl and yearned for unity and fame. He led the nation away from internal discord to foreign conquest, and he had the dream, and perhaps the prospect, of leading all Western Europe into the high championship of a Crusade...When he led the power of England across the Channel in continuation of the long revenge of history for Duke William's expedition he could count upon the support of a large part of what is now the French people... He reorganised the Fleet [and], like Alfred, built many vessels for the Royal Navy... The expeditionary army was picked and trained with special care... Agincourt ranks as the most heroic of all the land battles England has ever fought [and] made him the supreme figure in Europe.

Moreover, Churchill believed, Henry V was:

> ...entirely national in his outlook: he was the first king to use the English language in his letters and his messages home from the front; his triumphs were gained by English troops; his policy was sustained by a Parliament that could claim to speak for the English people... Henry stood, and with him his country, at the summit of the world.

Yet even Churchill had to admit, sadly, that Henry V had been the 'instrument of the religious and social persecution of the Lollards' and that, eventually, 'the long, costly campaigns' of the king's last years 'out-ran the financial resources of Island and gradually cooled its martial ardour'.[6]

The Venetian chronicler Gasparo Zancarulo, when describing Henry V's extraordinary victory at Agincourt, felt moved to dub him '*quel magnifico Enrigo*': Henry the Magnificent! Not only did the king triumph against overwhelming odds in the field at Agincourt in October 1415, moreover, he went on to conquer Normandy and, by 1422, had taken English arms as far south as the Loire. Throughout, he never suffered a single military defeat in person and, under the terms of the Treaty of Troyes, he gained virtually everything he had ever hoped to achieve in France. Yet his military record is far from unblemished. The siege of Harfleur in the autumn of 1415 could easily have gone wrong; it took longer than anticipated and, before the town finally sur-rendered, dysentery had seriously depleted the king's force; and, in 1416, heroic resistance by Harfleur's garrison and a naval victory in the Channel by Henry V's brother John Duke of Bedford were required in order to prevent the town's recapture by the French. The king's deci-sion to march from Harfleur to Calais in October 1415, with a depleted and disease-ridden army, was very much a gamble. As for Agincourt, although an exhausted, hungry and heavily out-numbered English army did indeed rout a fresh and well-provisioned French force, vic-tory resulted more from French folly than Henry V's generalship; moreover, while the battle's outcome certainly raised England's pres-tige abroad and the king received a hero's welcome at home, his great success in the field proved futile from a purely military viewpoint and, in 1417, Henry V had to begin all over again. Even between 1417 and 1420 the English king took great risks; he was much aided by the polit-ical situation in France; and, as for the Treaty of Troyes, it resulted not from Agincourt nor even the conquest of Normandy but, rather, from the entirely fortuitous Anglo-Burgundian alliance occasioned by the murder of John the Fearless. Following the treaty, moreover, the king's brother Thomas Duke of Clarence was defeated and killed at Baugé in March 1421; the prolonged sieges of Melun (July–November 1420) and Meaux (October 1421–May 1422) not only sapped Henry V's energy but also highlighted altogether more resolute and determined French resistance than hitherto; and, in the end, his last campaign largely petered out once the English king succumbed to disease. Even at the height of his success Henry V controlled no more than a third of France and, from a military viewpoint at least, he was probably fortunate to die prematurely while his warrior reputation remained relatively intact.

Clearly, Henry V was a military commander of real distinction; he enjoyed enthusiastic backing from most of his nobility for most of the time; and his captains and troops, by and large, seem to have been deeply devoted to him. Before Henry V's reign, moreover, no royal army had ever been kept in continuous service, in the pay of the crown and on foreign soil, for as long as his force was during the years 1417 to 1422. Throughout, too, he sought to maintain strict but fair discipline among his troops, setting up a sophisticated system of muster and review, dealing firmly with deserters, and putting in place regulations to control brigandage and looting as well as protect noncombatants from the ravages of war. Yet, despite the king's best intentions, even strong measures such as his 1419 Ordinances of War could never be fully effective: desertion remained a problem, and became worse as the years went by, nor could pillage and rapine be entirely prevented (especially since soldiers' pay was frequently in arrears, a significant number of troops were pardoned criminals and English garrisons often had little choice but to live off the land). Increasingly, too, fighting men longed for the war to end and the recruitment of new troops became more and more difficult as time went by: indeed, as early as March 1419, an English serviceman ended a letter home from Normandy with the heart-felt prayer that 'we may soon come out of this unlusty soldier's life into the life of England'.

Not only was Henry V an outstandingly able and successful general, he also created the most impressive royal fleet of any Plantagenet king. Indeed, he was probably the first English monarch seriously to recognise the importance of seapower, albeit as an essentially defensive weapon designed primarily to protect native coastlines and shipping and help facilitate the transport of men, equipment and supplies across the Channel to France. At his accession in 1413 the crown possessed just six ships but, by August 1417, the king had built up a balanced royal fleet of about thirty-four or thirty-five vessels (some bought, some captured, and a few specifically commissioned by himself). Moreover, although he never achieved complete control of the Channel, English naval squadrons patrolled the seas during every campaigning season 1415–1421, defeated the Franco-Genoese flotilla blockading Harfleur in August 1416, and emerged triumphant from another confrontation with enemy ships in July 1417. Henry V, in fact, seems to have been a master of naval as well as most other aspects of military strategy. By 1421, however, with the French naval bases of Harfleur and Rouen securely in the king's hands and the whole northern coastline of France and the Low Countries firmly controlled either by himself or Philip of Burgundy, any French threat to English ports and shipping had virtually disappeared. Since Henry V's financial problems were mounting as well, and the cost of maintaining ships in seaworthy condition was considerable, even before the king's death the royal fleet was beginning to be neglected and, during Henry VI's minority, most of the vessels were either sold off or left to rot. Certainly, Henry V cannot be credited with 'the foundation of the English Navy'.

If Henry V was to pursue his French ambitions free of distraction at home he clearly needed not only to maintain peace and stability in England but also protect his realm against any resurgence of Welsh resistance, preserve the only part of Ireland firmly in English hands (Dublin and its hinterland) from attack by native Irish clans and, most importantly, counter the ever-present threat to his northern border posed by the proud and independent kingdom of Scotland. By the summer of 1415 Wales, where he had learned so many invaluable military skills as a young man, had been largely reconciled to English rule and, as a result, many Welshmen even enlisted in the king's army and fought for him in France. John Talbot Lord Furnival, Henry V's lieutenant in Ireland from 1414 to 1419 was certainly a ruthless and successful military commander: indeed, according to an Irish annalist of the time, 'since the time of Herod came not anyone so wicked'. As a result of his savage measures, by the time Talbot sailed from Ireland to join the king in France in 1419, the borders of the English colony in Ireland were probably more secure than they had been for years (although he also left the lordship's finances in chaos and many of its inhabitants seething with resentment). The security of the Anglo-Scottish border, always a matter of great concern to medieval English kings, became even more crucial when England and France were at war since the long-standing and frequently renewed alliance between

Scotland and France was all too liable in such circumstances to trigger Scottish invasion of northern England. On the very eve of Henry V's departure for France in July 1415, for instance, Scottish raiders crossed the border and seriously harried adjoining English counties; in August 1417 came the so-called 'Foul Raid', a full-scale Scottish attack on Roxburgh and Berwick, eventually repulsed by John Duke of Bedford and Thomas Beaufort Duke of Exeter; and, for the next two years, southern Scotland in turn was subjected to almost constant English harassment. Scottish troops also supported the Dauphin Charles in France, most notably in helping to defeat Thomas Duke of Clarence at Baugé. Henry V, in response, persuaded the Lancastrians' long-time prisoner James I of Scotland to back him (in return for his release from incarceration in 1421) and, indeed, the Scottish king subsequently fought against his own subjects in France at the siege of Meaux. In the end Henry V did successfully defend and secure his northern border but only by encouraging such divisions within the Scottish ruling elite that the 'auld alliance' between Scotland and France took on a new lease of life.

Even though he spent more than half his reign in France, Henry V never put to one side the interests of his subjects in England; through-out, he continued to rule his kingdom, paying close attention to all aspects of government, and ensuring the firm and effective exercise of royal authority there whether he himself was present or not. Early on he set himself the all-important task of restoring political unity among England's ruling elite and, once accomplished, never lost sight of the need to maintain such harmony. To finance military campaigning on the scale and for the length of time Henry V did, moreover, was a major fiscal and administrative achievement. By making the existing financial system work more efficiently, and seeking to maximise yields from the crown's regular sources of income (most importantly, royal lands and customs duties), he made real progress in restoring the government's financial solvency; his eleven parliaments made regular and generous grants of taxation for defending the realm and financing his French campaigns; and, throughout, cooperation rather than confrontation was the hallmark of Henry V's relations with parliament. The king's personal stamp is very evident, too, in the measures undertaken to restore public order, and curtail the extent of violence and lawlessness, in England during the course of his reign: the success of his law

enforcement policies, moreover, is demonstrated by the relative infrequency of serious disorder at home during his long absences abroad
between 1415 and 1422. Nevertheless, there were clear limits to Henry
V's achievements on the domestic front. No new sources of revenue
were developed nor did much significant legislation reach the statute
book. The king was responsible for no judicial innovations; his arbitration in magnate disputes and curtailment of private aristocratic feuds,
although commendable, reflected his own self-interest as much as his
concern for the public weal and, anyway, proved but an ephemeral
phenomenon; and, although the level of provincial lawlessness did
indeed fall, this probably resulted as much from the regular diversion of
potential troublemakers into Henry V's armies as anything else. Even
before 1420, moreover, his relentless demands for men and money at
home to fuel protracted foreign campaigning had begun to become
increasingly unpopular and, once Troyes was concluded, the feeling
mounted (not least in parliament) that the French themselves, not the
English, should foot the bill for fighting what had now become a
purely internal war in France. In fact, although for most of his reign
Henry V did indeed demonstrate that the machinery of English
medieval government could be made to work, he had nothing new to
offer and, in his last years, there were already signs of an impending crisis that became even more evident after the king's death.

What of Henry V's rule of Normandy following his successful conquest of the duchy? Not surprisingly, his new Norman subjects were
required to take an oath of allegiance recognising the legitimacy of his
rule and, if they refused, local inhabitants were deprived of their
estates, forced to leave the province and compelled to seek refuge in
Valois-controlled territory (or accept the consequences if they did
not). From a very early stage of conquest, however, he took practical
steps to maintain the freedoms and privileges of all who did swear allegiance, employ Normans in a range of administrative posts and make
his rule as widely acceptable as he could (even providing ordinary folk
with a degree of protection against English garrisons). Yet, at the same
time, Henry V deliberately set out to encourage English settlement in
Normandy, most notably by granting many confiscated lands (ranging
from large estates to mere smallholdings in towns) to Englishmen
tempted to become colonists as well as soldiers in north-eastern
France. Clearly, then, the king aimed both to encourage and reward

Normans willing to accept his rule and, by ensuring a share in the benefits of conquest to Englishmen, also retain support at home for his French ventures. The fact that Normandy remained in Lancastrian hands until 1450 is perhaps a strong pointer to the degree of advantage he (and his successor) reaped from such a policy of conciliation and settlement. Yet, arguably, the loyalty of the many lesser Norman nobility and gentry who did accept Lancastrian rule could never be guaranteed and English possession of the duchy might have lasted even longer had the local aristocracy as a whole been dispossessed. Even during Henry V's own lifetime, moreover, not only did bands of Norman brigands continue to resist Lancastrian conquest and settlement but the crown's own servants may have left a good deal to be desired as well, as highlighted in a letter penned by John Duke of Bedford just five months after his brother's death. 'Many who call themselves our officers, bailiffs and captains', he reported on 31 January 1423:

...have committed and are committing great wrongs, excesses and abuses, taking advantage of their position to do so, to the prejudice of public welfare, such as: breaking into churches and stealing the goods therein; seizing and raping women, married and unmarried; cruelly beating the poor people, carrying off their horses with other beasts of burden and their seed corn; occupying the houses of churchmen, nobles and others against their will; demanding heavy tolls and quantities of merchandise at the city gates which they are supposed to guard; extorting levies of food from towns and parishes with law-abiding subjects; forcing men to perform more guard duties at towns and fortresses than is their obligation and making them pay huge sums if they go absent; seizing our poor subjects, beating them, judging them without trial and confining them to prisons or in their homes, robbing them of their goods, or seizing the same either without payment or else fixing the price.[7]

So effective was the 'eloquent persuasiveness' of Henry Beaufort Bishop of Winchester at the Council of Constance, Thomas Walsingham tells us, that he 'stirred up the lord cardinals to agreement and to prepare themselves for the election' of a new pope and, as a result, Pope Martin V was duly elected in November 1417. Thus ended the Great Schism which, since 1378, had seen two (more recently three!) rival popes all claiming to be the true successor of St Peter as bishop of Rome and spiritual head of Western Christendom. No doubt Beaufort in particular, and English delegates to the Council of Constance in general, did indeed play a significant role in resolving a crisis that had torn the Western European church apart for almost forty years but, throughout, they were clearly acting very much on Henry V's orders. No doubt, too, the English king genuinely did wish to see unity restored to the church, so it could focus its efforts more effectively on promoting religious reform, combatting heresy and, hopefully, backing his own long-term project of leading a new crusade. What he did not want, and consistently refused to tolerate even after Martin V's election, was papal interference in English affairs: hence his refusal to sanction Beaufort's elevation to cardinal, his retention of firm control of ecclesiastical appointments at home and his refusal to make any concessions to Rome that might adversely affect royal interests. Moreover, his close interest in the Council of Constance and its deliberations had overtly political as well as religious objectives. Constance was an imperial city; the council had originally convened there at the beginning of November 1414 in response to a summons issued by the Emperor Sigismund; and the emperor, perhaps even more vehemently than Henry V, pressed throughout for an end to the Great Schism and the election of a new (and undisputed) pope. Their common aims at Constance provided a powerful incentive for the two to become allies; Sigismund even made a rare imperial visit to England in 1416 and, during the lavish entertainments laid on for his illustrious guest, Henry V persuaded the emperor of the justice of his cause in France; and, although little of practical value resulted from the Treaty of Canterbury to which they both put their seals in August 1416, the English king's prestige and reputation in Western Europe were certainly advanced. During the deliberations in Constance itself, moreover, Henry V's delegates made the most of every opportunity to promote notions of English nationalism and justify the king's own essentially imperialist ambitions in France.

Henry V certainly took a close and active interest in the organisation of the English church and the quality of its spiritual life, as well as demonstrating an unflinching commitment to its protection from the cancer of heresy. Even if the extent of Lollardy, and the threat it posed to church and state, tended to be exaggerated by contemporary and near-contemporary commentators, there can be no doubt of the king's orthodox zeal when it came to searching out and suppressing religious dissent. Nor can his enthusiasm for religious reform seriously be called into question, particularly the reinvigoration of monastic life in early fifteenth-century England. Specifically, as Tito Livio reported, Henry V:

> ...had two religious houses built on the River Thames, one for the Carthusian Order, to which he gave the name of Bethlehem, and the other, which is known as Syon, for the nuns of St Brigit. He sought and obtained indulgences for both these religious houses from the pope and endowed them with many privileges and a great income.[8]

The last royal monastic foundations in England before the Reformation, both houses very much reflected the king's personal enthusiasm for spiritual fervour and asceticism: the Carthusians, in particular, were renowned for their austere religious practices and lifestyle. The foundation charters of both establishments, moreover, required that the monks and nuns pray for the king during his life, for his soul after death, for the souls of his ancestors and for the well-being of his kingdom. Henry V's powerful commitment to reform of the church is perhaps most evident during his final visit to England in 1421 when, on 7 May, he personally addressed a meeting of some sixty abbots and more than three hundred Benedictine monks at Westminster 'on the early religious observance of the monks, on the devotion of his ancestors and others in founding and endowing monasteries and upon the negligence and carelessness of the moderns'. Not only did he urge reform of the 'many abuses and excesses amongst the professors of the orders of the Black Monks of St Benedict in England', however, he also presented the assembled monks with thirteen proposals of his own designed to ensure stricter observance of the Benedictine rule. The king's proposals were in no way radical, though: indeed, they mainly serve to demonstrate his own unwavering belief in the efficacy of prayer and characteristically traditional vision of religious life. Even so, most of them were rejected.

Interestingly, Henry V's original summons to the Benedictines to meet at Westminster in May 1421 was composed not in Latin but in English and issued 'under the signet of the eagle' at Leicester on 25 March. Even as Prince of Wales he had begun to develop a real commitment to encouraging the use of the English language: he himself seems to have been most comfortable when speaking the vernacular; so were those closest to him and, after he became king, English rather than French probably became (for the first time) the main language of the royal court; and, increasingly, Henry V came to recognise the value of language as a weapon for promoting harmony and unity in the English nation. As early as 1412 he commissioned John Lydgate to translate a Latin history of the siege and destruction of Troy into English; in a preface to the resulting translation Lydgate specifically highlighted his own enthusiasm for rendering this 'noble story' in 'our tongue' so as to make it more widely available 'to high and low alike'; and, when dedicating the completed *Troy Book* to the king in 1421, he firmly equated the promotion of the English language with the evolution of a clearly identifiable English nation. As for Henry V himself, he seems to have enjoyed reading as well as speaking English; he could and did write not only in French and Latin but also in the vernacular; and, indeed, a number of royal letters survive in the king's own hand. From the time of his second invasion of France in 1417 if not before, moreover, Henry V deliberately promoted the use of English in government documents; he actively encouraged other institutions to employ the vernacular as well; and his success in expanding the scope of written English is never better demonstrated than by the decision of the London Brewers Company in 1422 to render even its formal proceedings in the vernacular. In modern days, so the company's records tell us, 'our mother tongue' has 'begun to be honourably enlarged and adorned', not least since 'our most excellent lord King Henry V' has, in his own letters, 'chosen to declare the secrets of his will' and, 'for the better understanding of his people', deliberately promoted 'the common idiom'; for 'which cause and many others' and in view of the fact that 'the greater part of the Lords and trusty Commons have begun to note down their deliberations in our mother tongue', the minute concludes, 'we also in our craft, following in their steps', have decided henceforth to employ the vernacular as well. Clearly, then, by the end of Henry V's reign English had indeed become a widely recognised, and acceptable, medium of written communication: indeed, it has even been suggested that the king's own personal mode of expression helped shape the chancery style of writing which eventually provided the basis of standard English.

The promotion of the vernacular during Henry V's reign no doubt contributed, too, to the growth of English patriotism, even the creation of an increasingly self-conscious English nation. In his own propaganda the king certainly put much stress on the notion of England as both a well-established island of saints (such as the tenth-century St Dunstan) and a land ruled since ancient times by kings. The *Gesta Henrici Quinti*, for instance, tells how, as part of the spectacular procession that greeted Henry V in London after his victory at Agincourt, there were represented 'twelve kings of the English succession, martyrs and confessors, with sceptres in their hands and their emblems of sanctity plain to see'. At the Council of Constance, in similar vein, royal envoys maintained that the English monarchy was not only uniquely ancient but also clearly superior to that of France 'in the antiquity of its faith, dignity and honour, and at least equal in all the divine gifts of regal power'. By 1417, moreover, the notion of England and its people as a nation was clearly well established, nicely demonstrated by the robust declaration at Constance that 'whether a nation be understood as a people marked off from others by blood relationship and habit of unity, or by peculiarities of language (the most sure and positive sign and essence of a nation in divine and human law), or whether nation be understood, as it should be, as a territory equal to that of the French nation, England is a real nation'. According to this astute commentator, indeed, England was a 'glorious kingdom'; it had an honourable and distinguished history; it possessed its own language; and, no less than France, it enjoyed real territorial integrity. Notions of English national identity and national unity under Henry V are nicely captured, too, in a sermon probably preached by a Benedictine monk in the early summer of 1421. There the king was portrayed as 'our peerless prince' and 'master mariner'; the realm was his 'fair ship'; and by controlling the rudder of the ship of state, and exhorting his people to 'all row together', he both could and did maintain the unity of the nation. Unfortunately, when Henry V was succeeded as 'master mariner' by his spectacularly ineffective and incompetent son Henry VI, England eventually lost not only its empire in France but also all semblance of unity at home: the result was the Wars of the Roses.

17

LEGACY

Even so enthusiastic a twentieth-century admirer of Henry V as Sir Winston Churchill concluded, in his *History of the English Speaking Peoples*, that 'the imposing Empire of Henry V was hollow and false'; indeed, when the king:

> ...revived the English claims to France he opened the greatest tragedy of our medieval history. Agincourt was a glittering victory, but the wasteful and useless campaigns that followed more than outweighed its military and moral value, and the miserable, destroying century that ensued casts its black shadow upon Henry's heroic triumph.[9]

Clearly, Henry V's sudden death with his work still far from complete resulted in a difficult, perhaps impossible, legacy for the Lancastrian dynasty. To make matters worse, his own final hopes and aspirations for the future, insofar as they can be gauged, left many questions unanswered, nor did he put in place practical provisions for the conduct of government during his infant son's minority. In his last will, written at Dover on 10 July 1421 as he prepared to leave England for the final time, Henry V's mind was focussed almost exclusively on his own eternal salvation: for instance, he made provision for the endowment of a chantry chapel in Westminster Abbey, where three masses per day were to be performed in perpetuity, as well as the purchase of a further 20,000 masses for himself to be celebrated soon after his death. Indeed, it has even been suggested that so heavy an investment in the purchase of paradise looks suspiciously like an urgent rescue operation for his soul! Yet the king's last will contained no provision for the upbringing and education of the child Catherine of Valois was already known to be carrying nor was there any reference to how government might be conducted in the event of a prolonged royal minority. Only in codicils added to his will on 26 August 1422 (just five days before his death) and orally at Bois de Vincennes as he lay dying did Henry V at last address such crucial matters. Perhaps fearing that his infant son and heir (born at Windsor on 6 December 1421) might even be barred from the succession in England let alone France, he now named his brother Humphrey Duke of Gloucester as Henry VI's chief guardian and protector; however, since custody of the child's person and control of his household were assigned to others, there was still plenty of potential for confusion and strife. On his death bed the king may also have made known his desire that Gloucester serve as regent in England, and his other brother John Duke of Bedford perform the same function in France, during Henry VI's minority. If so, this had even more potential for causing controversy and aristocratic friction, particularly as far as the government of England was concerned.

For the sake of the very political unity he himself had so vigorously promoted, if nothing else, Henry V's will and its hastily added codicils should have set out clearly his wishes regarding both his son personally and the conduct of government during the extended royal minority that must now inevitably follow his death. Instead, the king's sudden demise abroad and failure to put in place a firm structure for future administration at home resulted in several weeks of highly charged political squabbling and constitutional conflict, very much centred around Humphrey Duke of Gloucester. Whether or not Henry V had specifically expressed the desire that his younger brother become regent in England after his death, and he probably had, Gloucester himself certainly seems to have believed he had every right to such a role and that it should carry great powers and responsibilities. When parliament met in November 1422, however, the duke's many political opponents ensured his claim to the regency was decisively rejected. Instead, early in December, he was declared protector, an office giving him titular pre-eminence (at any rate so long as John Duke of Bedford, his elder brother and heir-presumptive to Henry VI, remained in France) but only very limited responsibilities: real power, in fact, was vested in a magnate council, of which Gloucester was a senior member but whose wishes could always be overruled by the collective decision of his fellow councillors. This was a moderate and sensible solution to a potentially grave political and constitutional crisis, and probably the best available in the circumstances, but it almost certainly went against Henry V's last wishes, fell far short of Gloucester's hopes, and merely patched up – rather than resolved – the personal animosities and rivalries within the ruling elite that had so marked the weeks since the second Lancastrian's death. Indeed, in the years that followed, Humphrey Duke of Gloucester was to challenge the constitutional settlement of 1422 at least twice, in 1424 and 1432, as well as frequently finding himself at odds with fellow members of the council.

During the minority of Henry VI (1422–1437) there certainly developed a bitter feud between Humphrey Duke of Gloucester and Henry Beaufort Bishop of Winchester (who was finally raised to the status of cardinal by the pope in 1427). The rivalry of these two powerful men, moreover, obviously provided the council with a considerable dilemma, not least in 1425 when it even threatened to thrust England into out-and-out civil strife. Other magnate feuds also surfaced from time to time, while the fragility of Henry V's achievements in the field of public order more generally soon became evident as well. Perhaps inevitably, since the decline in lawlessness under the second Lancastrian had very much reflected the king's own personal authority, there was an immediate slackening of central judicial control following his death and, although the minority government did not preside over a collapse of law and order in the country, the level of disorder almost certainly became significantly higher in the years after 1422 than it had been at any time since 1413. Even before Henry V's demise, moreover, crown/parliament relations and the royal finances had been showing real signs of strain and, clearly, his passing did nothing to improve an already deteriorating situation. Nevertheless, throughout the years of Henry VI's minority, the council certainly did demonstrate real resolution to function in a businesslike and impartial manner, even when confronted by major problems such as containing the Gloucester/Beaufort feud, keeping the government solvent and preserving law and order. What probably helped maintain conciliar unity more than anything else was a shared sense of loyalty to the memory of Henry V and determination to pass on untrammelled the authority he had exercised to his son once he came of age. Such a sense of devotion to the second Lancastrian's renown, and desire to celebrate his reputation as a great war leader, is equally evident in the eulogistic biographies (by Tito Livio and the anonymous Pseudo-Elmham) commissioned by Humphrey Duke of Gloucester and his circle. Similar sentiments also help explain architectural monuments to the king at Oxford University and in Westminster Abbey. The building of All Souls College, Oxford, was specifically commissioned by Archbishop Henry Chichele in 1438 'to pray for the king's and the archbishop's well-being while they live, and after their deaths for their souls and the souls of the most famous King Henry V, Thomas late Duke of Clarence, the dukes, earls, barons, knights, armigerous men and other noblemen and commoners who have ended their lives in the king's and his father's reign in the French wars'. As for the chantry chapel in Westminster Abbey, originally stipulated in Henry V's own last will, putting into effect such a grandiose architectural project certainly was a great tribute to his glorious campaigns and conquests.

What of Henry V's legacy in France? Despite the diplomatic ingenuity of its negotiators and the skilful propaganda of its promoters, the Treaty of Troyes was always very much a gamble and, in the end, it was a gamble that failed. Even in England the treaty received a distinctly mixed reception, particularly once its military and financial implications for the country began to become evident. In France it did not put an end to internal strife but, rather, virtually guaranteed the continuance of civil war for years to come, as the Dauphin Charles showed himself ever more doggedly determined (especially after his father's death in October 1422) to resist all attempts by Anglo-Burgundian forces to destroy him. Even had he lived Henry V might well have faced a mega-crisis at home before long and, in France, the truly daunting prospect of a long, hard and very expensive struggle to make English rule a permanent reality in northern France (let alone the dauphinist south). Indeed, there are signs that towards the end of his life the king himself was beginning to doubt the feasibility of ever winning the whole of France. His precise wishes regarding the future rule of France, no less than that of England, remain far from clear. Seemingly, he wanted John Duke of Bedford to take responsibility for the government of Normandy during Henry VI's minority and, on his death bed, may well have advised his closest companions to make the retention of Normandy in English hands their top priority. Seemingly, too, he may have urged the need to preserve the Anglo-Burgundian alliance at all costs, avoid any negotiations with the dauphin and firmly uphold his dynasty's right to the Valois throne. Most English chroniclers also suggest that Henry V wished Bedford to become regent in France although, interestingly, Thomas Walsingham learned that his expressed preference was for Philip the Good Duke of Burgundy to assume the regency for as long as Charles VI lasted. In the event, John Duke of Bedford did become regent and, clearly, both he and the minority council in England had but one priority following Henry V's death and his son's succession: continuing the second Lancastrian's programme of conquest in France, securing Henry VI's possession of the Valois throne and, eventually, engineering his coronation in Paris in December 1431 (when young Henry did, indeed, become the only English monarch ever to be crowned king of France). Yet the burden of maintaining Henry V's legacy across the Channel increased rather than decreased as the years went by, particularly following Bedford's death, the collapse of the Anglo-Burgundian alliance and the final fall of Paris to Charles VII in the mid-1430s. Most fatal of all came the end of Henry VI's minority in 1437: thereafter, it took him just fifteen years of personal rule to lose virtually the whole of the English empire in France.

Clearly, in the end, neither Henry V's brother John Duke of Bedford nor his son Henry VI proved able to turn the dual monarchy of England and France into a permanent reality: yet it did take the French almost thirty years to win back what the second Lancastrian had built up in less than seven. Had he lived, could Henry V have succeeded where his successors failed? Inevitably, this has been much debated. At one extreme, it has been argued that, given time, Henry V might well have completed the conquest of France; the dauphinists, by 1422, had virtually abandoned all hope and a further sustained military pounding could have finished them off once and for all; and, whereas Bedford could only delay ultimate English failure across the Channel, such was the force of Henry V's personality, his brilliance as a military commander and his capacity to adapt to changing circumstances if required, he might indeed have secured – and retained – the French crown once Charles VI was dead. Yet, so the king's critics would have us believe, only Henry V's premature death saved him from inevitable failure; the Anglo-Burgundian alliance, very much a by-product of the murder of John the Fearless, was bound to fall apart in the end; and most Frenchmen, including the majority of Burgundians, had far stronger natural (and increasingly national) affiliations with Valois loyalists than the English and, once Charles VI had gone, had more reason to support his son's succession (as Charles VII) than that of a Lancastrian king. The Treaty of Troyes, and its long-term viability, have always been at the hub of the debate and, on balance, the case for regarding it as fatally flawed are compelling. In 1420, arguably, Henry V could have chosen to offer himself as a powerful mediator between the Dauphin Charles and Philip of Burgundy and, had he done so, he might have helped bring the French civil war to an end and even secured both his inherited lands and the territories he himself had conquered across the Channel in a settlement along the lines of the Treaty of Bretigny. Instead, by putting his seal to Troyes, he committed England to being a participant in an on-going French internal struggle for years to come; large parts of the Valois realm adamantly refused to recognise the treaty; and, as a result, Henry V probably was fortunate to die suddenly before his reputation became irrevocably tarnished. His legacy, in the last analysis, was bleak; by the later 1450s not only had his son failed dismally in France but England itself had dissolved into civil war; and the Wars of the Roses, before long, brought the deposition of Henry VI, the usurpation of the Yorkist Edward IV and the end of the Lancastrian dynasty.

NOTES

PART I: HENRY V IN HISTORY

1 W.C. Sellar and R.J.Yeatman, *1066 and All That* (Penguin edn, 1960), pp.52-3.
2 J. Farman, *The Very Bloody History of Britain* (Red Fox edn, 1992), p.49.
3 *Gesta Henrici Quinti*, ed. and transl. F. Taylor and J.S. Roskell (1975), especially pp.3, 79, 101, 181.
4 Thomas Elmham, *Liber Metricus de Henrico Quinto*, in *Memorials of Henry V*, ed. C.A. Cole (1858), especially pp.79-82.
5 Tito Livio, *Vita Henrici Quinti*, ed. T. Hearne (1716), especially pp.2-3, 12. See also A. Curry, *The Battle of Agincourt: Sources and Interpretations* (2000), p.62; *Chronicles of the Wars of the Roses 1377–1485*, ed. E. Hallam (1998), p.130.
6 Pseudo-Elmham, *Vita et Gesta Henrici Quinci*, ed. T. Hearne (1727), especially pp.12-15. See also A.J. Church, *Henry V* (1889), pp.44-5; A. Gransden, *Historical Writing in England c.1307 to the Early Sixteenth Century* (1982), p.214.
7 Thomas Walsingham, *St Albans Chronicle 1406–1420*, ed. V.H. Galbraith (1937); *Historia Anglicana 1272–1422*, ed. H.T. Riley, Vol. 2 (1864); *Ypodigma Neustriae*, ed. H.T. Riley (1876), especially p.3. See also Curry, *Agincourt Sources*, p.52; Hallam, *Chronicles*, pp.158-60.
8 *The Chronicle of Adam Usk 1377–1421*, ed. and transl. C. Given Wilson (1997), especially pp.270-1.
9 'Chronicle of John Strecche for the Reign of Henry V (1414–1422)', ed. F. Taylor, *Bulletin of the John Rylands Library*, 16 (1932). See also *England under the Lancastrians*, ed. J.H. Flemming (1921), pp.46, 31.
10 Monk of Westminster, *Versus Rythmici in Laudem Regis Henrici Quinti*, in *Memorials of Henry V*, ed. C.A. Cole (1858); Thomas Otterbourne, *Chronica Regum Anglie*, Vol. 1, ed. T. Hearne (1732); *Ingulph's Chronicle of the Abbey of Croyland*, ed. and transl. H.T. Riley (1854).
11 *Brut or Chronicles of England*, ed. F.W.D. Brie (1908); *An English Chronicle of the Reigns of Richard II, Henry IV, Henry V and Henry VI*, ed. J.S. Davies (1856).
12 *Cleopatra CIV*, in *Chronicles of London*, ed. C.L. Kingsford (1905); *Gregory's Chronicle*, in *Historical Collections of a Citizen of London*, ed. J. Gairdner (1876).
13 *English Historical Documents 1327–1485*, ed. A.R. Myers (1969), pp.214-5
14 John Page, 'The Siege of Rouen', in Gairdner, *Historical Collections*, pp.24, 25
15 Thomas Hoccleve, *The Regement of Princes*, ed. F.J. Furnivall (1897); John Lydgate, *Troy Book*, ed. H. Bergen (1906), *Siege of Thebes*, ed. A. Erdmann (1911)
16 'The First Version of Hardyng's Chronicle', ed. C.L. Kingsford, *English Historical Review*, 27 (1912); William Worcester, *Boke of Noblesse addressed to King Edward IV on his invasion of France in 1475*, ed. J.G. Nichols (1860), especially pp.40-1.
17 C. Allmand, *Society at War: The Experience of England and France during the Hundred Years War* (1973), p.130.
18 Curry, *Agincourt Sources*, p.442
19 P.S. Lewis, *Later Medieval France* (1968), p.63.
20 *Chronique du Religieux de Saint-Denys*, ed. L. Bellaguet, Vols 5 and 6 (1852–54), especially Vol. 5, p.565, Vol. 6, pp.48, 163, 165, 381. See also M.W. Labarge, *Henry V: The Cautious Conqueror* (1975), p.186; D. Seward, *Henry V as Warlord* (1987), pp.108-9, 148; Curry, *Agincourt Sources*, p.337.
21 Jean Juvenal des Ursins, *Histoire de Charles VI, roy de France*, ed. J.F. Michaud and J.-J.F. Poujoulet (1836).
22 Jean Chartier, *Chronique de Charles VII, roi de France*, ed. V. de Viriville (1858); Alain Chartier, *Le Quadrilogue Invectif*, in *Fifteenth-Century English Translations of Alain Chartier's La Traité de L'Esperance and Le Quadrilogue Invectif*, ed. M.S. Blayney (1974); Robert Blondel, *Oeuvres*, ed. A. Heron (1891); *Parisian Journal 1405–1449*, ed. and transl. J. Shirley (1968), especially p.146.
23 *Chronique Normande de Pierre Cochon*, ed. C. de Robillard de Beaurepaire (1870); *Chronique de Perceval de Cagny*, ed. H. Moranville (1902); *Memoires de Pierre de Fenin*, ed. E. Dupont (1837), especially p.186; Thomas Basin, *Histoire de Charles VII*, ed. C. Samaran (1964), Vol. 1, especially p.79. See also Seward, *Henry V*, p.209 and C.L. Kingsford, *Henry V: The Typical Medieval Hero* (1901), p.391.

24 *Froissart Chronicles*, ed. and transl. G. Brereton (Penguin edn, 1968), p.37; Enguerrand de Monstrelet, *The Chronicles*, ed. and transl. T. Johnes, 2 vols (1853), especially Vol. 1, pp.1, 484-5; *The Chronicles of Enguerrand de Monstrelet*, in *Contemporary Chronicles of the Hundred Years War*, ed. and transl. P.E. Thompson (1966), especially pp.18, 292.

25 Georges Chastellain, *Oeuvres*, ed. K. de Lettenhove (1863), Vol. 1, especially p.221. See also Seward, *Henry V*, p.204.

26 Jean le Fevre, *Chronique*, ed. F. Morand, 2 vols (1876, 1881); Jean Waurin, *Recueil des Croniques et Anchiennes Istories de la Grant Bretaigne, à present nomme Engleterre, 1399–1422*, ed. W. Hardy (1868).

27 *Johannis Rossi Antiquarii Warwicensis Historia Regum Angliae*, ed. T. Hearne (1745), pp.207-9; Robert Fabyan, *The New Chronicles of England and of France*, ed. H. Ellis (1811), especially p.577; Curry, *Agincourt Sources*, pp.223-30 (Polydore Vergil).

28 *The First English Life of Henry V*, ed. C.L. Kingsford (1911), especially pp.4, 185

29 Edward Hall, *The Union of the Two Noble Families of Lancaster and York* (1550, Scolar Press 1970), especially f.xlix.

30 Richard Grafton, *Chronicle or History of England*, ed. H. Ellis (1809); Robert Redmayne, *Vita Henrici Quinti*, in *Memorials of Henry V*, ed. C.A. Cole (1858); *Holinshed's Chronicle As Used in Shakespeare's Plays*, ed. A. and J. Nicholl (1927), especially p.89; John Stow, *The Annales of England* (1592)

31 The full text of *The Famous Victories of Henry V* can be found in G. Bullough, *Narrative and Dramatic Sources of Shakespeare*, Vol. 4 (1996). See also Curry, *Agincourt Sources*, pp.316-21, especially p.316.

32 William Shakespeare, *King Henry IV Part I*, especially Act 1 Scene 2; *King Henry IV Part 2*, especially Act 5 Scene 5; *King Henry V*, especially Act 1 Scene 1, Act 3 Scenes 1 and 3, and Act 4 Scene 3.

33 John Speed, *The History of Great Britaine* (1611); Michael Drayton, 'The Bataille of Agincourt', in *The Works of Michael Drayton*, Vol. 3, ed. J.W. Hebel (1932); *Foedera, conventiones, literae, et cujuscunque generis acta publica*, ed. Thomas Rymer, Vol. 9 (1709); Thomas Goodwin, *The History of the Reign of Henry the Fifth, King of England* (1704).

34 Paul Rapin de Thoyras, *History of England*, transl. N. Tindall (1728–32), Vol. 1; David Hume, *History of England from the Invasion of Julius Caesar to the Accession of Henry VII* (1762); William Hazlitt, *Characters of Shakespeare's Plays* (1817); N. Harris Nicolas, *History of the Battle of Agincourt* (1827); J.R. Green, *A Short History of the English People* (1874); J.H. Ramsay, *Lancaster and York* (1892), Vol. 1.

35 William Stubbs, *Constitutional History of England*, Vol. 3 (1878), especially pp.74, 77.

36 A.J. Church, *Henry V* (1889), especially pp.154-5.

37 C.L. Kingsford, *Henry V: The Typical Medieval Hero* (1901), especially pp.390, 401.

38 E.M.W. Tillyard, *Shakespeare's History Plays* (1944); L.C. Knights, *Shakespeare: The Histories* (1962); John Sutherland, 'Henry V, war criminal?', in John Sutherland and Cedric Watts, *Henry V, War Criminal? and Other Shakespeare Puzzles* (2000).

39 John Harvey, *The Plantagenets* (1948); David Douglas, Introduction to Edouard Perroy, *The Hundred Years War* (1951); Richard Vaughan, *John the Fearless* (1966); Kenneth Fowler, *The Age of Plantagenet and Valois* (1967); John Palmer, 'The War Aims of the Protagonists and Negotiations for Peace', in *The Hundred Years War*, ed. K. Fowler (1971); Maurice Keen, *England in the Later Middle Ages* (1973); Charles Ross, 'Henry V of England', in *Encyclopaedia Brittanica*, 5th edn (1974); C.S.L. Davies, 'Henry VIII and Henry V: the Wars in France' in *The End of the Middle Ages?*, ed. J.L. Watts (1998); A.J. Pollard, *Late Medieval England 1399–1509* (2000); Michael Hicks, *English Political Culture in the Fifteenth Century* (2002).

40 J.H. Wylie and W.T. Waugh, *The Reign of Henry the Fifth*, 3 vols (1914–29), especially Vol. 3, p.426; R.B. Mowat, *Henry V* (1919), especially p.292.

41 Edouard Perroy, *La Guerre de Cent Ans* (1945), translated into English as *The Hundred Years War* (1951), especially pp.235-6.

42 K.B. McFarlane, 'The Lancastrian Kings', in *Cambridge Medieval History*, Vol. 8 (1936) and *Lancastrian Kings and Lollard Knights* (1972), especially 'Henry V: A Personal Portrait' (a lecture originally written, and delivered, in 1954); E.F. Jacob, *Henry V and the Invasion of France* (1947) and *The Fifteenth Century 1399–1485* (1961), especially p.201.

43 Harold F. Hutchison, *Henry V* (1967); Peter Earle, *The Life and Times of Henry V* (1975, edn), especially p.114; Margaret Wade Labarge, *Henry V: The Cautious Conqueror* (1975), especially p.190.

44 *Henry V: The Practice of Kingship*, ed. G.L. Harriss (1985), 'Introduction: the Exemplar of Kingship', 'The King and his Magnates', 'The Management of Parliament', 'Financial Policy' and 'Conclusion', especially pp.28, 201, 209-10; Edward Powell, 'The Restoration of Law and Order', in Harriss, *Henry V*, and *Kingship, Law and Society: Criminal Justice in the Reign of Henry V* (1989), especially p.275.

45 Desmond Seward, *Henry V as Warlord* (1987), especially pp.214-18; T.B. Pugh, *Henry V and the Southampton Plot* (1988), especially 'The Place of Henry V in English History', pp.137-46.

46 Christopher Allmand, *Henry V* (1992), especially pp.437, 443. See also C. Allmand, *Henry V* (Historical Association pamphlet, 1968); 'Henry V the Soldier and the War in France', in Harriss, *Henry V*; and *The Hundred Years War: England and France at War c.1300–1450* (1988).

47 Anne Curry, *The Hundred Years War* (1993); 'Henry V: A Life and Reign', in *Agincourt 1415*, ed. A. Curry (2000); and *The Battle of Agincourt: Sources and Interpretations* (2000).

PART II: LIFE AND REIGN OF HENRY V

1 Kingsford, *Henry V*, p.17 (Jean Creton and Thomas Otterbourne); Brie, *Brut*, p.545
2 Paul Strohm, *England's Empty Throne: Usurpation and the Language of Legitimation 1399–1422* (1998), p.118 (Pseudo-Elmham).
3 Kingsford, *First English Life*, pp.11–13.
4 Thompson, *Hundred Years War*, pp.264–5.
5 Usk, *Chronicle*, p.243.
6 Kingsford, *First English Life*, p.17.
7 Kingsford, *Henry V*, pp.88–90 *(Book Named the Governor)*.
8 Hallam, *Chronicles*, p.119 (Tito Livio).
9 Myers, *English Historical Documents*, p.274.
10 Hallam, *Chronicles*, p.112.
11 *Gesta Henrici Quinti*, p.5.
12 Usk, *Chronicle*, p.247.
13 *Gesta Henrici Quinti*, p.7.
14 Church, *Henry V*, pp.100-101 and Strohm, *England's Empty Throne*, pp.75-6 (Walsingham).
15 Usk, *Chronicle*, p.267.
16 Strohm, *England's Empty Throne*, especially pp.65-86.
17 *Gesta Henrici Quinti*, p.19; Davies, *English Chronicle*, p.40; Usk, *Chronicle*, p.255; Myers, *English Historical Documents*, p.210 (Walsingham); Thompson, *Hundred Years War*, p.268 (Monstrelet); Pugh, *Henry V and the Southampton Plot*, pp.172-3 (Cambridge's confession).
18 Myers, *English Historical Documents*, p.274.
19 Jacob, *Henry V and the Invasion of France*, p.187.
20 *Gesta Henrici Quinti*, pp.17, 181; Usk, *Chronicle*, p.253; Hallam, *Chronicles*, p.122 (Tito Livio).
21 Flemming, *Lancastrians*, p.29 (Monk of St Denis); Curry, *Agincourt Sources*, p.134 (Juvenal des Ursins); Johnes, *Monstrelet*, Vol. 1, p.329.
22 Myers, *English Historical Documents*, p.208, Flemming, *Lancastrians*, p.30 and Hallam, *Chronicles*, pp.122, 124.
23 *Gesta Henrici Quinti*, p.35.
24 Usk, *Chronicle*, pp.255-7; Kingsford, *Chronicles of London*, p.119 (Cleopatra CIV); Thompson, *Hundred Years War*, p.271 (Monstrelet); Curry, *Agincourt Sources*, p.101 (Monk of St Denis).
25 Curry, *Agincourt Sources*, p.441.
26 Curry, *Agincourt Sources*, pp.42 (Thomas Elmham), 101 (Monk of St Denis), 56 (Tito Livio).
27 Curry, *Agincourt Sources*, pp.43 (Thomas Elmham), 129 (Juvenal des Ursins), 104-5 (Monk of St Denis).
28 Curry, *Agincourt Sources*, pp.45-6 (Thomas Elmham); Thompson, *Hundred Years War*, p.275 (Monstrelet); Brie, *Brut*, p.378.
29 Curry, *Agincourt Sources*, pp.59, 62 (Tito Livio), 47 (Thomas Elmham), 52 (Walsingham).
30 Curry, *Agincourt Sources*, p.130.
31 Curry, *Agincourt Sources*, p.47 (Thomas Elmham); *Gesta Henrici Quinti*, p.91; Curry, *Agincourt Sources*, pp.52 (Walsingham), 186 (Anonymous Norman Chronicler).
32 *Gesta Henrici Quinti*, pp.91, 93; Curry, *Agincourt Sources*, pp.62 (Tito Livio), 108 (Monk of St Denis); Allmand, *Society at War*, p.110 (Jean Waurin).
33 Curry, *Agincourt Sources*, p.47 (Thomas Elmham); *Gesta Henrici Quinti*, p.97.
34 Curry, *Agincourt Sources*, pp.62 (Tito Livio), 131 (Juvenal des Ursins), 108, 337-8 (Monk of St Denis).
35 Thompson, *Hundred Years War*, pp.280-1 (Monstrelet); Curry, *Agincourt Sources*, pp.63 (Tito Livio), 266-7 (Brut).
36 Usk, *Chronicle*, pp.259, 261, 263; *Gesta Henrici Quinti*, p.113; Curry, *Agincourt Sources*, p.268 (Walsingham).
37 Brie, *Brut*, p.380; Hallam, *Chronicles*, pp.136, 140 (Tito Livio); *Gesta Henrici Quinti*, p.175.
38 *Gesta Henrici Quinti*, pp.135, 145, 147, 149.
39 Usk, *Chronicle*, p.265; *Gesta Henrici Quinti*, pp.157, 173, 175, 177, 179, 181.
40 Myers, *English Historical Documents*, p.219.

41 Seward, *Henry V*, p.101.

42 Kingsford, *First English Life*, pp.96, 92.

43 Johnes, *Monstrelet*,Vol. 1, pp.370-1; Flemming, *Lancastrians*, pp.46-7 (John Strecche).

44 Myers, *English Historical Documents*, pp.220-22 (John Page).

45 Hallam, *Chronicles*, p.147 (Tito Livio); Flemming, *Lancastrians*, pp.46-7 (John Strecche).

46 Flemming, *Lancastrians*, p.54.

47 Myers, *English Historical Documents*, p.225 (Juvenal des Ursins); Kingsford, *First English Life,* p.153.

48 Flemming, *Lancastrians*, p.57.

49 Myers, *English Historical Documents*, pp.225-6.

50 Shirley, *Parisian Journal*, p.151; Seward, *Henry V*, p.148 (Monstrelet).

51 Flemming, *Lancastrians*, pp.59-60 and Seward, *Henry V*, p.151 (Juvenal des Ursins); Gransden, *Historical Writing*, p.407 (John Strecche).

52 Shirley, *Parisian Journal*, pp.153-4; Thompson, *Hundred Years War*, pp.288-9 (Monstrelet); Seward, *Henry V*, p.154 (Chastellain).

53 Myers, *English Historical Documents*, p.229 (John Strecche); Johnes, *Monstrelet*,Vol. 1, p.453.

54 Myers, *English Historical Documents*, pp.228-9 (Dauphin's manifesto, 31 January 1421), 230 (John Harding); Usk, *Chronicle*, pp.269, 271.

55 Flemming, *Lancastrians*, pp.65-6 (Monk of St Denis); Johnes, *Monstrelet*,Vol. 1, p.475; Shirley, *Parisian Journal*, p.167.

56 Myers, *English Historical Documents*, pp.230-1 and Mowat, *Henry V*, p.281 (Pseudo-Elmham); Hallam, *Chronicles*, p.158 (Walsingham).

57 Gransden, *Historical Writing*, pp.216-7 (Pseudo-Elmham); Shirley, *Parisian Journal*, p.178; Flemming, *Lancastrians*, pp.67-8 (London Records).

PART III: HENRY V IN RETROSPECT

1 W.S. Churchill, *A History of the English Speaking Peoples* (1958),Vol. 2, pp.315, 322-3.

2 M. Keen, *The Laws of War in the Late Middle Ages (1965)* and *Chivalry* (1984), especially p.253.

3 Church, *Henry V*, p.105.

4 *Gesta Henrici Quinti*, p.155

5 Kingsford, *First English Life*, pp.132-4.

6 Churchill, *English Speaking Peoples*,Vol. 2, pp.316-8, 320, 322, 324.

7 Seward, *Henry V*, pp.206-7.

8 Hallam, *Chronicles*, p.122

9 Churchill, *English Speaking Peoples*,Vol. 2, p.323.

BIBLIOGRAPHY

Allmand, C., *Henry V* (Historical Association pamphlet, 1968)

Allmand, C., *Society at War: The Experience of England and France during the Hundred Years War* (1973)

Allmand, C., *Lancastrian Normandy 1415–1450* (1983)

Allmand, C., 'Henry V the Soldier and the War in France', in *Henry V: The Practice of Kingship*, ed. G.L. Harriss (1985)

Allmand, C., *The Hundred Years War: England and France at War c.1300–1450* (1988)

Allmand, C., *Henry V* (1992)

Basin, Thomas, *Histoire de Charles VII*, ed. C. Samaran, Vol. 1 (1944)

Blondel, Robert, *Oeuvres*, ed. A. Heron (1891)

Brut or Chronicles of England, ed. F.W.D. Brie (1908)

Bullough, G., *Narrative and Dramatic Sources of Shakespeare*, Vol. 4 (1962)

Cagny, Perceval de, *Chronique de Perceval de Cagny*, ed. H. Moranville (1902)

Catto, J., 'The King's Servants' and 'Religious Change under Henry V, in *Henry V: The Practice of Kingship*, ed. G.L. Harriss (1985)

Chartier, Alain, *Le Quadrilogue Invectif*, in *Fifteenth-Century English Translations of Alain Chartier's Le Traité de L'Esperance and Le Quadrilogue Invectif*, ed. M.S. Blayney (1974)

Chartier, Jean, *Chronique de Charles VII, roi de France*, ed. V. de Viriville (1858)

Chastellain, Georges, *Oeuvres*, ed. K. de Lettenhove, Vol. 1 (1863)

Chronicle of London from 1089 to 1483, eds N.H. Nicolas and E. Tyrrell (1827)

Chronicles of London, ed. J. Gairdner (1905)

Chronicles of the Wars of the Roses 1377–1485, ed. E. Hallam (1988)

Church, A.J., *Henry V* (1889)

Churchill, W.S., *A History of the English Speaking Peoples*, 4 vols (1958)

Cochon, Pierre, *Chronique Normande de Pierre Cochon*, ed. C. de Robillard de Beaurepaire (1870)

Curry, A., *The Hundred Years War* (1993)

Curry, A. (ed.), *Agincourt 1415* (2000)

Curry, A., 'Henry V: a Life and Reign', in *Agincourt 1415*, ed. A. Curry (2000)

Curry, A., *The Battle of Agincourt: Sources and Interpretations* (2000)

Davies, C.S.L., 'Henry VIII and Henry V: the Wars in France', in *The End of the Middle Ages?*, ed. J.L. Watts (1998)

Dockray, K., 'Patriotism, Pride and Paranoia: England and the English in the Fifteenth Century', *The Ricardian*, 110 (1990)

Dockray, K., *William Shakespeare, the Wars of the Roses and the Historians* (2002)

Drayton, M., 'The Battaille of Agincourt', in *The Works of Michael Drayton*, ed. J.W. Hebel (1932)

Earle, P., *The Life and Times of Henry V* (1972)

Elmham, Thomas, *Liber Metricus de Henrico Quinto*, in *Memorials of Henry V*, ed. C.A. Cole (1858)

English Chronicle of the Reigns of Richard II, Henry IV, Henry V and Henry VI, ed. J.S. Davies (1856)

English Historical Documents 1327–1485, ed. A.R. Myers (1969)

Fabian, R., *The New Chronicles of England and of France*, ed. H. Ellis (1811)

Famous Victories of Henry V, in G. Bullough, *Narrative and Dramatic Sources of Shakespeare*, Vol. 4 (1962)

Farman, J., *The Very Bloody History of Britain* (1992)

Fenin, Pierre, *Memoires de Pierre de Fenin*, ed. E. Dupont (1837)

First English Life of Henry V, ed. C.L. Kingsford (1911)

Flemming, J.H. (ed.), *England under the Lancastrians* (1921)

Foedera, conventiones, literae, et cujuscunque generis acta publica, ed. T. Rymer, Vol. 9 (1709)

Fowler, K., *The Age of Plantagenet and Valois* (1967)

Fowler, K. (ed.), *The Hundred Years War* (1971)

Froissart, Jean, *Froissart's Chronicles*, ed. G. Brereton (1968)

Gesta Henrici Quinti, ed. F. Taylor and J.S. Roskell (1975)

Goodwin, T., *The History of the Reign of Henry the Fifth, King of England* (1704)

Grafton, R., *Chronicle or History of England*, ed. H. Ellis (1809)

Gransden, A., *Historical Writing in England c.1307 to the Early Sixteenth Century* (1982)

Great Chronicle of London, ed. A.H. Thomas and I.D. Thornley (1938)

Green, J.R., *A Short History of the English People* (1874)

Griffiths, R.A., *The Reign of King Henry VI* (1981)

Griffiths, R.A. and J. Cannon, *The Oxford Illustrated History of the English Monarchy* (1988)

Griffiths, R.A., 'Henry of Monmouth, Henry V of England; Local Esteem and National Reputation', *Monmouthshire Antiquary*, 19 (2003)

Hall, E., *The Union of the Two Noble Families of Lancaster and York* (1970)

Harding, John, 'The First Version of Hardyng's Chronicle', ed. C.L. Kingsford, *English Historical Review*, 27 (1912) and *Chronicle of John Hardyng*, ed. H. Ellis (1812)

Harriss, G.L. (ed.), *Henry V: The Practice of Kingship* (1985)

Harriss, G.L., 'Introduction: the Exemplar of Kingship', 'The King and his Magnates', 'The Management of Parliament', 'Financial Policy' and 'Conclusion', in *Henry V: The Practice of Kingship*, ed. G.L. Harriss (1985)

Harriss, G.L., *Cardinal Beaufort* (1988)

Harvey, J., *The Plantagenets* (1948)

Hazlitt, W. *Characters of Shakespeare's Plays* (1817)

Hicks, M., *Who's Who in Late Medieval England* (1991)

Hicks, M., *English Political Culture in the Fifteenth Century* (2002)

Historical Collections of a Citizen of London, ed. J. Gairdner (1876)

Historical Poems of the Fourteenth and Fifteenth Centuries, ed. R.H. Robbins (1959)

Hoccleve, Thomas, *The Regement of Princes*, ed. F.J. Furnivall (1897)

Holinshed, R., *Holinshed's Chronicle As Used In Shakespeare's Plays*, ed. A. and J. Nicholl (1927)

Hume, D., *History of England from the Invasion of Julius Caesar to the Accession of Henry VII* (1762)

Hutchison, H.F., *Henry V* (1967)

Ingulph's Chronicle of the Abbey of Croyland, ed. H.T. Riley (1854)

Jacob, E.F., *Henry V and the Invasion of France* (1947)

Jacob, E.F., *The Fifteenth Century 1399–1485* (1961)

Juvenal des Ursins, Jean, *Histoire de Charles VI, roy de France*, ed. J.F. Michaud and J.-J.F. Poujoulet (1836)

Keen, M., *The Laws of War in the Late Middle Ages* (1965)

Keen, M., *England in the Later Middle Ages* (1973)

Keen, M., *Chivalry* (1984)

Keen, M., 'Diplomacy', in *Henry V: The Practice of Kingship*, ed. G.L. Harriss (1985)

Kingsford, C.L., *Henry V: The Typical Medieval Hero* (1901)

Kingsford, C.L., 'The Early Biographies of Henry V, *English Historical Review*, 25 (1910)

Kingsford, C.L., *English Historical Literature in the Fifteenth Century* (1913)

Kingsford, C.L., *Prejudice and Promise in Fifteenth Century England* (1925)

Kirby, J.L., *Henry IV of England* (1970)

Knights, L.C., *Shakespeare: the Histories* (1962)

Knowles, C.H., 'Henry V and the Historians', *Presenting Monmouthshire*, 21 (1966)

Krochalis, J.E., 'The Books and Reading of Henry V and his Circle', *Chaucer Review*, 23 (1988)

Labarge, M.W., *Henry V: The Cautious Conqueror* (1975)

Lander, J.R., *Conflict and Stability in Fifteenth Century England* (1969)

Lewis, P.S., *Later Medieval France* (1968)

Livio, Tito, *Vita Henrici Quinti*, ed. T. Hearne (1716)

Lydgate, John, *Troy Book*, ed. H. Bergen (1906)

Lydgate, John, *Siege of Thebes*, ed. A. Erdmann (1911)

Massey, R., 'The Land Settlement in Lancastrian Normandy', in *Property and Politics: Essays in Later Medieval English History*, ed. A.J. Pollard (1984)

McFarlane, K.B., 'The Lancastrian Kings', in *Cambridge Medieval History*, Vol. 8 (1936)

McFarlane, K.B., *Lancastrian Kings and Lollard Knights* (1972)

McFarlane, K.B., 'Henry V: A Personal Portrait', in *Lancastrian Kings and Lollard Knights* (1972)

McKisack, M., *Medieval History in the Tudor Age* (1971)

McNiven, P., 'Prince Henry and the English Political Crisis of 1412', *History*, 65 (1980)

Memorials of Henry V, ed. C.A. Cole (1858)

Milner, J.D., 'The English Enterprise in France, 1412–13', in *Trade, Devotion and Governance: Papers in Later Medieval History*, ed. D.J. Clayton, R.G. Davies and P. McNiven (1984)

Monk of Saint-Denis, *Chronique du Religieux de Saint-Denys*, ed. L. Bellaguet, Vols 5 and 6 (1852–54)

Monk of Westminster, *Versus Rythmici in Laudem Regis Henrici Quinti*, in *Memorials of Henry V*, ed. C.A. Cole (1858)

Monstrelet, Enguerrand de, *The Chronicles*, ed. T. Johnes, 2 vols (1853)

Monstrelet, Enguerrand de, *The Chronicles of Enguerrand de Monstrelet*, in *Contemporary Chronicles of the*

Hundred Years War, ed. P.E. Thompson (1966)

Morgan, D., 'The household retinue of Henry V and the ethos of English public life', in *Concepts and Patterns of Service in the Later Middle Ages*, ed. A. Curry and E. Matthew (2000)

Moseley, C.W.R., *Shakespeare's History Plays* (1988)

Mowat, R.B., *Henry V* (1919)

Newhall, R.A., *The English Conquest of Normandy 1416–24* (1924)

Nicolas, N.H., *History of the Battle of Agincourt* (1827)

Norwich, J.J., *Shakespeare's Kings* (1999)

Otterbourne, Thomas, *Chronica Regum Anglie*, ed. T. Hearne, Vol. 1 (1732)

Page, John, 'The Siege of Rouen', in *Historical Collections of a Citizen of London*, ed. J. Gairdner (1876)

Palmer, J., 'The War Aims of the Protagonists and Negotiations for Peace', in *The Hundred Years War*, ed. K. Fowler (1971)

Parisian Journal 1405–1449, ed. J. Shirley (1968)

Perroy, E., *The Hundred Years War* (1951)

Pollard, A.J., *Late Medieval England 1399–1509* (2000)

Powell, E., 'The Restoration of Law and Order', in *Henry V: The Practice of Kingship*, ed. G.L. Harriss (1985)

Powell, E., *Kingship, Law and Society: Criminal Justice in the Reign of Henry V* (1989)

Pseudo-Elmham, *Vita et Gesta Henrici Quinti*, ed. T. Hearne (1727)

Pugh, T.B., 'The Southampton Plot of 1415', in *Kings and Nobles in the Later Middle Ages*, ed. R.A. Griffiths and J. Sherborne (1986)

Pugh, T.B., *Henry V and the Southampton Plot* (1988)

Pugh, T.B., 'The Place of Henry V in English History', in *Henry V and the Southampton Plot* (1988)

Ramsay, J.H., *Lancaster and York*, Vol. 1 (1892)

Rapin de Thoyras, P., *History of England* (1728–32)

Redmayne, R., *Vita Henrici Quinti*, in *Memorials of Henry V*, ed. C.A. Cole (1858)

Richmond, C., 'The War at Sea', in *The Hundred Years War*, ed. K. Fowler (1971)

Ross, C., 'Henry V of England', in *Encyclopaedia Brittanica*, 5th edn (1974)

Rotuli Parliamentorum, ed. J. Stracey and others, Vols 2 and 3 (1767)

Rous, J., *Johannis Rossi Antiquarii Warwicensis Historia Regum Angliae*, ed. T. Hearne (1745)

Saccio, P., *Shakespeare's English Kings* (1977)

Saul, N., 'Henry V and the Dual Monarchy', *History Today*, 36 (1986)

Scattergood, V.J., *Politics and Poetry in the Fifteenth Century* (1971)

Sellar, W.C. and R.J. Yeatman, *1066 and All That* (1930)

Seward, D., *Henry V as Warlord* (1987)

Shakespeare, W., *King Henry IV Part 1*, ed. A.R. Humphreys (New Arden edn, 1960)

Shakespeare, W., *King Henry IV Part 2*, ed. A.R. Humphreys (New Arden edn, 1966)

Shakespeare, W., *King Henry V*, ed. J.H. Walter (New Arden edn, 1955)

Speed, J., *The History of Great Britaine* (1611)

Stow, J., *The Annales of England* (1592)

Strecche, John, 'Chronicle of John Strecche for the Reign of Henry V (1414–1422)', ed. F. Taylor, *Bulletin of the John Rylands Library*, 16 (1932)

Strohm, P., *England's Empty Throne: Usurpation and the Language of Legitimation 1399–1422* (1998)

Strong, P. and F., 'The Last Will and Codicils of Henry V', *English Historical Review*, 96 (1981)

Stubbs, W., *Constitutional History of England*, Vol. 3 (1878)

Sutherland, J., 'Henry V, war criminal?', in Sutherland, J. and Watts, C., *Henry V, War Criminal? and Other Shakespeare Puzzles* (2000)

Tillyard, E.M.W., *Shakespeare's History Plays* (1944)

Usk, Adam, *The Chronicle of Adam Usk 1377–1421*, ed. C. Given-Wilson (1997)

Vale, M.G.W., *Charles VII* (1974)

Vaughan, R., *John the Fearless* (1966)

Vaughan, R., *Philip the Good* (1970)

Walsingham, Thomas, *Historia Anglicana 1272–1422*, ed. H.T. Riley, Vol. 2 (1864)

Walsingham, Thomas, *Ypodigma Neustriae*, ed. H.T. Riley (1876)

Walsingham, Thomas, *St Albans Chronicle 1406–1420*, ed. V.H. Galbraith (1937)

Waurin, Jean, *Recueil des Croniques et Anchiennes Istories de la Grant Bretaigne, à present nomme Engleterre, 1399–1422*, ed. W. Hardy (1868)

Weiss, R., *Humanism in England during the Fifteenth Century* (1957)

Worcester, William, *Boke of Noblesse addressed to King Edward IV on his invasion of France in 1475*, ed. J.G. Nichols (1860)

Wylie, J.H. and W.T. Waugh, *The Reign of Henry the Fifth*, 3 vols (1914–29)

LIST OF ILLUSTRATIONS

Page 82 Coronation of Henry IV's second queen Joan of Navarre in Westminster Abbey, February 1403. Although Henry V and his stepmother enjoyed a cordial relationship for years, this did not prevent the queen dowager's sudden arrest and imprisonment in the autumn of 1419, a ruthless and wilful act of injustice occasioned by sheer royal greed.

Page 84 The battle of Shrewsbury, 21 July 1403. Although only sixteen years old, Henry V (as Prince of Wales) fought bravely and received a severe wound in the face at Shrewsbury: indeed, he was probably lucky to survive the action.

Page 101 Richard Beauchamp, an early companion-in-arms of Prince Henry of Monmouth, dubbed a knight by Henry IV following the battle of Shrewsbury, 1403.

Page 109 The betrayal of the Lollard conspiracy of 1413/4 to Henry V.

Page 116 Richard Beauchamp Earl of Warwick's appointment as captain of Calais by Henry V, February 1414.

Page 130 Richard Beauchamp's appointment as an envoy to the Council of Constance by Henry V, October 1414. Henry V took a close personal interest in the deliberations of the council (which eventually, in November 1417, secured the election of Pope Martin V and the ending of the Great Schism) and his delegates acted very much in accordance with the king's instructions.

Page 166 Fighting at sea, possibly the battle of the Seine, August 1416. As a result of this naval victory by Henry V's brother John Duke of Bedford, the French blockade of Harfleur was ended and the way opened up for the king's subsequent invasion and conquest of Normandy.

Page 176 The siege of Rouen, July 1418 to January 1419. The capitulation of the 'master city of all Normandy' on 19 January 1419, after a long and implacable blockade by Henry V, made the duchy's conquest by the king virtually inevitable.

Page 185 Marriage of Henry V and Catherine of Valois in the parish church of St John, Troyes, 2 June 1420, a direct result of the Treaty of Troyes ratified less than a fortnight earlier on 21 May.

Page 201 The birth of Henry VI at Windsor, 6 December 1421.

Page 204 Richard Beauchamp Earl of Warwick becomes Henry VI's tutor following the death of Henry V.

Page 206 The coronation of Henry VI in Westminster Abbey, 6 November 1429.

Page 208 The coronation of Henry VI, the only English monarch ever to be crowned king of France in Paris, 16 December 1431.

All pictures are courtesy of the Tempus Archive.

INDEX

English Monarchs

A series of biographies of the kings and queens of England by acknowledged experts in the field.

Published

David Bates, *William the Conqueror*
'As expertly woven as the Bayeux Tapestry' *BBC History Magazine*

Keith Dockray, *Henry V*

Michael Hicks, *Edward V: The Prince in the Tower*
'The first time in ages that a publisher has sent me a book that I actually want to read! Congratulations' *David Starkey*

Michael Hicks, *Richard III*
'A most important book by the greatest living expert on Richard... makes for compulsive reading' *BBC History Magazine*

Ryan Lavelle, *Aethelred II*

M.K. Lawson, *Cnut: England's Viking King*
'An exhaustive review of the original sources... excellent'
English Historical Review

Richard Rex, *Elizabeth I: Fortune's Bastard?*
'polished' *History Today*

Forthcoming

Douglas Biggs, *Henry IV*
Emma Mason, *William II: Rufus, the Red King*
W.M. Ormrod, *Edward III*
A.J. Pollard, *Henry VI*

Further titles are in preparation

If you are interested in purchasing other books published by Tempus, or in case you have difficulty finding any Tempus books in your local bookshop, you can also place orders directly through our website

www.tempus-publishing.com

or from

BOOKPOST, Freepost, PO Box 29,
Douglas, Isle of Man IM99 1BQ
Tel 01624 836000
email bookshop@enterprise.net

DU	07/04
US	1/06
BC	7/05